THE
AFGHAN
PARADOX

GENNARO BUONOCORE

The image of the cover page was taken by US Navy Commander Michael Freidberg during the course of a Shura in the Saraw district of the Uruzgan province, southeastern Afghanistan on 20 January, 2013.

The picture depicts some of the 200-plus pairs of shoes left by the Shura participants outside the meeting hall.

When the Shura was suddenly moved outdoors, the chaotic scene that ensued became symbolic. The incredible "dance" of dozens of men hopping around wearing only one shoe was the ultimate representation of Afghanistan's paradox.

1 May 2014

The opinions expressed in this book do not represent the position of the United States Navy, the US Department of Defense or of the Government of the United States of America.

Copyright © 2014 by Jackson Hill Press

ALL RIGHTS RESERVED
No part of this publication may be reproduced, stored in a retrieval system or transmitted, in any form or by any means—electronic, mechanical, photocopying, recording or otherwise—without prior written permission, except for the inclusion of brief quotations in a review.

For information about this title or to order books and/or electronic media, contact the publisher.
  Jackson Hill Press
  Rancho Santa Margarita, California
  www.jacksonhillpress.com
  (949) 533-4050

Printed in the United States of America

Dedication

To My Children

"When you're wounded and left on Afghanistan's plains.
And the women come out to cut up what remains,
Jest roll to your rifle and blow out your brains
An' go to your Gawd like a soldier."

The Young British Soldier by Rudyard Kipling
(1865–1936)

Gennaro Buonocore

Contents

Introduction	vii
(ROI) Rules of Engagement	1
Afghan Rugs, Afghan Stories	7
Nothing but the Truth	13
Life Is a Movie	29
The Rumor Mill and Afghan Society	39
War and Its Story Makers	55
On Sex and the Afghans	81
On Afghan Courage	123
Afghans' Use of Humor	143
Combat Narratives	169
The Lost Afghan Diary	185
The Social Scientist	231
The Accidental Angel	243
Time	261
Conclusion	273
Acknowledgments	277
About the Author	279

INTRODUCTION

Metaphor

> A statement that is seemingly contradictory or opposed to common sense and yet is perhaps true. An argument that apparently derives self-contradictory conclusions by valid deduction from acceptable premises. One (as a person, situation, or action) having seemingly contradictory qualities or phases. A figure of narrative that describes a subject by asserting that it is, on some point of comparison, the same as another otherwise unrelated object.
> — Merriam-Webster dictionary of English

The social geometry of the world can always be found in dialogue, and dialogues are always immortalized in people's stories.

Back in Italy, we say, *La storia siamo noi*. It conceptually translates into *we are the story, therefore, we make history*, figuratively meaning that history is made by countless personal threads woven into a magnificent carpet.

I have a competitive advantage in the storymaking and storytelling field. As a native of Naples, I grew up in a reality where the fabric of Southern Italian society is permeated with thousand of stories that come alive through the *sceneggiata* (the Neapolitan play) or the region's internationally acclaimed music.

The *sceneggiatas* and Neapolitan music are romantic and tragic at the same time. For Neapolitans, life is a privilege—it is not a right or an expectation.

Life for Afghans is much the same. I was, therefore, well positioned to understand Afghanistan and its favorite brand of stories: the dance between life and death. This dance is at the center of both cultures, and the stories about it are so embellished that historical truth becomes murky. Intrigue and conspiracy theories enthrall the listeners and give way to a new reality where even the most fantastic hypothesis gets accepted as matter of fact.

Afghan history is a *sceneggiata,* an entertaining mix of real events, folk tales, propaganda stories, myths and discussion points. The acknowledgment that truth is just a relative matter is accepted by everybody as a useful educational instrument. Naturally, the one-eyed Mullah Omar could not start the Taliban uprising against warring *mujahidins* (holy warriors) because of economic and sectarian reasons. That would have been too secular and not romantic at all. He had to do it to avenge the kidnapping and rape of two young girls who were martyred by a brutal warlord. Whether it is true or not, it feels a lot nobler, more pious, less *realpolitik;* it is now commonly accepted as part of Afghanistan history.

What is Past is Prologue is carved in the marble of the pedestal outside the National Archives in Washington, DC. A picture of the elegant carving makes an ideal image wallpaper for anybody's preferred electronic device. A personal reminder that failing to abide by this tenet of wisdom has frequently gotten people into serious trouble.

The United States Congress had decided on a place where millions and millions of documents and pieces of evidence could be stored to help preserve memory in the hope that memory would help us lead a better life.

The majority of us, at the end of the day, are not so naïve. We are curious about everyone's past whether we are embarking on a love story or a business merger. We want to know about our mates' pasts and their family histories in order to know what we are getting ourselves into.

We check on the credit records of our tenants or future business partners to detect whether they are suitable for us. Due-diligence processes in business can take so long that often mergers or investments fail to go through just because of timing issues. Socially, whether in racial or political interactions, we hold grudges and stereotypes that are deeply rooted in history. We might forgive, but we do not forget that easily. We rarely give second chances, because we tend to believe that what happened once will happen twice. We believe that who has betrayed once will betray again.

Historian Giambattista Vico formulated the *Corsi e Ricorsi Storici theory* (Occurrences and Recurrences of History), the theory for which things that have happened in the past are bound to happen again if similar conditions are repeated. The philosophy behind *occurrences and recurrences* reinforces the notion that repeating the same actions expecting a different outcome might be the definition of insanity.

So, what happened with our Afghanistan campaign? We rushed through due diligences and we spent more than 12 years there. For most people, it felt like an eternity, but, for all intents and purposes, we literally rushed through it. We came to the land, fought, died, killed, but we did not stop and listen.

Military observers might appreciate that, had we really *listened* to Afghan history, we might have come to the conclusion that the only two courses of action in Afghanistan were either the Roman *Tabula Rasa* or not getting involved at all.

Regardless of whether enough due diligence was done before getting involved in Afghanistan, we did eventually commit to a war there.

If Vico is correct, we have a duty to learn from our presence in Afghanistan. It is all about the lesson that should be learned once a fateful decision has been taken.

With a style perhaps unique to modern warfare and unique to the West, we went in with all of our might and became quickly impatient. We were caught in the never-ending Afghan paradox.

Writing this book has taken many different directions during the course of two years. I felt like I had to write a summary of my experiences and the stories I had heard in Afghanistan, but, while I was writing it all down, the book did not mean much to me. I was writing like a Westerner.

I was writing matter of fact. There were no personal anecdotes—just the crude facts—and Afghanistan stories are not just about crude facts.

I needed to write and listen to the countless stories that are being narrated without giving in to a natural inclination to move on quickly, move to the next thing. This comes necessarily with the ability to slow down to our Afghan hosts' time—a difficult feat given the colossal gap in the way the West and Afghanistan experience our lives and the way we communicate.

In Afghanistan, there are *Quissa Mar* (Storymakers) and *Quissa Khwan* (Storytellers). Anybody who sets foot in Afghanistan, no matter where from, is asked to be one of the two. This is the way Afghans communicate. This book is a collection of stories from a number of *Quissa Mar* and *Quissa Khwan*.

In the book, I will also touch on the dynamic between story-making versus plain reporting and whether *enriching* the stories with subjective details (an Afghan tradition) might be ethical or fair.

A good story, after all, needs to be emphatic, and military stories carry the most weight in the history of the world. Stories of bravery, of great victories, of valor, inspire and unite people of different backgrounds and social status. Afghan stories often talk of war.

I encourage the reader to take the time to relax, brew a cup of smoky *chai* (tea), and read the stories without giving in to the tendency to rush through them, judge, decide, or to move on.

In some areas of Afghanistan, villagers get stuck in their homes because of the harshness of the winter months. Their only entertainment is the word, the spoken one. Hundreds of stories are recounted around an animal-dung fire, often the only source of heat. With no electricity or running water, it is a simple life where concepts, such as democracy or nation building, have no meaning. Only the stories have meaning.

TAKE YOUR TIME—stories, especially good ones, take time to be properly savored, and this book has some confusing stories, some superficial ones and some real gems. Just as the Afghanistan paradox, they all tie together in one manner or another.

Gennaro Buonocore
Tarin Kowt, Uruzgan, 20 December, 2012

xii • *The Afghan Paradox*

Drawing by Meranda Keller

(ROI) Rules of Engagement

> *"Within four months their shells and rockets had damaged the capital more severely than had the war between the mujahidin guerrillas and the Soviet-backed communist regime."*
> — Afghanistan Uneasy Peace. National Geographic. October 1993

More than rules of engagement, what follows are discussion points attempting to dispel myths about Afghanistan and Western involvement in that land. Naturally, these points are not dogmas, but they constitute opinions about Afghanistan which have, for good reason, been voiced loudly by many. They should help set the stage for the reading of the book, as these are the arguments that are most often heard when operating in Afghanistan.

1. Afghans bear the primary responsibility for their tragedies, their successes, their achievements and their failures. They are as much victims as perpetrators. The NATO coalition and the United States Armed Forces did not bomb Afghanistan back to medieval time. Afghanistan was already in medieval time, and almost all the damage to the infrastructure, social fabric and major cities (urbanization and viability) was done by the Afghans and not by foreigners, not even

the Russians. Kabul, for example, was literally destroyed by Afghan *mujahidin* after the Soviets withdrew.

2. Observations about the nature of armed struggles highlight that local problems are not generally solvable through traditional civil-military means because they are fundamentally problems of politics, sociology, economics and related cross-loyalties that the traditional Western civil-military approach is not always equipped to solve. If the West involves itself in nation building (Western styled) in countries like Afghanistan, Somalia, Yemen or Mali, then ten years might be a short time, indeed, to achieve any measurable results (connects to point five).

3. In a modern society like ours where, because of democratic evolution and media presence, the military wins a war only if CNN says it did, appropriate communication might be a cheaper instrument of war than a *Hellfire* missile and maybe even more effective than an *MQ-9 Reaper UAV* drone. We cannot kill everybody to victory (connects to point six).

4. Afghanistan, just like Yemen or Somalia, is, yes, in need of economic, political and social stability, but, because of its medieval tribal structure, its ability to absorb the kind of development assistance we currently offer is questionable. We might be finally modifying our policy of exporting our Western democratic-styled approach to nation building and communication, but currently the language of the societies where we are waging war is still fundamentally different from the communications machinery that modern societies field in the course of military operations.

5. In the subject of communication in Afghanistan, the Western military coalition has taken a long time to start relating properly. *Troop cards*, for example, are a summary of portable useful information about a number of subjects such as hosts' language, culture and tradition. Almost every coalition service member is issued one. We first went into Afghanistan in 2001. *Troop cards* were distributed to coalition personnel by 2003. Our Afghan allies received their *troop cards*, the tools needed to understand Western customs, in September 2012, nine years later. Western communication in Afghanistan has failed on most fronts.

6. A number of people advocate *Tabula Rasa* in Afghanistan. *Tabula Rasa* (blank slate), in the lingo of Roman military strategy, translates to the total annihilation of the opponent, bringing a territory back to a time before it was first populated, eradicating a potential threat for good by canceling the source: the human being and its legacy. During the Roman senate deliberations on the course of action with regard to Carthage in the final Punic War (149–146 BC) a prominent Roman, who had been involved in the constant struggle against Carthage, became a proponent of sorting out the century-old struggle with that Phoenician city across the Mediterranean with a radical solution—*Cartago delenda est* (Carthage has to be destroyed). When consulted to give his personal analysis, as one of the country's experts during Rome's final push into modern-day Tunisia, he closed his speech with words that left no space for misunderstanding: *Ceterum autem censeo Carthaginem esse delendam* (Furthermore, I believe that Carthage must be destroyed). Carthage was eventually razed to the ground, its population massacred, with the survivors transformed into

slavery, its grounds covered in salt. Carthage ceased being a threat for Rome once and for all, with only a few ruins on the edges of modern *Sidi-bou-Said* bearing testimony of its past grandeur.

One can just imagine a US military commander, in his testimony on Afghanistan to the US Congress, being prompted to express his expert opinion on the strategic posture for that war and the members hearing this sort of answer: "Look, honorable gentlemen, given the short time we have been engaged in this fight and the limited amount of military assets we have devoted so far to it, we should commit at least 200,000 additional personnel for the final push to crush the insurgency, and, furthermore, I believe that Afghanistan must be destroyed...." Most people would really love to witness the scene; they might even pay good money to be there and see it live, in person—the looks on the members' faces and the fury of the media. Afghanistan will never be a *tabula rasa*. Rome did not have the scrutiny of International Humanitarian Law and of the media outlets and their 24-hour news cycle. So, once and for all, let's stop advocating the total annihilation of the citizenry of Afghanistan; it will never happen.

7. Another myth to be dispelled is that the Afghans have never experienced before the misery of the past ten years. During the Soviet invasion, Afghanistan lost one million lives, two million driven from villages, with more than five million made refugees in Pakistan. In all, half of the nation's population was killed, disabled or uprooted. It is estimated that the total number of deaths since October 7, 2001 hovers around

63,000, including civilians and military personnel. To put this number in perspective there have been the same number of civilian deaths in Syria since April 2001. There have been 52,000 deaths in Mexico's war against the *narcos* since 2006, and six years of continuing conflict in Congo have claimed 3.8 million lives, nearly half of them children. In three years, between 1945 and 1948, with World War II already ended, the Allied occupiers in Germany suffered as high as 700 deaths while attempting to stamp out Nazi "insurgents."

8. A great number of Afghans are profiting from the Western military involvement in their own land; so are a number of Western corporations and individuals. Afghanistan is, after all, economically better off than ever before. However, economic growth might have brought in the typical economic disparity caused by capitalism.

9. *Mujahidin* are not only *holy warriors*. There were plenty of men who took part in the struggle under that banner who were only thugs and criminals, just as not every insurgent now is a Taliban.

10. Rationality mandates that war should be waged only if the outcome is somewhat foreseen and quantified. The opponents' willingness to fight should never be discounted, and, if, amongst all options, one is not prepared to exercise violence to its full extent, then one shall seek other ways to resolve the conflict at hand. Military personnel gets instructed to never point a weapon in the direction of anything they are not intending to fire upon.

11. The biggest obstacle to Afghanistan's development is Islam and the lack of sizeable natural resources for self-reliance. A closer analysis of all the other Muslim countries across the globe should not encourage the vision of a democratic and prosperous Islamic Republic of Afghanistan.

Drawing by Meranda Keller

Afghan Rugs, Afghan Stories

Afghan rug is a type of hand-woven…textile traditionally made in Afghanistan. Many of the Afghan rugs are also woven by Afghan refugees who reside in Pakistan and Iran. In any case, Afghan rugs are genuine, charming and usually phenomenally inexpensive. One of the most exotic and distinctive of all oriental rugs is the Shindand or Adraskan (named after local Afghan towns), woven in the Herat area, in western Afghanistan. Strangely elongated human and animal figures are their signature look. Another staple of Afghanistan is Baluchi rugs, most notably, Baluchi prayer rugs. They are made by Afghanistan's Baloch people, also in the southwestern part of the country. Most of the weavers in Afghanistan are the Ersari Turkmen, but other smaller groups, such as Chub Bash and Kizil Ayaks, are also in the line of weaving rugs. In addition, Uzbeks, Kyrgyz, Kazakhs and Arabs label their rugs according to their ethnic group. Various vegetable and other natural dyes are used to produce the rich colors. The rugs are mostly of medium sizes. Many patterns and colors are used, but the traditional and most typical is that of the octagonal elephant's foot (Bukhara) print, often with a red background. The weavers also produce other trappings of the nomadic lifestyle, including tent bags and ceremonial pieces.
— Afghan Rug—Wikipedia

Buying an Afghan rug from a vendor just off Chicken Street, in central Kabul, is the experience of a lifetime. As soon as one enters this treasure cove of a shop, one gets immediately offered a cup of *chai*. Shopkeepers who specialize in rugs are storytellers and hold a deep knowledge of Afghan geography, traditions and craft. Rugs in Afghanistan are not just craftworks, they are entertainment.

Rugs are brought to your feet, and there are so many, of all colors and shapes, that the visual sense can go on overload. Ask the shopkeeper, and he will have a different enthralling story for each one of them.

Afghan rugs and Afghan stories are of the same fabric. In an Afghan carpet, every detail is both important and unimportant, every image consistent and inconsistent. The result is hypnotizing. One could literally stare at the rug for hours and keep discovering new details.

The texture of stories about Afghanistan is the same. Some might be funny, some might be too intense, some outright disturbing, and a few are inspirational. So is Afghanistan: intense, disturbing, inspirational and comic.

There are as many rug types as there are books and movies about Afghanistan. All of them constitute universal depiction of a paradoxical reality. Among the great number of books which have been authored by both Westerners and Afghans, a few can be considered true masterpieces. There are also a number of movies about Afghanistan, and, again, these are filmed and directed by foreigners and Afghans alike. When one thinks of filmed entertainment works of art, one might quickly mention *The Kite Runner*, a 2007 movie directed by Marc Forster and based on a book by Khaled Hosseini, but there are a number of little-known motion pictures like *Lions for Lambs* by Robert Redford or Russian works of art like *9th Company*.

These movies illustrate the tragic failures of foreign military involvement in Afghanistan. *Lions for Lambs* tells of the choice of two young American students who decide to serve their nation and die during the war against the backdrop of Washington DC's political maneuvering and media dynamics. The movie *9th Company* depicts the cruel and devastating reality of the Soviet experience.

The actors are the greatest storytellers, the set is Afghanistan. Giants like Meryl Streep, Robert Redford and Tom Cruise have nothing over little-known Arthur Smolyaninov, Aleksey Chadov and Konstantin Kryukov. Their mission is fully accomplished. Viewers are transported back into the plush office of a lawmaker, a cold Afghan mountain or the dusty barracks of the crumbling Red Army.

On the literary side, James Albert Michener (1907–1997) was a prolific American author, a storymaker, who used to produce entertaining sagas that escorted readers across various continents, generations and native cultures. Michener made his stories memorable by filling them with historical anecdotes.

When finished reading one of Michener's stories, the reader could feel somewhat knowledgeable of the land he had been taken to by the author. Most importantly, a reader would slow down to fully take in the colorful description. One would leave the daily routine of personal life to smell the campfires, touch the warm sand of the desert and daydream about the exhilarating rhythm of a tribal dance. The reader would find himself immediately projected out of a snowy New York night into the heat of Kandahar or the bustling crowd of Kabul's great bazaar.

The offering of *chai* or a *hookah* (instrument for smoking flavored tobacco) and its scented aroma by the carpet seller is an invitation to slow down and fully take in all details. The visual details of the carpets are as important as attentively listening to the stories behind each rug. The never-ending price negotiation is just one of the rituals that take place in those precious moments of life.

Back in our homes or in cinemas, when we find ourselves engrossed in a book, when we feel like we have stopped breathing while watching a very poignant scene, or when we are listening to a great story, we make a conscious, natural choice to slow down. Even when we strive to get to the end of the story, because we believe it possesses the climax, we flavor every page, every frame and every word.

In 1963, Random House published James Michener's novel *Caravans*. It is a marvelous story of love, passion and death. In *Caravans*, a young State Department employee gets exposed to the social and historical puzzle of Afghanistan during his diplomatic billet in Kabul. The protagonist has to travel Afghanistan while searching for a missing American woman who had left the United States to marry a local. The book depicts the Afghanistan of the '50s. During the young diplomat's adventurous exploration, he gets immersed in his host nation's troublesome history. The missing woman is the embodiment of the Afghan paradox, a troublesome combination of passion, irrationality and color.

The diplomat's journey is both a romantic one and an excursion into the tragedy of human conflicts, but, all through the revisiting of the country's bloody past, the picture of a razed Afghanistan never appears. This is an important detail because its date (1963) testifies to an Afghan resilience that constantly gets questioned, a resilience that is that land's best asset and the most underestimated factor by Westerners. The book romantically describes a land that has been a center of war yet never annihilated.

In Afghanistan, conflict is perpetually present but constantly punctuated by the frequency of conversations, the storytelling, the *shuras* (dialogues) and the philosophical discoveries over interminable cups of *chai*. All of these are activities that populate novels like *Caravans* with the typical theme of continuous verbal exchange. An everpresent narrative that recounts the region's extreme resiliency and love of both life and of the "beautiful death." The same narrative one finds in the carpet stores all over Afghanistan.

The author in a carpet store, Kabul

Nothing but the Truth

> *"We cannot capture hearts and minds.*
> *We must engage them; we must listen to them,*
> *one heart and one mind at a time—over time."*
> — US Navy ADM Mike Mullen,
> Chairman of the Joint Chiefs of Staff
> From an article in *Joint Forces Quarterly*
> Issue 55, 4th Quarter 2009

I have had the dubious fortune to go to Afghanistan a number of times. I have not always liked it. Experiences have been dramatically different whether I was on a military mission or on a civilian humanitarian-assistance project. Whether I have found myself in green, peaceful *Hazara-jat* or in medieval *Uruzgan,* the theme has been a constant one of paradoxical beauty and contradicting perceptions.

Every single trip has been a mixture of curiosity, amazement and repulsion. The majority of the visits have been without the burden of wearing a military uniform. There is no doubt in affirming that, in Afghanistan, a uniform makes one a target and restricts freedom of movement. When visiting locals or sites as a civilian, dressed in a *salwhar kameez* (a pajama-looking local garb), sporting a beard and a traditional *pakol* (tajik-styled hat), one is allowed to go to markets and restaurants, drive around freely and accept the hospitality of the Afghan hosts without the benefit or liability of a curious second look.

Dwellings of Afghan middle and upper classes are definitely comfortable or outright plush. Water and electricity supply might be sporadic at best, but interiors look exotic, with lots of carpets and carved wooden furniture. At any level of Afghan society, kitchens do not compare in the least even with the most modest Western household. They pale in comparison with our standards for health and practicality. Afghan lower classes' abodes are modest to downright filthy. They all seem to have at least two to five old posters of European alpine scenery on their makeshift walls. With the exception of the poorest dwellings, they all look like royal palaces in comparison with the lodgings that some of the military personnel have to endure while serving in that land, be they Afghans or Westerners.

On one of my Afghan visits, I was dispatched there as a public affairs officer by the United States Navy. The US Navy has a first-class public affairs community with a very poignant motto: *Nil Nisi Verum* (Nothing but the Truth). The statement, taken in its absolute meaning, is deeply promising, honorable, and powerful. It reflects the nature of the service, the branding of a nation and a branch of its armed forces that seeks to embody *Honor*, *Courage* and *Commitment*. Without sounding propagandistic, I can attest to the fact that this community abides by a standing order of *Maximum Disclosure, Minimum Delay,* which is a very delicate service for defense stakeholders when dealing with matters of national security. I have personally witnessed a healthier relationship with truth in the public affairs component of the United States Navy than in the commercial media sector.

The people of the United States and their media have always had a very interesting relationship with truth.

Etched in the marble wall of the main lobby at the United States' Central Intelligence Agency, there is an inscription from the New Testament's John 8:32, which reads: *…and ye shall know the truth, and the truth shall make you free.* The notion that truth and freedom are closely correlated is an American tenet.

Once, on my way to Afghanistan, I decided to spend a few more days than usual while transiting in Dubai, the glitzy Arab Emirate. This time, instead of rushing through, I took the opportunity to have dinner with one of my university colleagues who is of Middle Eastern descent and living there. Over three hours of delightful Lebanese food, most philosophical aspects of life were visited, commented on and debated. It is amazing how, for most cultures, the most important negotiations and the most insightful philosophical debates always take place around the serving of food.

Waiting for the Ariana Afghan Airlines flight to Kabul, and its very inconvenient middle-of-the-night flight, there is nothing more relaxing than spending the hours preceding the crazy stampede that they call check-in in the company of a few old schoolmates while philosophizing about life.

My friends are Lebanese Christians who had immigrated to the United Kingdom via Egypt. Neapolitans and Lebanese share Greco-Phoenician roots and a passion for interminable meals, laughter and conversations. Just as most Afghans do. Most Americans don't.

During this dinner, among many conversation topics, the subject of truth came up. Much debate ensued about the cultural definition of absolute truth and the perceived subjective recognition that comes with upholding it. The deliciousness of the *tabouleh* (a type of salad) and of the *dolmades* (grapevine leaves stuffed with rice and minced meat) provided great taste alternatives to my friends' pontifications. The average Middle Easterner seems to believe that the fixation with absolute truth is a very Anglo-Saxon trait.

The Anglo-Saxon fixation with defining truth is considered a legacy of the *Reformation* and the *Enlightenment* that engulfed Europe. Both movements were seen as the historical reaction to the Church of Rome's arrogant claim over absolute truth. But this fixation with truth is not a claim that Arabs concern themselves with. There is only one truth, which is the belief in the omnipotence of Allah; the rest is conversation, the rest is gossip.

At the dinner table, it was strongly advocated that, if Middle-Easterners might indeed believe that mottos like *Nil Nisi Verum* carry too big of a responsibility for the average Arab to bear, it is also very plausible that the average Afghan would not even comprehend the basic conceptual meaning of *Nothing but the Truth*.

The average Arab, man or woman, is a fatalist in the awareness that he/she has lied more than once in life without having to confess, correct deeds or beg for forgiveness. *Nil Nisi Verum* might end up constituting a very uncomfortable tenet when applying it to one's everyday life, especially when one tries to perfectly abide by the standard it claims.

Nil Nisi Verum to an Arab is just a symbolic image like a sword of light or world peace. One of my philosopher friends swore that the motto brought this image to mind: a blond-haired, blue-eyed gallant naval officer looking proudly at the horizon underneath a stars and stripes banner. They all agreed that the message evoked strong images, but, aside from that, it meant something absolutely abstract to them, something pious and admirable, but inhuman and unachievable. Truth to an Arab is subjective—somebody's truth might be somebody else's lie.

Therefore, *Nil Nisi Verum* or *Ye shall know the truth* and *the truth shall set you free* means nothing to the average Afghan and, that day I learned, very little to the average Middle Easterner. It means even less to the *Helmand* poppy grower. To him, truth is not even an issue to be debated over a dinner with his friends. That kind of debating is a luxury for rich men; he is too busy protecting his crop and the livelihood of his family. His truths are his belief in myths, traditions and how he gets his fourteen-year-old daughter to marry a wealthy cousin.

An accomplished Los Angeles-based psychotherapist whom I have known for the past 21 years states: "Truth is a vibration, it is not a belief or thought, it is recognized by its energy quality, it is the same vibration all through the cosmos. With each time you allow yourself to experience truth, you will get better at recognizing all the moments you deceive even yourself."

Even spiritually motivated Afghans cannot relate to this kind of definition. Their lies are, at times, infantile by Western standards, their defense mechanism too strong to *better recognize all the moments when they are deceiving even themselves.*

When it comes to Western truth, I find it very defined by public perception and mass media.

Wasn't it an American Armed Forces officer who stated something to the tune of "You have won a war only when CNN says you did..."? Thus, does truth vary accordingly to the mouth of the communicator and the ear of its beholder, or do absolute truths exist?

In James Allen's booklet titled *As a Man Thinketh*, we read that a man is what and how he thinks. His moral backbone, his honor, his character are defined by his thoughts. *As a Man thinketh in his heart, so is he*—his mind is his temple, it is his garden, and, by tending it or dilapidating it, he either makes or unmakes himself. He either cares for his soul and honors the Divinity within, or he destroys himself. Any man or woman possesses his/her own truth. Thoughts are subjective; so is truth, then.

An Afghan's entire thought process is monopolized by the preoccupation of survival. The majority of his thoughts are concentrated on the now and on how his family is going to eat next.

The Greeks often mentioned *phronesis* (practical wisdom). We often talk about knowledge and common sense, but *phronesis* implies the ability to figure out what to do, at the same time, knowing what is worth doing and, most importantly, worth telling. Traveling around the world and having to deal with a vast number of individuals coming from completely different cultures and social classes teaches us that individuals think according to the way they have been brought up. The natural correlation between causes and effects varies according to geography, ethnicity, religion and a variety of other social factors.

Storymaking and storytelling, without the filter of the double-edged "Anglo-Saxon" fixation with the truth, are therefore the ideal instruments for a social comprehension of alien societies. By trying to establish, at an earlier stage, a closer human connection with a potential enemy, any socially conscious military personnel aims to appeal to the natural unwillingness of the human being *to pull the trigger*. When we are trying to avoid being shot at, we are willing to listen. Why do we stop doing so as soon as we feel the danger has evaporated?

Empathy and a willingness to listen are necessary ingredients to a great story—that is why: In the beginning was the Word. The Word was with God, and the Word was God. (John 1:1)

Operating both as a civilian and as a military officer, I have adopted the application of societal intelligence gathering and analysis applied to the art (for it is an art and not a precise science) of defining who the appropriate stakeholders are when trying to deliver the most effective message in a timely fashion. I have found this method very successful when having to communicate anywhere around the world. I have also had plenty of experience with the manipulation of truth or just plain deceit.

I worked in Wall Street for many years, and the experience might be, in itself, considered a rite of passage with regard to flexible approaches in representing the truth. However, it was my negotiation with a manager of the Kabul *Marastoon* (Afghan Red Crescent Center for Long-Term Care) that became my ultimate initiation, for I finally comprehended that I was culturally predisposed to manipulating the truth, a capacity that the Afghans define as the ability *to play the game*.

This is a *game* that can be as innocent as going through the ritualistic dance of negotiating a price and pretending not to carry any money, or more cunning in order to obtain monetary or safety-related advantages. The "encounter" with the manager of the *Marastoon* revealed that I could not only *play the game* but was quite good at it, too. The Western translation for the Afghan proverb that defines the initiation would be: It takes an excellent bullshitter to recognize when another bullshitter is in action. I will describe the *sceneggiata* initiation that played between the two of us in another chapter.

Many people in the "civilized" world would assert that they are not comfortable with liberal interpretations of the truth. Westerners claim to have a clear grasp of what constitutes truth and what doesn't. But the portrayals of life are seldom accurate or exact pictures. Life is not black and white.

One might meet bankers who would never lie to a client but readily embrace creative accounting. One might chat with her child's Sunday school teacher, a divorced lovely lady, who doubles as an exotic dancer at nights. Or we might vote for a particular pillar of morality who wouldn't resign from office when a journalist uncovers a history of embezzlement. Finally, how many military leaders do we see giving up their careers only when the illicit affair has finally come to light? I am one of those Westerners who aren't too judgmental against "truth massaging" when used as a facilitator of effective communication. When truth gets omitted in order for egos to stay unengaged and beneficial agreements reached, it is, in my opinion, an acceptable practice.

For the entire world's inhabitants to tell the truth would be a dream. But, in practice, it is just that.

In Afghanistan, those who are comfortable dealing with truth "masseuses" have an invaluable competitive advantage. This willingness to *play the game* does not deliver the absolute ability to navigate Afghan communication, but it qualifies an individual to being considered almost as an equal.

Many pieces of literature, traditions and historical texts romanticize and herald *Pashtunwali* as a noble and pure behavioral code that defines the mighty tribes of the "Land of the Afghans." The code might be constantly publicized but not universally applied in that land.

The *Code* or the *Way of the Pashtun,* promotes self-respect, independence, justice, hospitality, love, forgiveness, revenge and tolerance toward all other human beings with particular reference to strangers and guests. Every Pashto (42 percent of the Afghan population plus a lot more in Pashtunistan [the area between Afghanistan and Pakistan] and North Waziristan) has a duty to abide by and apply it.

In the *Code,* where self-respect, independence, justice, hospitality, love, forgiveness, revenge and tolerance are the pillars of human conduct, there is absolutely no mention of truth, manipulation of the truth or the appropriate use of deceit. In behavioral terms, truth and deceit are not issues that need to be defined and therefore regulated.

Again, life is not black and white, and truth can be subjective. Bear with me and with the following story that does not have only Afghans as protagonists.

In September 2007, I escorted three North American volunteers around *Hazara-jat*. The group was composed of two Americans, a Methodist minister, a female member of his congregation with extensive humanitarian experience, and a Canadian entrepreneur.

After an emotionally charged but uneventful mission, during the course of which I had worried only on two separate occasions, we headed to the Kabul International Airport for the group's return home.

The first time I had worried was when I drove our ubiquitous white Toyota minivan off the road in a remote village somewhere between the Bagrami (the road that connects Kabul and Bagram Air Base) and Bahmyan. The trip was planned with little intelligence gathering. With a few notable exceptions, civilian organizations tend to disregard the warning emails they receive from Kabul-based foreign embassies.

A few of these "cables" are genuinely useful, but most deliver the warning after an event has taken place and then the majority of them carry the same narrative:

There are strong indications and intelligence reports indicating that a white Toyota minivan might be driving around Kabul laden with explosives and searching for opportunities of chance. Avoid getting into close proximity with a vehicle of such description.

In Afghanistan, the warning corresponds to an advice to levitate and use "cloud cruising" in order to commute from A to B. The basic nuisance is that white Toyota minivans are the most common vehicle in Afghanistan. Literally, an estimated two million Toyota minivans are jammed into Afghanistan. The majority of them are indeed white.

We were not levitating or flying in the clouds when we were driving one of the two million Afghan Toyota white minivans, the only one that was not laden with explosives but with weird looking *koregee* (foreigners). Despite the fact that the men were donning convincing *shalwar khamiz* and that the female member was wearing a turquoise *chadri* (all-covering veil), we might have looked completely out of place.

I was truly driving like a madman, skillfully in my own estimation of my driving abilities, attempting to avoid deep, water-filled potholes. I just felt like I was driving as any good Afghan would, except they know that roadside water-filled ditches should be avoided and not driven through. I completely got the important lesson just after I hit one of those ditches.

With the vehicle completely immobilized, I asked everybody in the van to stay quiet and to avoid talking either among themselves or to any approaching villagers—"Just smile and look innocent"—I stepped out of the vehicle to face the incoming crowd of *Pashtun* villagers, which was growing around us by the minute. One of them, a man in his 20s, kept stroking my beard, calling me *uncle* in his native dialect, and asking continuously if I was doing fine and where I was from.

Looking at his questioning eyes, which were growing increasingly suspicious, I had to make a move. So I went for broke: "*Man Araby ast*" (I am an Arab), I said in my uncertain Dari. Was I lying? Oh yes! Was I worried? Oh yes! I had images of being dragged away with the people I was meant to protect and making it into the next Taliban propaganda video. My answer seemed to satisfy the Pashto's curiosity.

Arabs who can be found in Afghanistan are either traders, preachers, military of the coalition or Al Qaeda operatives. Afghans' feelings about their Arab cousins are mixed, as Arabs are said to often overstay their welcome.

Also, the language barrier between Pashtuns and Arabs is strong. Afghans who are educated in *madrassas* (religious schools) memorize the Holy Quran, that being their only exposure to Arabic.

So, Pashtuns, even the Taliban, do not particularly care for Arabs. We might believe they are fierce allies, but the reality is that most Islamist Arabs, with their ruthless interpretation of the *Sharia*, have overextended their stay in Pashtunistan. The other complicating factor to Afghan-Islamists relations is that most Arab fighters have lost their funding sources and, code of hospitality or not, anywhere around the world, there is nothing worse than a persistent, self-celebrating, petulant and broke guest.

A lot of Afghans call their Arab cousins *goats* and crack jokes at their purist arrogance and their *Wahabist* religious fundamentalism.

However, I thought that the chance of meeting one of his fellow Sunni believers might spoil the villager's afternoon a lot less than the burden of having to give hospitality to an infidel *Amerikani*.

I was also hoping that being an Arab might justify my terrible Dari and even get me an invitation to the guy's *qualla* (walled compound), with the added benefit of some good sweetened *chai* and some fresh *naan* (bread). Fear was really making me feel hungry.

While I was starting to feel good about my quick thinking and the apparent success of my deceit, the Canadian entrepreneur jumps out of the van with a forced big grin stamped on his face, opens his arms and, in his best British Columbian accent, shouts: "Hey guys, what's up? We are Canadians!!"

For a quick second, both of us—the villager and I—found ourselves rolling our eyes in unison. We must have thought, the villager in Pashto and I in Italian: *"You must be freaking kidding me!"* If there ever will be a war zone hall of fame of the most moronic episodes, this one might well rank among the top ten.

Clearly, Canadians do not appear to know how to *play the game.*

I am still alive so the story has a good ending and I am sure that the villagers are still recounting their side of the story and laughing their heads off thinking of the moronic *koregees* who ended up entertaining them that afternoon.

The willingness to deceive one to obtain an advantage, such as security or, in that case, the gift of life, becomes, with time and repeated exercise, a default mechanism. When one has learned to use *the art of deceit* successfully, it becomes a tool that activates automatically every time one believes it is time to employ it. In Afghanistan it has become the default, therefore automatic, response to perceived threats. Individuals trying to protect themselves against a perceived threat resort to deception automatically.

The second time I had to seriously worry during this mission was when the group, by now feeling so secure in their knowledge of the territory to be qualified Afghanistan experts, decided to get rid of the local garb and don again the obligatory University of Kansas sweatshirts and go shopping in Kabul's main *bazaar* (market). The Kabul bazaar is a sight to behold, and, after the experience, I was told by volunteers that they absolutely loved the experience. I am glad they did. I did not. I was too busy watching over their *koregee* buttocks to really take in the sights, the colors and busy market life. What is it with this baseball caps and university sweatshirts middle-age withdrawal crisis? I find the sight of a 53-year-old man wearing a university ball cap and fleece already a sign of emotional instability and wishing to parade your collegiate allegiance in the middle of an Asian war zone a sign of mental illness. With all the funny t-shirts that can be decorated on demand, someone should come up with one that states: *Please, shoot me or kidnap me, I am an infidel foreigner* and supply one to each middle-aged university graduate wishing to travel to Kabul and commit suicide.

In any case, I witnessed three people who had vehemently argued about their belief that absolute truth really does exist and that telling the truth is always preferable to coming up with a lie, even if benign, swearing to Afghan knife and spice traders that they had expended all of their money to negotiate more favorable prices. Claiming that they were leaving Afghanistan a few hours after the visit to the *bazaar* (we were scheduled to depart in three days) there would be no chance for them to get back to the shop to buy the merchandise. Isn't the truth always preferable to a lie?

The third and final time I had to worry on this trip was during the Kabul airport's *sceneggiata*. In order to best recount it, I have chosen an excerpt from the diary of the female member of the group that she was most gracious in sharing with me in 2012:

During our visit to Afghanistan, our team member, K (the Methodist pastor), has read a number of books, including the Holy Quran, the biography of Mother Teresa and the football saga

Saturday Night Live. He also purchased a small prayer rug for his spiritual adviser back home and has no more room in his suitcase. He has asked me to bring back his books in my extra bag. Happy to oblige I toss them in my suitcase, along with clothing worn for the past ten days, shoes, lingerie and a couple of books of my own.

It is time to leave. Our Afghan interpreter drives us to the airport, and we begin the lengthy process of clearing customs. We move, men and women separately, through repeated body and luggage inspections. Finally, we are reunited in an area where a uniformed military official begins reexamination of each bag.

Something is terribly wrong. The suitcase with K's books and my dirty laundry has created havoc. The official, voice rising, arms waving, eyes bulging, face purple beneath his dark beard, is tearing off through the contents of my suitcase. In one shaking hand he holds the Holy Quran… He speaks in Dari to our interpreter. We have offended Allah, the esteemed government of Karzai, the Islamic nation of Afghanistan and the entire Muslim world—an offense especially egregious during the Holy month of Ramadan. The suitcase and its contents will be confiscated, and we will be punished. The Sacred Book has been contaminated due to its proximity to the mundane trappings of life. The Holy Quran must be always protected and shielded from the ordinary. It should be wrapped in green silk, accorded the utmost respect and carried separately. We are in serious trouble.

Our team leader, the ever-savvy Gennaro, enters the fray. Profusely apologizing and begging forgiveness, expressing the innocence of our actions, he offers baksheesh—would the honorable inspector consider five dollars as adequate atonement for our transgressions? Without missing a beat, the official's face is wreathed in smiles. He pockets the money, gently places the Holy Book back in *the suitcase and waves us through the line. All is forgiven. We are free to board our flight to India.*

My recollection of the story is not as dramatic and, contrary to the statement of the female volunteer, I do not consider myself particularly savvy, but one thing I know is that the Kabul airport episode saw the typical naïvety of the average American humanitarian worker interact with the average Afghan in a position of relative power—an individual who was used to *playing the game*. I will elaborate about the inaccuracy of my colleague's story later in the book. I should add that I have the utmost respect for the three individuals in the story, and I count the Methodist pastor as one of the most important people in my life.

The author and the three humanitarian volunteers
Kabul 2007

LIFE IS A MOVIE

"Flourish like a flower, but may your life be longer."
— Afghan greeting when offering flowers

It was a typical London day. From my position on the dealing floor, located on the third floor of a modern building on Upper Thames Street, London, I could see the relentless drizzle and the wet asphalt of a side street. I was one of the few dealers who sat by the glass wall. For people like me, the day would have meaning. I could witness the changing of time.

In other trading rooms, I had started working with the early morning darkness and would leave my daily routine under the cover of the evening's dusk. This time, seniority had warranted me a "spot in the sun."

That particular day, the frenzy of trading was particularly intense. The firm was the leading underwriter of a massive bond issuance on behalf of a Russian energy company. Bonds had to be placed fast, on a *first come, first served* basis. Desks covering clients, financial institutions, divided in precise geographical areas, were competing against each other acquiring "orders to purchase" from their clients. The race for the reputation of most successful desk but, most importantly, for sales commissions, was in full swing.

In the expectation that the offering would be over-subscribed and that clients' orders would be only partially filled, we would ask customers to inflate their order size in order to see their actual demand met. The offering was huge by 1998 standards, more than 1 billion *Deutsche Marks* worth of bonds.

We had gone into work with the nervous expectations of fans going to watch their preferred team's World Cup final. Now that I think about it, it was the feeling of someone playing rather than watching the most important game of the decade.

My team of 12 went to work frenetically. It took no more than 50 minutes for the Italy and Switzerland desk to collect 2.8 billion *Deutsche Marks* in orders, almost three times the size of the available offering. Dealers from other desks were looking at us, stunned. Southern European ingenuity had again triumphed over German and Scandinavian zealousness. We felt exhilarated, adrenaline still rushing. I looked at my deputy. I could not believe what had just happened. It looked like, with our bonus, we could both afford new Ferraris.

"Piero, what the hell just happened? Have you ever seen 2.8 billion *Deutsche Marks*? We just asked for the craziest amount I have ever seen. I don't even know what it would look like."

"Gennaro, life is a movie," Piero answered, trying, as usual, to control his excitement. From that day on, *life is a movie* would always be mentioned by us to describe the absolute absurdity of the financial leverage of the system and the complexity of the products we were creating and marketing.

Life is a movie is the only appropriate way Piero could justify the utter madness and the irrelevancy of our professions. He had no war-zone experiences—the world of international capital markets was his trench—but he and a few more of us ended up developing our own sort of *post traumatic stress disorder (PTSD)* because of the dissociation created by the deception of our so called professions and the day-to-day life of ordinary citizens. We were institutional fixed-income salesmen; we were masters of the universe.

In his book *Bombardiers,* a novel about institutional fixed-income salesmen, Po Bronson has the protagonist describe one of First Boston's top brokers in this manner: "…according to Sid Geeder, who did this better than anyone, success was only a question of how much they could lie before they felt guilty and then how much guilt they could take before they suffered psychological malfunction."

Banker's PTSD or not, my former deputy eventually moved to another organization that he proceeded to sue because he believed he had been denied a well-deserved multi-million dollar bonus, a premium he had received the year before and was, therefore, expecting again because of his performance. Such a bonus, by the way, should have been the fair compensation for unloading on the bank's clients a higher than the average amount of "toxic waste" securities, which normally ends up doing more damage to society that the average improvised explosive device. My colleague lost his "whistleblower" lawsuit. The firm, however, got into trouble on other occasions. *Life is indeed a movie.*

Life is a movie is a great detachment statement. It is simple justification for a lot of things that we find ourselves doing yet have difficulties reconciling with. If passively living, it is better to consider ourselves as spectators of a movie that unfolds irrespective of our wills. As active protagonists, it is even better to consider ourselves actors in this massive comedy or tragedy called life.

Where is the correlation between a number of Wall Streeters and the average Afghan civil servant? They both start using *life is a movie* as a way to cope, but, when it becomes a way of life, they find it difficult to let go for the sake of potential, yet uncertain, betterment. The corrupt Afghan governor replies with fatalistic acceptance to accusations of bribery—*I am just an actor in this movie called Afghanistan.*

Life is a movie—is what my friend Yasin Mohammad Farid would say as his way of anesthetizing the horrors he has witnessed over the years—the senseless killings, the random mortar rounds, children lacking bedding in poorly financed *marastoons* or frostbitten in remote orphanages. Life must not be real if anything, and I mean anything, can be taken away in a fraction of a second by a rudimentary improvised explosive device. How can this be real if the person you were talking to a few minutes before and who was worried about the usual matters of life is now just a thing, a bloody piece of cloth and blackened flesh?

Playing the game, being part of the movie is the moral justification behind the deception perpetrated by Afghans. The same can be found in the West. Life narratives between Westerners and Afghans are naturally different, and so might be the reasons the parties deceive.

The following description of life's narratives might be stereotypical, but no less argumentative, in having to decide whose *life is a movie*-styled deception might be more acceptable. There is no right or wrong in the following argument, which I heard from a US NGO employee in Paghman.

Afghans and other people of war like Kosovoans, Congolese or Sudanese have not been cocooned like the average Westerner, who worries about his malfunctioning pool filter, his child's college costs or how he is going to fill his SUV because his credit card bills are mounting.

The everyday fears of a debt-ridden American teacher living well above his means are massively different from the average Afghan *muallim* (teacher). The first one might not be making the end-of-the-month car payment; the latter worries about having to wake up with a bunch of NATO special forces personnel bursting through his door at three in the morning and violating the sanctity of his women's *otaaq-ekhaw* (bedroom). The first one worries about the way it might look if he loses his car to a collection agency; the latter is worried about losing his honor forever—honor which to him is everything. It is even worth filling his white Toyota minivan with explosives so that he can restore it.

They both might be culpable of abusing their fiduciary positions, but some would argue that, at present, the Afghan party risks more with regard to punishment.

Average people in the West worry about their kids getting too much homework, or too little, they worry about their children to the point of reading the list of child molesters in the area before they close escrow on their dream homes. They do not let the children walk to school anymore.

On the other hand, Mohammed Ahmad remembers the time that his seven-year-old baby, Nelofer, the light of his eyes, lost her own beautiful green ones because she had played, yet again, with a *green parrot*, one of those terrible little mines that look like toys and that are littering farmland from the time of the *Rusky* (Russians).

Average people in the West donate toys to shelters and to the poor so that no child goes without toys. They even worry that these toys could be made with toxic plastics or could be small enough to choke a baby.

Mohammed Ahmad concerns himself with having to pick up his child's eyes as these kids never learn to distrust the PFM-1, or Ïðîòèâîïåõîòíàÿ Ôóãàñíàÿ Ìèíà (anti-personnel cluster bombs) because, to his little girl, who has no toys, these anti-personnel mines are too attractive, as they look like mechanical green parrots. She keeps wondering if she can make them fly again.

Mohammed Ahmad has to worry which one of the three closest hospitals, in a range of ten miles, will provide the best care or, by Western standards, the least bad. When the moment he dreaded finally came, he had to rush to the local medical post, which had nothing to help his little child. So he rushed to the closest military Forward Operating Base (FOB), which directed him to Kandahar's NATO Hospital.

It was outside those heavily guarded walls that he ended up waiting for three days. He was crouching holding his little bloodied baby just outside the base's gate because he could not understand a word of what those guards were saying, and they did not know what to do with this crazy dad and his blind child.

Nie je niè, èo môžeme urobit (there is nothing we can do)—Mohammed's dad kept hearing from the Slovak sergeant and, while the NATO soldier kept asking himself why the hell he is guarding this damn gate instead of eating his mother's *kapustnica* (traditional Slovak dish) at his parent's little, but tidy, apartment in *Nitra*, Mohammed's dad kept thinking that his child's pain would eventually fade—at the end of the day, his little baby had been luckier than Faizal, who had come back from that hospital in a cab, a corpse. The dad kept reassuring himself that his beautiful child was indeed still alive and that life always gets better because, like all good movies, it is just a movie. *Inshallah* (Gods willing). The script has already been written.

Life is a movie—must have thought the Pakistani policeman, in a video released by the *Talib of Lashkar-e-Taiba*, as he was genuinely smiling while talking to a number of bearded men wearing black turbans just before his head was removed with a single sword blow. Was he fully aware of his condition? Was he trying to deceive his nemesis by hiding his fear, or was he deceiving himself to exorcise that fear? Was he just laughing about the thought that his movie was naturally coming to its end? *Inshallah.* The script has already been written.

There are plenty of people from all over the world who are very liberal with the adoption and interpretation of the *life is a movie* concept. They come from all regions and social classes—from Italian politicians to Russian presidents, from Norwegian housewives to Wall Street bankers, from military officers to cab drivers and from Arab merchants to Afghan warlords. These are all actors in the greatest blockbuster of all the world's history.

All actors might, willingly or unwillingly, play the roles of complete detachment from mutually beneficial reality for different reasons: shame, personal profiteering, pathology, narcissism; a few lie to act the part just in order to cope.

Most people dealing with the Afghans have been in direct contact with two categories of actors.

A consistent proportion tries to profit and gain monetary advantage by means of deceit. This is an activity that is considered an allowed cunning instrument at the disposal of the smart operator to sway people's action into one's favor. Greed is definitely the motivator behind those Afghans who are trying to take advantage of the sudden foreign influx of easy money. Whether in the form of *baksheesh* (bribe) or pure extortion, it gets practiced by all strata of society but primarily by bureaucrats and warlords.

The second category, which constitutes the majority of Afghans, deceives to cope. From innocent gambles such as inviting you to lunch while having almost no food at home, to telling you what they think you want to hear so that no harm can be caused. Afghans are naturally conditioned to pay lip service and, in the past seven years, westerners operating in Afghanistan appear to be paid to receive it.

Life had to be a movie for any visitor of Washington, DC on Thursday, June 28, 2012.

That week, all eyes and ears of the citizens of the United States were focused on the Supreme Court ruling on whether to uphold the so-called *Obamacare,* the Presidential plan to introduce universal health care. To an attentive citizen, that week will always be the week of *United States v. Alvarez.*

In the opinion of many observers, that week the Court's most important decision was to uphold a citizen's right to lie. In the case of *United States v. Alvarez,* the Court decided to strike down, in a six to three ruling, the Stolen Valor Act of 2005—a law that declared it a federal misdemeanor to falsely impersonate a decorated military officer.

In other words, *one could not lie pretending to be a member of the military, decorated or not, in public, in private and even in a whisper.* The Court ruled that this law restricts freedom of speech and dangerously impinges on an individual's constitutionally guaranteed right to lie.

If in Afghanistan truth manipulation is just a tradition, in the United States of America, the modern cradle of democracy, the willingness to lie is a constitutionally guaranteed right. This is why this world is really a beautiful affair, a masterful movie.

Kabul cityscape courtesy of Penelope Price

The Rumor Mill and Afghan Society

RUMOR MILL
"A group or network of persons who originate or promulgate gossip and other unsubstantiated claims."
— HTTP://EN.WIKTIONARY.ORG

United States Department of Defense Joint Publication 1-02 defines Psychological Operations as: *planned operations to convey selected information and indicators to audiences to influence their emotions, motives, objective reasoning, and ultimately the behavior of governments, organizations, groups and individuals.*

In asymmetric warfare, the Afghans have a few things to teach us with regard to Information Operations (IO). They are masters of deception and profound connoisseurs of the narrative that gets their compatriots worked up into a fighting frenzy.

The national *rumor mill* is incredibly efficient when needed to rouse the masses. Western IO's tools are too heavily regulated and scrutinized in their content. The scrutiny of military supervision is just too established to be bypassed. When the IO message gets combined with an unclear understanding of the target audience, it becomes a very weak weapon.

Even in mainstream media, where the message should be simply accurate and truthful, news consumption differs greatly between Muslims and "unbelievers." "Unbelievers" tend to love snippets. They have little time to spare, and, even if attracted by it, they get generally turned off when the story seems too unrealistic and preposterous. Afghans and Muslims in general love elaborated and incredible narratives.

On August 27, 2012, NATO reported that the Taliban had beheaded 17 people, including two women, in a remote corner of southern Afghanistan, apparently for attending a dancing party, an activity that is against Taliban law.

The NATO press release cited *Musa Qala's* District Chief Neyamatullah Khan in confirming that the victims were killed as a result of a crackdown on government informers but, most importantly, the men were killed as a result of two Taliban leaders arguing over the women.

The Taliban spokesman, Qari Muhhamad Yusuf Ahmadi, replied that the two women had gotten the men fighting against each other to the point of chopping each others' heads off. The Taliban version of the story could not really explain how the last man standing had decapitated himself, but that would not really matter. The point is that a story about men decapitating each other in a terrible fight to the death, just like gladiators, and all of it because of the bewitching influence of two women is a much more appreciated tale for the Afghan listener. It provides years and years of *Quissa khwan* (storytelling) for the men of the region.

On December 22, 2012, the English version of the Taliban's *Islamic Emirate of Afghanistan* propaganda website *Shahamat* reported that three *mujahidin* had destroyed 12 NATO tanks. There are almost no tanks in Afghanistan, but that is not the point; the point is that Afghans with Taliban sympathies loved the story anyway and found in it a confirmation of the invincibility of the holy warriors. They found in it another proof that the sword of Islam is just too powerful for the "unbeliever."

The Afghan rumor mill for kinetic purposes starts with the most outlandish and fantastic accusation.

Its effectiveness is easily achieved by the *Quissa Mar* once he grasps the nature of the listening crowd and the Afghan male's mind.—*Five little girls have been kidnapped by American infidels who have taken them to a remote base and have repeatedly raped them while forcing them to witness the horrible desecration of Holy Qurans. The unbelievers defecated on the Holy Books before burning them. They are keeping the poor girls as sexual slaves, and they are being kept at what the infidel calls FOB Ice…*

Why is this story so appealing to the average Afghan male? Because it appeals to different sources of the avengers' masculine pride: the fighting spirit, the male bravado, the purity of the religious, the curiosity of the youngster and the rage of fathers and brothers. These avengers are Afghans who are both naïve and reactive. They are prone to participate in shows of force in order to defend their beliefs and prove their masculinity. These males, no matter what their age is, behave like a bunch of eight-year-olds. Once they hear the story, with its lurid details, they do not even bother to check it out, as their best friend recounted it and he has heard it from the *imam*.

Death to the infidels!—They start chanting together as they turn off their radios that had been blasting an Indian song about a man's desperate love for an unreachable woman of higher financial means—the harmonic melody that makes the young men's blood boil and swells their strengths with words that they can't understand.

A crowd of 2,000, not the 20,000 that could be mustered in a real emergency *jihad* but enough to do real damage, approaches menacingly the base manned by a few hundred Italian *Bersaglieri* (Italian light infantrymen). A few more bystanders realize that the scene is getting exciting, so they decide to shut their shops and to join their *baradar* (brothers).

They are only getting snippets of the horrible story from the crowd's excited mouths, but they go along anyway because, God forbid, they ever joined the infidels *Bersaglieri* holed up inside the forward operating base where the girls are being kept in chains. They finally understand what those infidels were up to with their secretive behavior.

The great majority of these poor young Italian military personnel, in the wrong place at the wrong time, are from *Casoria*, *Casavatore* and *Casal de' Principi*, in the Naples province, one of Italy's poorest areas with 40 percent unemployment and a *camorra's* kingdom. They have joined the military because the armed forces were the only way out.

They are between 20 and 30 years old and, like their Slovak partners in Kandahar, are wondering why they find themselves in a God-forsaken place called *Farah* instead of walking, arm in arm, with their *ciaccarelle* (cuties) on the sun-soaked *via Partenope*, finally free from Naples' automobile noise.

These kids might come from thousands of miles away but are as naïve about life as the boys facing them. They just left the protective embrace of their mothers, families and community, and the fear of the unknown can get them as jumpy as the boys outside the wire, but real excitement for them comes only when their football team is playing the deceitful archrival—the *Northerners*.

They were told they were going to Afghanistan to help the very people who were now shouting at them from outside the wire. Were they deceived by their commanding officers?

Back at their barracks in Salerno, they had watched Enzo Monteleone's movie *El Alamein—The Line of Fire*, because the Italian military still believes in its glorious defeats rather than its few successes. After watching the mandatory movie, which was meant to rally their spirits into emulating the glorious discipline of their unfortunate World War II brothers, they had left the screening with the words of the protagonist permanently stamped in their memory: *Death is only beautiful in schools' history books; in real life it is pitiful; it stinks of charred flesh.* The words were pronounced after a particularly bloody encounter with the British, who were now fighting alongside them in Afghanistan. *World history is the greatest movie.*

They know about the latest rumor, the one that is inflaming the crowd, and they are thinking: *Who makes up these freak stories? These American kids can act like nuts, especially when they take pictures posing with the corpses, but would they ever take advantage of little girls? Why don't these crazies out there go and take it out on the Americans instead of threatening us?*

The crowd gets rowdier—*Ma perche non se ne tornano a casa? Sta a vedere che qualcuno adesso si fa male* (But why don't they just go back home? Just look, someone might end up getting hurt). American flags get burned. Stones are hurled by a few Afghan youngsters wearing Italian football shirts.

The stones come in with wide arches and hit the soft roofs of the tents just inside the perimeter walls. The boys from the *Mezzogiorno* (the Italian South), under their heavy Kevlar helmets and their cockerel feathers, are wondering why so much anger is coming from the same people they have traded friendly banter with until the day before.

Some of the kids throwing stones even play in the football team they have challenged numerous times before. Claudio recognizes Atatullah in the crowd and swears to himself to kick his butt next time he shows up at the base with his duffel bag full of Pakistani pirated DVDs.

All of the boys are keeping a worried eye on the crowd and on their female colleague Rosaria, who appears to be the calmest of all, while manning the heavy-caliber machine gun on the *ralla* (the turret) of the *Lince* armored vehicle. The men admire Rosaria's *balls*.

Suddenly, as a signal, one AK47 shot gets fired and ricochets right in front of Rosaria, the shot is followed by many others. It looks like they are coming from everywhere, although many of them might be directed vertically, straight in the air. Who knows? The noise is infernal, eyes get blurry, the smoke and smell of cordite intoxicates.

Il nervosone (the nervous one), Massimiliano, who has been the most homesick of the entire group, opens fire with his AR70/90 machine gun. Its 5.56 millimeters rounds are not aimed vertically, up in the air. They tear through the legs of two older men and through the little body of Qandigul, the four-year-old mascot of the camp's football team.

She was so popular with all the soldiers, with her great smile and great singing voice, always ready to sing a lullaby when prompted for the benefit of the female soldiers bearing the gift of a doll, crayons or hair bands.

Little Qandigul had joined her dad in the crowd because it was a fun and exciting thing to do. As usual, her patient father had tried to order her back to the house, but she was always a strong-headed little girl, stomping her miniscule feet with her little plastic flip flops. She was the love of his life and could do no wrong. Even the Italians had come to love her stubbornness when she sternly refused to hand the ball back once she had gone to pick it up during breaks in the game.

A father, suddenly older, much older than his 28 years of age, is staring at the limp body of his little girl, gripped by a speechless grief. There is no more anger in him, no more vengeful feelings toward the infidels' arrogance, no more desire to show his masculine bravado. He can no longer hear the gunfire. The chants, the shouts, and the story about the American rapists have dissolved into the dusty air. Where has little Qandigul, father's light of his life, gone? It has dissipated in a millisecond with the smile of a beautiful four-year-old who had just started to learn how to write: *yak, du, sey, chaar, panj, shash* (one, two, three, four, five). Her little plastic flip flops are left behind on the cold dirt outside an Italian base.

The mandatory ISAF investigation ensues, and ARSIC (Afghan Regional Security Integration Command) West directs the Italian CIMIC (Civil Military Cooperation) cell to divert more cash to those projects that had been sitting for so long on the desks of the PRT (Provincial Reconstruction Team) because of dwindling funds. The two clinics, the electric station and the spaghetti factory are finally being funded, and Qandigul's father will meet with General Antinori's entourage that will make sure his pain is soothed with adequate compensation. Just another day in Afghanistan. A day like thousands of others.

Qandigul will be remembered by her family and by her neighbors for many years. They will recount stories of a sweet, vivacious little beauty with bright eyes and flowery flip flops who died in the war with the infidels. Her dad and mom will have another daughter, two years later, and she will have the same *laqab* (nickname) Qandigul—the Sugar-flower.

Massimiliano is headed home, just as he wished, but he will never talk to anyone about war; he will never again want to think of the firefight. War will be with him forever. He will not be like one of those soldiers who get stuck in a camp outside the range of real fire for a full year, in Kuwait, for example. They spend the long tedious time staring at tents and containers and taking pictures of themselves in full battle gear. Those who come back home and wear t-shirts that say: *500 kilometers—The race to Baghdad*—but have never been once in the Iraqi capital.

They will have war stories to tell. Massimiliano will not.

They will proudly display their "war" pictures to their friends and family and will start their stories with *when I was at war…* Massimiliano, with a real war in his heart that he cannot manage to make disappear, will never start a phrase with that premise or Qandigul will, yet again, come and visit him in his nightmares.

In the episode of FOB Ice, deceit has influenced and somewhat served a number of people. Those actors who employed the tool believe it is historically and morally justified, for it leads to a number of justified outcomes. Justification is subjective. The Afghan *Warlord Inc.*, for example, stands to benefit from instability. Money, especially coalition money, flows easily into areas considered troublesome and insecure. The Afghan rumor mill is the primary tool for those who take advantage of the political economy shifts created by instability. Regional power brokers get more influence, funding and authority by taking advantage of the need to quell instability.

In the transition to Afghan hands, many local strongmen or downright criminals and smugglers stand to benefit from the Western reaction to secure a security-unstable area. Deceit might even be shaping the new power structure of Afghanistan, and it might be justified not only as a warfare tool but also as an economic-development tool. If deceit brings security and development over the long term, is it justified?

Is deception an acceptable instrument for the fulfillment of legitimate societal objectives defined as such by local or national interest? Who referees when the defense of one has to be seconded to the interest of others? A certain strongman, whose family has ruled over a particular area for longer than any recent Afghan central government, might oversee the land using policies that foreigners consider controversial. During this period of ISAF presence, he will have faced an enormous amount of scrutiny from anticorruption pressure groups, yet he might claim that the well-being of the families he rules over dictate the rules of engagement and that the end justifies the means.

What is good for the nation as a whole in the international environment constitutes national interest. What is good for the nation as a whole in domestic affairs constitutes public interest.

As mentioned, it is important to fully understand the nature of an audience before crafting messages aimed at *influencing the target's emotions, motives, objective reasoning, and ultimately the behavior of governments, organizations, groups and individuals.*

For the past ten years, we have attempted to study Afghan society in detail. Here is my offer of a snippet. An entire other book could be written about the human mapping of Afghanistan, however, the following are general observations that should quickly get to the point, borrowing not only from personal experience, but also using a very intelligent graphic depiction of allegiance in Afghan society that is a product of the United States military community.

An old Somali proverb regarding societal allegiance in that land recites: *Me and my nation against the world, me and my tribe against my nation, me and my family against my tribe, me and my brother against my family, me against my brother.* The same can be said of Afghan society.

The following two graphic illustrations are extracted from an excellent booklet titled *Afghanistan Smart Book* and produced by the United States TRADOC Culture Center based in Sierra Vista, Arizona, in cooperation with the Defense Intelligence Agency. The *Afghanistan Smart Book* is an unclassified publication on Afghanistan that gets distributed to military personnel who are operating in the theater. The literal reproduction parts of the booklet might be prohibited for commercial purposes, but the choice of including it without editing is a testament to the excellent job TRADOC did in this case.

AFGHAN IDENTITY
Loyalty and Decision-Making

Least Important → Most Important

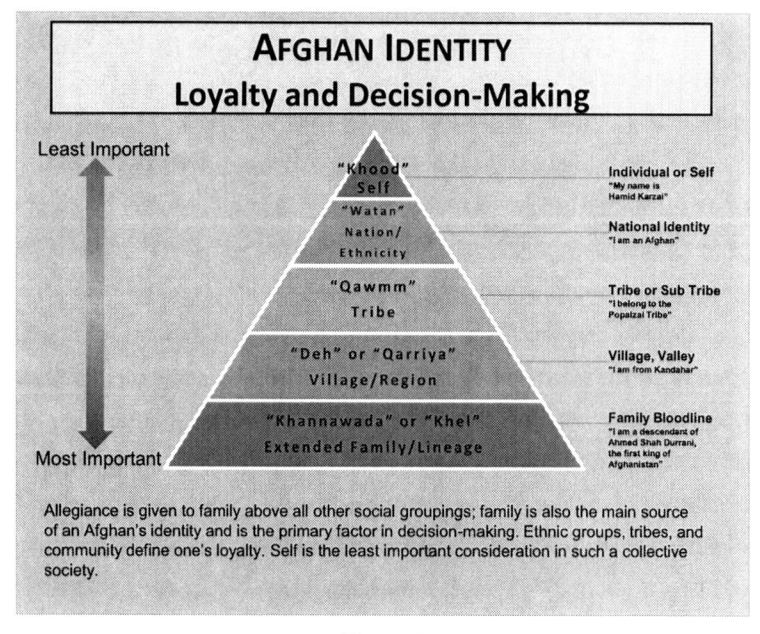

- "Khood" Self — Individual or Self — "My name is Hamid Karzai"
- "Watan" Nation/Ethnicity — National Identity — "I am an Afghan"
- "Qawmm" Tribe — Tribe or Sub Tribe — "I belong to the Popalzai Tribe"
- "Deh" or "Qarriya" Village/Region — Village, Valley — "I am from Kandahar"
- "Khannawada" or "Khel" Extended Family/Lineage — Family Bloodline — "I am a descendant of Ahmed Shah Durrani, the first king of Afghanistan"

Allegiance is given to family above all other social groupings; family is also the main source of an Afghan's identity and is the primary factor in decision-making. Ethnic groups, tribes, and community define one's loyalty. Self is the least important consideration in such a collective society.

Figure A

AMERICAN IDENTITY

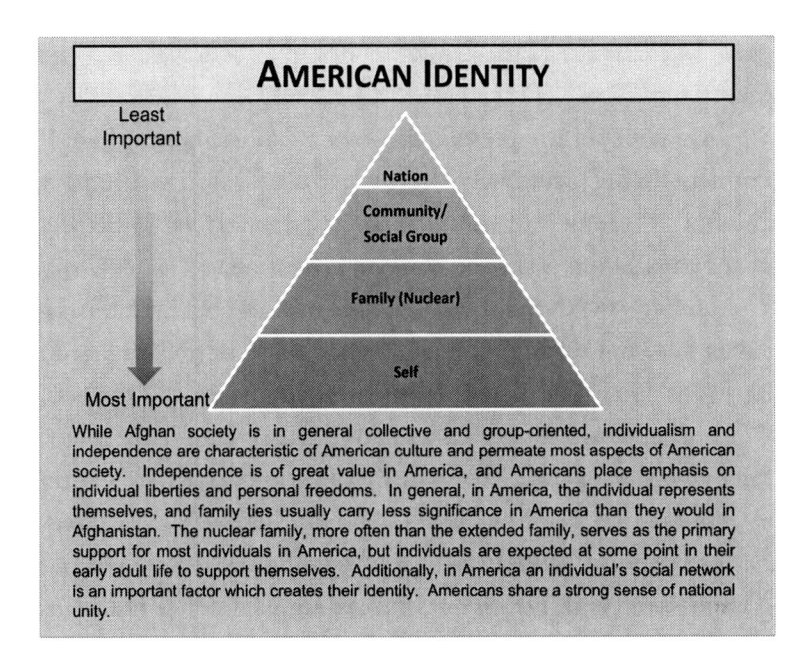

Least Important → Most Important:
- Nation
- Community/Social Group
- Family (Nuclear)
- Self

While Afghan society is in general collective and group-oriented, individualism and independence are characteristic of American culture and permeate most aspects of American society. Independence is of great value in America, and Americans place emphasis on individual liberties and personal freedoms. In general, in America, the individual represents themselves, and family ties usually carry less significance in America than they would in Afghanistan. The nuclear family, more often than the extended family, serves as the primary support for most individuals in America, but individuals are expected at some point in their early adult life to support themselves. Additionally, in America an individual's social network is an important factor which creates their identity. Americans share a strong sense of national unity.

Figure B

I have personally read a number of books on Afghanistan history and culture, and the TRADOC booklet might have easily surpassed them all. These tables effectively depict the pyramid of the Afghan loyalty structure (Figure A) as opposed to its US equivalent (Figure B), and images are worth a thousand words. Looking at the pyramid, how would one define what is good for the Afghan nation as a whole in the international environment?

An individual talking about his fascination for national anthems described his interest in being able to detect a nation's soul by just listening to the melody and the verbiage of its anthem. The anthem—he affirms—describes the spirit of a nation.

The warrior hymn, the *Star Spangled Banner*, tells of a people ready to fight against all odds to defeat tyranny. In the great battle hymn of the United States of America, there is no mention of God.

Afghanistan is represented by the *Milli Tharana,* which is not a hymn but a compromise. It is a mish-mash, a melting pot attempt. It is sung in Pashto, the language spoken by 35 percent of the population, with the obligated mention of *God is Great.* The anthem mentions the names of most of the Afghanistan tribes so as not to short change anybody and in the attempt to represent 35 to 47 different ethnicities, languages and dialects.

The anthem itself, which very few Afghans outside the armed forces listen to or sing, tries to unify the interests and allegiances by representing *Pashtuns, Tajiks, Uzbeks, Turkmens, Nuristanis, Baluchs, Aimaqs, Quizilbashs, Brahuis, Wakhis, Farsiwans* and *Hindu-Sikhs.* Within each one of these ethnicities, one finds tens of tribes and families. If a national anthem is a representation of a national spirit, how does one define public interest within Afghanistan?

In a *minestrone* like Afghanistan, the *wastah,* the taking care of each other, has been the only real instrument of public-interest implementation within the tribal structure and the strength of family allegiance for the past two millennia.

In Afghanistan, how applicable is the Western concept of a centralized democracy that acts as a guarantor for equal representation, power sharing, security development and a uniform judicial apparatus?

When the finest minds in the West decided that we had to be involved in shaping the building of a new national Afghanistan, were they deceiving themselves? Were they deceiving taxpayers, or were they just incredibly optimistic to the point of insanity?

Ancient Romans had tried to expand their "democracy" into the rest of the known world, and mighty Rome had the willingness to stay in the fight for centuries at a time. Rome was willing to either totally eradicate another culture, as in the case of Carthage, or to just stay clear of trouble, as in the case of Northern England, the Anglia north of the Adrian Wall. And Rome failed at it.

Bearing witness to the mighty Romans' failure, how did we think we could accomplish the arduous task within ten years?

In Afghanistan, or as Western military personnel say, *downrange,* duplicity is omnipresent. In government ministries, in the headquarters of major international organizations and within the field offices of international development agencies, we are just paying each other lip service. Westerners are being told what they want to hear because they are not considered feasible long-term partners by the Afghans. We all know that, sooner or later, we are going to leave. We are telling Afghans that we believe they are ready to take over security and that we will stand by to help them should they get in rough waters, yet we do not believe either of the two statements.

Even those who have fully endorsed the mission of our military in that land deeply recognize that we will not stay in Afghanistan in perpetuity. Knowing the precipitous timing to which the American public opinion is addicted, we even expect to anticipate a pullout with respect to the date that has been made public. The reason for our withdrawal is not because we lost the war or because it is too expensive or because we believe the Taliban will never take power again. The truth is that we will be, one day, gone because we just do not belong there.

In villages, I have yet to meet a single humanitarian worker, a single military officer or a diplomat who is willing to give this news, to an Afghan, straight—*we are leaving because a long-term engagement of this kind is impossible to sell to today's Western public. Friends, you are now on your own; call us back when you have discovered oil or when a few crazies who want to blow us up happen to take residence again in your land.*—We all think of it, yet we can't tell our Afghan partners. Is this not duplicity?

The simple truth might have been relayed at higher levels between governments as early as 2010 but, as late as the middle of 2012, the people in the villages, the farmers, the illiterate foot soldiers in the Afghan National Army or the Afghan National Police, are hearing a different story. Afghanistan is made by villages and not by Kabul. Suddenly, at the beginning of 2013, we delivered the news we always knew we were going to come out with sooner or later.

Kabul, at the end of 2012, felt like what Saigon must have felt like during the dying days of America's final mass involvement in Vietnam. Most NGOs and International Organizations were in demobilization mode. However, one can still meet a few die-hard crazy humanitarians who, I am convinced, will remain in Afghanistan no matter what. It is difficult to say what the percentage is of those heroes, but they are certainly a small minority of the operators on the ground.

Deeply the Afghans knew the truth, the reality of recurrent history, before we even confirmed it to them. They do know where we stand and they are *playing the game*. After all, they have already played it with the Macedonians, the Arabs, the Mongols, the British and the Russians. The Americans and NATO are just one other "empire," that have happened to rush through their history and failed to definitely shape its course.

With Vico's *circularity of history*, the nature of a self-repeating cycle of events is in full motion. We will be gone like many other *koregees,* and the Afghan families will remain and will go back to what they have done for the past two thousand years—they will go back to their stories.

We might believe we have given these families a glimpse at modern development and democratic freedom, but, in reality, we might have just added a few more good stories to their historical repertoire. For many in the big cities, especially the younger generations, these will be tales of disappointment, betrayed expectations and of longing for distant liberal ideals. For many villagers in remote areas, those who are repulsed by both us, the *Goats,* and by the Taliban, those who shy away from the temptations of modernity and want to be left alone, the memory of this war will be somewhat confused with the memory of other invaders.

The sequence of events and timelines between the Westerner's war and the Russian invasion might be blurred in the future memory of the villagers and in the stories that will be made up for generations to come. The stories of glorious fights between the proud villagers and the boys from South Dakota will be mixed with the tales of victories against the boys from Siberia.

In 2007, at a fireside get-together, I listened to the story of an intelligence officer who had operated in the *Korengaal Valley.* A few years prior, he had gone along to a number of *shuras* with local villagers and realized that a lot of the locals hadn't even realized that the Russians had gone. They thought that some of these weird *koregees* had come from Vladivostok or Smolensk and were surprised when none of them were willing to sell them their issued weapons or ammunitions. They had been able to barter anything with the *koregee* soldiers before. They could not understand why the Russian soldiers were not willing to part with their weapons anymore.

54 • *The Afghan Paradox*

In 2012, a Tribal Engagement military officer told me that when he had gone into a village on the border between the Uruzgan and the Zabul provinces, the local elders had enquired as to where the visiting soldiers were coming from, and, when they were told the place was America, the villagers claimed they did not know where or what it was. They asked whether America was one of Pakistan's districts. Two of them had traveled to Pakistan in the past and had recounted the incredible vastness of that land.

How many years, decades or centuries would it really take to settle that misunderstanding?

Drawing by Meranda Keller

War and Its Story Makers

> *"...I say to you: that we are in a battle and that more than half of this battle is taking place in the battlefield of the media. And that we are in a media battle in a race for the hearts and minds of our Umma."*
> — Ayman al-Zawahiri to Abu Musab al-Zarqawi, 9 July 2005

Not everyone wants to be a storymaker. Even storytelling does not come natural to many.

I have tried, for the past 46 years, to get stories out of my father. My dad has 75 years worth of material that he keeps guarding jealously; he would be a wealth of information, yet he is reluctant to say much. Every once in a while, unexpectedly, he reminisces loudly, and his children become an eager public. We all want to know the reasons behind the way we were brought up, our traditions, our legacy; we want him to gift us his past. The gift, however, does not come easily due to his shyness and introvert character.

My father lived through a World War as a child, ended up with his extended family in an Allied concentration camp for internally displaced refugees after his own dad had led the family out of the hell of Monte Cassino. I often pry him to get details of his experience, and the few times my father opens up about it, he almost chokes at the memory of the corpses of young German paratroopers lying by the sides of the roads with newspaper pages covering their faces in a final show of piety. Dad remembers the same kids forcibly entering his family's house, and, when Grandma had faked a heart attack to distract them, the German soldier had told her: "*Mom, do not worry; we mean no harm; we want to go home.*"

After the devastating experience of war, Dad went on to live the dream, *la dolce vita*, of post-war Italy. He built businesses, made money and lost it; he traveled the world as much as he could, but he is very parsimonious when having to give out too many details about this great life of his.

I asked a great number of people to contribute stories for this book—a former USAID (United States Agency for International Development) employee, a US Army Human Terrain social scientist, an Italian Army Civil Affairs officer with a few Iraq and Afghanistan tours under his belt, a Canadian journalist who is very much involved with Afghan women's rights, a number of Western humanitarian volunteers, Afghan writers, politicians, poets and members of my Afghan staff. Each one of them brought up different reasons, but most of them declined to contribute with one of their stories.

It is not that people have no stories to tell; the point is that storymaking is an art and is not anybody's talent.

It is traveling that one meets the most interesting characters. One should never discount the importance of casual encounters. Anybody, and I mean anybody, has something to teach. On a coast-to-coast flight in the United States, I sat by a 94-year-old man accompanied by his 72-year-old son.

They had bought fried chicken before they boarded the plane. I was literally starving, and the aroma was killing me. I jokingly offered to buy the chicken from them and got rebuked, but it was this casual ice-breaker that gave me the chance to start a conversation with the older man.

I am ninety-four years old, and I crashed twice—he started. *What do you mean?*—I asked—*Plane crashes?*—I was already thinking of getting out of the aircraft as he said, *yes, I was shot down twice over North Africa in 1942.* Now, that was interesting! I pressed for more details. Nothing more was offered. How selfish was that? Any aviator who survives being shot down twice has been endowed by the Creator with a great story to tell again and again. I mean I really believe that fate bestowed on the old man an obligation to tell the tale, yet he turned his face straight and became lost in his thoughts.

The 75-year-old son must have sensed my disappointment and chimed in, confirming that it had been impossible even for him to get anything more than *I was shot down twice over North Africa in 1942* out of his dad over the years. The majority of people like to hear other people recounting their stories. There is something that I call *relationships overload,* which is what I call when someone just shuts off to the outside world, but I understand that, in most cases, this condition is just short lived.

One can experience many encounters and storytelling staying in the same place during the course of an entire life. Motion pictures and reading help the mind in that case. A minority of individuals embark on frequent geographical *quests* to gather these human interactions. *Gather* might be the appropriate verb.

It was in April 2006 that I found myself on yet another of my frequent quests to seek human stories. This time it was in Kabul, Afghanistan.

In my opinion, the *quests* to gather the best stories, the stories that, in the Western world, get recounted to friends at the bar or in social settings, those quests that offer material for numerous stories, stories that are very entertaining and spark laughter, tears and interesting conversations, do not tell of *mojitos* at the beach bar of the Ritz Carlton in Dubai or of the roar of Formula One cars in Monte Carlo.

The *quests* that give us stories people want to hear about have to do with experiences that listeners would like to live but have no intention to pursue because of fear or pure laziness.

They might be *quests* that entail sleeping outside in distant lands' freezing weather, while in danger of being robbed; or environments where, over the course of six very long days, one ends up discovering orifices one never thought possible because of feeling compelled to accept a lunch invitation at a street *kabob* vendor on a trip back from Bagram Air Field to Kabul's city center.

Quests like these create great stories, and some of these stories eventually become jokes. Some of these jokes get grosser and even more fantastic and funnier with the passing of time. One recounts them frequently while trying to get the listener to live the scene as if he were the protagonist. Just a spectator with the benefit of no real danger posed—as entertaining as going to the movies without the discomfort of leaving one's family room's couch.

Quests and storymaking go hand-in-hand, and stories are the juice of life. What would life be without exploration? Most explorers go through the same experiences, almost like a rite of passage. The first common rite of passage for Afghanistan quest seekers is diarrhea.

So if good stories can be dramatic, those that might be preferable for nights out with friends are the very funny ones. Like a story that details how one would be feeling, while stuck in Kabul's traffic, a very important man for his staff, sitting next to a driver in a minivan full of *chadri* (the all-covering Afghan light blue veil) clad women, with his bowels aching from either an amoeba or *Montezuma's Revenge* or whatever these street vendors' *kabobs* can give to the delicate Westerner's digestive system.

The very important man sets sight on the InterContinental Hotel that looms at Kabul's dusty horizon as if in a thirsty legionnaire's mirage of an oasis in the Great Eastern Erg desert. The very important man directs the driver to get there fast, please, very fast. The sounds coming from the man's stomach are now clearly audible by everybody in the van. Yet the very important man has no more shame, and he is truly contemplating to relieve himself into his trousers. Every sudden stop in Kabul's choking traffic is an excruciating moment and a test of his will. The driver protests that the InterContinental Hotel security guards will never let the van in. The VIP looks at the driver with the last few remnants of authority that his diminishing social status still affords and answers: *You think so? Watch me!* He is now considering relieving himself just behind the guard post if the guards prove to be too zealous. There is no shame in meeting extreme circumstances with exceptional actions. Even the absence of toilet paper is the last thing on the VIP's mind. The *chalkhi dori* (gate guards) at the base of the steep climb to the heaven of the InterContinental take just one look at the crazy-eyed VIP *koregee* (foreigner), and that look speaks loudly to the drama that is unfolding, so they let the van through. The driver was wrong, the VIP right, as usual. The satisfaction of being proved right is not what is on the VIP's mind, anyway.

The chairman of the board of directors of Physiotherapy and Rehabilitation Support for Afghanistan, one of the oldest nongovernmental Afghan organizations, exactly three hours after having conferred at high level, with a great show of expertise and Western professionalism with the Secretary General of the Afghan Red Crescent, is re-enacting the legendary Jeff Daniels toilet scene from *Dumb and Dumber* in the plush surroundings of the InterContinental Hotel restrooms. Stomach bugs know no social status. A *Tajik* peasant, a stunning actress, a French general or the President of the United States are all the same when diarrhea occurs. Diarrhea is a social equalizer. Afghanistan is a generous host when it comes to its equal opportunity policy of stomach-bug allocation.

Then, a *Quissa Mar* might always trump the funny story with a black-humor finale. One might state that the VIP did more damage to the hotel than the Taliban's attack four years earlier. I have personally witnessed children and women laughing to the story. Hard-earned social status re-dimensioned by poop talk is as internationally appreciated as pizza!

Once the *quissa mar* has finished mimicking the entire story so that the listener can visually picture the ridicule in the drama, the people in the audience will be disheveled, with tears of laughter streaming out of their eyes, whether they are middle-aged British stockbrokers, American teenagers or *Tajik* and *Hazara* women. I have witnessed the story recounted and mimicked to these exact audiences, and the result has been consistent. The hilarious reality of an "important" man on the point of being embarrassed for pooping his pants is global. Especially when listeners can identify themselves with a similar episode. Who can deny having, at least once in their lives, risked soiling their underwear? Almost everyone has stared at the abyss, and most avoided falling in it. Laughter is also a sign of relief from preoccupation. Authority gets greatly diminished by a simple, irresistible, sudden bowel movement. Re-dimensioning human rankings by very common physiological needs makes comedy, and comedy is a great pacifier.

The best stories come from explorations, and we call these experiences *quests* because this is what they are: a constant searching of one's own soul. Some can find themselves by searching inside; I personally envy those individuals. I wish I could be one of those who can travel thousands of miles in the course of a transcendental meditation session or an hour of *bikram yoga*.

On a hot Arizona afternoon, one of those hot yoga sessions can make any hard man crumble. It is either the sheer physical exertion or the claim by your female yoga partner that the session makes her feels like she is traveling through the jungles of Borneo among tigers and rare birds that makes you feel like you are just sweating your exhausted butt off in a stinking hot yoga studio in Scottsdale, and that's it. If you are one of those who do not feel like you have been in Borneo and you head to the bar next door to the studio to down five cold Coronas, one after the other, and that actually feels like heaven, then you might be ready for the Kabul *quest*.

When we try to have deep conversations while sipping espressos in a dusty Forward Operating Base (FOB) somewhere in rural Afghanistan or Iraq, we state that we envy these people who can stay still. They can touch the center of their own being by just standing in the middle of an incense-filled sanctuary or by staring at their children. We philosophize, genuinely wishing we could be one of those, but deeply we know it is just not us. Restless souls are just that—restless souls. The souls feel like they are resting only when time is being taken to recount the *quest*. *Quissa Mar* might be individuals of chaos, but they rest their souls in describing dramatic action and idyllic scenes. We are those who manage to find inner peace in the middle of social conflict: Iraq, Tunisia, Guatemala, and, why not?—Naples, Italy.

Yes, Naples, Italy. I come from an area of Naples with the same population density as Kolkata. Even Kabul, with its traffic and improvised explosive devices, is quieter. When human beings coexist on top of each other, the noise of their voices never quells; it is a constant murmur. If one wakes up at three in the morning in Portici, a city annex to Naples, of 100,000 inhabitants per square kilometer, one can hear *a voce de' criature* (the creatures' humming), this constant, relentless whispering tune constituted by the reverberation of thousands of voices trapped in a labyrinth of Neapolitan stones—humanity's echo.

A Neapolitan song recites: *Napule e' a voce de' creature ca saglie chianu chianu, e tu sai ca nun si sule.* (Naples is the creatures' humming, which rises steadily so that you know you are not alone). I left Portici when I was ten, and I have felt alone since. I have been searching for the *voce de' criature* ever since. When I hear it, I can hear my soul speak. My soul does not speak to me in the silence of *bikram yoga*. It does in the mayhem of Tunis' main bazaar, in Kabul's traffic and in the chants of Tarin Kowt's *muezzin*.

Quissa Mar are into soul quests; their better stories do not come from their minds but from their souls.

I have come to the conclusion that most Westerners end up doing humanitarian work in war-ravaged areas to be able to hear their own restless souls. I am one of them. Our souls have stories to tell; they are great sounding boards. If we allow the soul to be vocal outside the confines of our physical bodies, if we unleash its ability to talk, we make history.

Just before I landed in Kabul for the first time, I thought *What better magnifying lens a talking soul than the vociferous, boastful, poor, ravaged Afghanistan?* Kabul's messy streets talk to me. I have heard the same impression from many people who are hooked on the *Crossroads of Central Asia*. There are plenty of Afghan junkies, not in the sense that they are the drug addicts of the '60s, but they tend to be a number of NGO workers, a few diplomats and journalists who, once they get in that land, they can't leave anymore. Definitely Afghanistan is puzzling, and its inhabitants enthrall, confuse, enchant or repulse most of the Westerners who come in contact with them.

After returning home from Afghanistan, people wanted to know about my experiences with these people from a country smaller than Texas who, over the past 30 years, have managed to get more press time than most of the other world nations. After my initial trips there, I had to think very hard when asked what I thought of the Afghans. Words used to escape me when trying to describe the people I had met.

Initially and superficially, nothing more would come to my mind other than "they are peaceful people who have a terrible love of war." At social get-togethers back in the United States or in Europe, I found it easy to describe the Afghans as real-life *Klingons*. I could swear that, especially in rural *Pasthunistan,* a lot of those I had met, be they farmers or warlords, even looked and sounded like Star Trek's *Klingons*.

During some of my first rural *shuras,* I really felt like pulling the stunt of jumping up and shouting—*beam me, up Scottie*—in my switched-off cellular phone. I imagined the puzzled look on the villagers' faces and the embarrassment of my translators. I never did it, but the thought keeps reoccurring every single time.

My initiation into the *Quissa Mar* game came during one of my first negotiation meetings with a local civil servant. The level of corruption in Afghanistan is stunning by any standards.

Mid-level bureaucrats are often illiterate but hold allegiances that keep them in employment. In this instance, I was asked to mediate with the manager of the Kabul *Marastoon* on behalf of an NGO. A *Marastoon* is a center for long-term shelter managed by the Afghan Red Crescent.

After the usual initial pleasantries, as soon as I met the man in the *Marastoon*'s main courtyard, he launched into a diatribe. He was claiming that the Western male volunteers were trying to Christianize the center's residents and, even worse, they were trying to sexually compromise the honor of the mentally handicapped and almost toothless female patients of the *crazy house*—the mental health section of the *Marastoon*. The man had secured statements from two female residents who had confirmed the allegations. He held a stern, serious gaze while offering his speech, but he kept avoiding eye contact with me. The stories became more and more fantastic and outlandish by the minute. Suddenly, it dawned on me that, not only was I immensely enjoying his stories but, most importantly, I was not his intended audience. His audience was the great number of residents who had come to listen and were crouching or standing in a circle around the two of us, my interpreter and his minder.

He must have thought I might have been one of the mentally challenged residents because I kept looking at him and smiling. I had the weirdest feeling in me—one of gratefulness, as I kept admiring the man. I was witnessing a real Afghan *Quissa Mar*. I was finally experiencing the typical dance of Afghan deceit in its most creative and artistic form. The only true part of the man's story was that the NGO team had visited the *crazy house* for about 30 minutes, two days before. Therefore, this wasn't even manipulation of truth—it was a complete re-invention of reality.

I kept staring at the *Quissa Mar* and thinking: *This guy is the Raphael, the Picasso, of bullshit!*

He was good. I could not help but admire him. The more I questioned the veracity of his stories and allegations, the more he came up with amazingly minute details to prove that his tale was veracious. All the residents around us had bought into the story. They believed it, and they were proud that this man was standing up for the honor of these defenseless women. While the interpreter kept translating the *sceneggiata*, the *Marastoon* director's staff kept nodding vigorously, completely sold on the fact that one of my volunteers, married back home to a former Kansas State University's cheerleader, was sexually molesting a sixty-year-old, severely handicapped resident of their mental health facility.

I tried to glimpse at the "victimized" woman who was standing in the surrounding crowd. Just glimpsed because I didn't want to be accused of lusting over her, and she kept staring at the floor, drooling and muttering the same thing over and over again—*here comes the queen.* The guy facing me but not looking at me was the Salvador Dali, the *genio impresionante* (the impressive genius) of mass persuasion; he might not have known me but he knew his people well, and his story was sticking.

He managed to speak for half an hour without more than three looks in my general direction. My respectful silence and my willingness to listen were empowering him, and I felt like he gradually relaxed. We started dancing, and he realized I could do it without the risk of degenerating. When he pretended to get very animated and belligerent, I would think—*Man! General Martok here loves to argue*—and would let him vent. When all was said and done, after a two-hour show, we shook hands. I had the volunteers reassigned to another facility, and the *Marastoon* manager allowed my organization access to needed supplies. I apologized profusely if "his people's" sensitivities had been hurt. He saved face and looked like a hero to his constituency, a sort of *Salâ ad-Dîn* of the *Marastoon,* and I went away feeling that I had not given up too much. There is no reason for pride when negotiating with a *Quissa Mar.* The important thing was that, from that moment on, the man knew that *I could play his game,* and he insisted only on dealing with me. A lot got accomplished that period.

Then the more I met Afghans like the *Marastoon Klingon,* the more it made me reflect on the fact that, actually, most humans find a way to spar in one way or another. It does not often lead to warfare, but if we think of forums such as sports, political debates and religious preferences, they are either arenas for dissent or reasons for arguments.

With regard to sparring that leads to lethal consequences, rhetoric teaches us that modern wars are fought in the name of peace, yet we have to admit war is truly fought for war's own sake. Much is written about the nature of warfare, and plenty of self-defined "experts" have talked about the lethal consequences of conflict and about ways to get rid of them once and for all. None of the Afghans I have talked to would attest that there are, in fact, solutions to the tendency of human beings to take each other out. Most Afghans are experts about war. If we want to know more about a particular subject, we consult the subject-matter experts. Those who are frank at admitting this terrible love for conflict are the individuals we should rely on to fully penetrate this timeless force in human history, for they have made of conflict management and resolution a *raison d'etre.* Warriors have no reason to exist without an enemy. The enemy and the pursuit of victory over the opponent give the warrior meaning. A warrior without war is nothing. The average Afghan male without war is nothing.

How can one truly appreciate peace without fully understanding or even embracing the social usefulness of conflict? How can one personally develop any clear understanding of destruction by relying only on theories from history books, statistics, doctoral theses and socio-analytical case studies? A few weeks deeply embedded into the Afghan rural scene exposes any traveler to the nature of warfare.

After a number of encounters with *Quissa Mar,* Afghan men can become any foreign warrior's soul mates. Warriors, whether they are invaders or defendants, infidels or believers, end up discovering an unexpected kinship with each other. *Quissa Mar* are the safe-keepers of the warring oral tradition; they are the diplomats, the negotiators, the emissaries who always precede the bout. Most battles in Afghanistan were never fought. They are averted with a switch of allegiance or a compromise. There is a lot of space between shouting and shooting. Afghans work hard at increasing that space. They possess a deep appreciation of a familiarly dramatic dance—the eternal waltz of love and destruction. The dance of Venus and Mars, of *Ethos* and *Thanatos*—a dance that both the Afghans and foreign warriors love to the point of giving up all they should hold dear: wives, daughters, sons and relatives. They give it all up because all they know is that they have to keep dancing to feel alive.

The biggest question that people in the West keep asking me is whether Afghans are inherently peaceful or aggressive. My answer is that the majority of Afghans, especially males, are inherently aggressive. The *Quissa Mar* repertoire is overwhelmingly made up by conflict narrative. Asking the same question to different Afghanistan veterans might yield different answers.

The social-libertarian leaning NGO worker from Copenhagen might tell you that the average Afghan is a peace lover and is definitely tired of the devastation that has affected his land. Ask the British Royal Marine, from Dagenham, who just came back from a four-month combat tour in *Helmand* and you will hear a number of colorful cockney expletives accompanying his depiction of Afghan innate and incurable aggressiveness. Both, the Danish humanitarian worker and the English warrior will offer *Quissa Mar* material to support their views. The stories from both might be convincing.

Like with most vital decisions, the answer to this basic question is not in the story itself but in the way the listener metabolizes it and makes up his mind. The listeners' learned behaviors, upbringing, education and spiritual beliefs are all deciphers that actualize the story. It is a deeply personal perception that assigns a meaning to a story. An Afghan *Quissa Mar* is a profound *connoisseur* of his listeners; foreigners have often formulated communication for Afghan consumers based on American-styled narrative—straight to the point, concise and devoid of flowery inventions. At the end of the day, in story-making and storytelling, it is the listeners who make up their own mind and react accordingly to their experience and beliefs.

In December 2012, I had been serving as the public affairs officer for SEAL Team Four, a US Naval Special Warfare unit assigned to support the Afghan Special Forces in the Afghan southeast's Uruzgan province. Two days before Christmas, the Team's commanding officer passed to a better life. Our official statement was curt, bearing little detail surrounding the death and the SEAL's life. Hardly any Afghan media outlet "picked up" the news. A few days later, two fantastic stories began circulating. The first one was that the Commander had perished while flying with Secretary of State Hillary Clinton on a mission to Iran. His plane had crash-landed in Iran and had caused his death and the Secretary's head trauma. They had both been evacuated with the cooperation of the Iranian government, and the story was somewhat confirmed by the Secretary's announced admittance into a US hospital. The second story was that the commander had killed himself and that he was the one in charge of the team that had killed Osama Bin Laden. The story, broadcast all over Afghanistan and Pakistan on line media, clearly stated in the same paragraph that the Commander was in charge of SEAL Team Four and that SEAL Team Six had conducted the Osama Bin Laden operation—a flagrant contradiction that no Afghan picked on.

For the next three days, a number of Afghan interpreters kept stopping me in the camp cafeteria, ecstatic about their association with a man whose commanding officer had personally killed Bin Laden and had sneaked out of Tarin Kowt to assist Mrs. Clinton on her top-secret negotiations with Mahmoud Ahmadinejad. The interesting part was that they were not really interested in what I had to say about it. They were deaf to my denials and to my assertions that the stories were just too idiotic. I came up with precise facts and my personal testimony, all of it to no avail—they had already made up their mind. Any other rendering of my Commander's death was just too banal for them to relay to their friends and families.

The Afghans suffer from a typical human condition—that of being constantly passionate about the dynamics of human confrontation. They can spend countless hours engaged in this jousting—they love it. When one is passionate about something, time ceases to be important. Time stalls, the clock stops ticking. *Quissa Mar* make up stories about their world's love for the Gods of War. They craft tales catering to the eternal superhuman myths of insatiable horror and renewed hopes. Such myths display, on one hand, their lack of human dimension by employing an incessant narrative of cruelty, devastation, rape and annihilation and, on the other hand, a lesson for the soul when the cruel stories are culminated by a beautiful outcome of redemption, like peace that can finally blossom with its healing force. The myth of annihilation feels so inhuman, yet is pursued by human beings with continuous occurrence.

The described philosophical posture of the *Quissa Mar*'s stories is not solely rooted in the Islamic credo. There is plenty of Judeo-Christian literature that celebrates the inevitability of the *yin-yang*. There is plenty in the Scriptures about the equilibrium between opposite forces. The Holy Texts are not only about peace. In the Old Testament, in *Ecclesiastes,* one of the three Jewish *Ketuvim* (the Writings), Chapter 3, recites: There's a right time for everything, There's an opportune time to do things, a right time for everything on the earth: a right time for birth and another for death, a right time to plant and another to reap, a right time to kill and another to heal, a right time to destroy and another to construct, a right time to cry and another to laugh, a right time to lament and another to cheer, a right time to make love and another to abstain, a right time to embrace and another to part, a right time to search and another to count your losses, a right time to hold on and another to let go, a right time to rip out and another to mend, a right time to shut up and another to speak up, a right time to love and another to hate, a right time to wage war and another to make peace. But in the end, does it really make a difference what anyone does? I've had a good look at what God has given us to do—busywork, mostly. True, God made everything beautiful in itself and in its time—but he's left us in the dark, so we can never know what God is up to, whether he's coming or going. I've decided that there's nothing better to do than go ahead and have a good time and get the most we can out of life. That's it—eat, drink, and make the most of your job. It's God's gift. I've also concluded that whatever God does, that's the way it's going to be, always. No addition, no subtraction. God's done it, and that's it. That's so we'll quit asking questions and simply worship in holy fear. Whatever was is. Whatever will be is. That's how it always is with God.

In Afghanistan, the inevitability of the *yin-yang* is just accepted. It is the necessary ingredient of life. There is no pretense of searching for absolute peace or absolute goodness. Some things are not preferable yet accepted; good and bad are accepted as eternally linked. As humans, we all seem to need gods and beliefs as much we need friends and enemies. Affiliation and, again, empathy become so important that other needs seem to be secondary. Poverty and lack of comforts are almost forgotten when they are conditions shared by many, when the common purpose subsumes the individual necessity.

The sublime symbol of humans' inherent fear is a need for security that closely correlates to our need for friends and allies. In Afghanistan, the same factor motivates the desire for the existence of an enemy. Enemies in Afghanistan are as socially important as allies because freedom from fear, in that land, is not often achieved by embracing love but often by perpetrating a destructive act. Attacking and defeating the enemy is the expression of the desire to overcome such fear with a spectacular show of consistency and power—the ultimate power to decide between life and death, the power to transfer one's own fear onto another. Once all enemies and allies have been identified, war can take place—and war is the ultimate Afghan ritual to banish fear.

Acts of unnecessary cruelty and lack of proportion are common not only among Afghans but Western troops, too. I would bet that those Marines who filmed themselves while urinating on insurgent corpses might be engaging in an unconscious ritual of defeating personal fears—their own styled exorcism of war. The willingness to film oneself while perpetrating an abominable act might be seen as a desire to immortalize a moment when fear was finally dominated for good—as one could frame that moment forever.

Are Afghans—these veterans of horror—a people inherently fearful or fearless? This is the other question often asked by the people back home. My personal opinion is that the average Afghan, male or female, revels in their ability to subdue fear. When one picks up a fight with these people, how does one instill fear in the opponent without the massive use of horror? My views on this subject are influenced by my conversations with a number of Afghans, especially males, whose majority assured me that they need enemies because they deeply believe that peace mollifies the soul. Life is better, more intense and great when it is short and lived with the full waves of a passion that only the sublime clash of love and hate can create. A swift honorable death in a *jihad's* battle is preferred to a long life of idle poverty and monotony.

Dulce et decorum est pro patria mori (it is sweet and honorable to die for your nation)—the Romans told their barbarian foes of the Republic and the Imperial *beautiful* death for something higher than oneself. They taunted their adversaries, scaring them out of a fight, before it even took place. In the initial scene of the movie *Gladiator* by director British Ridley Scott, a Roman army faces the Germanics who have refused an offer to terms. The Roman lines are ready to "unleash hell," and General Maximus, the Roman commander, is walking through them with final words of encouragement. His Chief of Staff greets him and asks a common question in that era—*Will they fight?* That was the nature of ancient warfare with the initial fight of wills. The Romans would make sure all enemies knew that they were ready to fight to the death. If you belonged to a tribe who had a different inclination, you better back down and agree to terms. Both Americans and Afghans employ the same technique, and they are ready to call each other's bluffs. Just one kind of Afghan does not know when to back down—the naïve one.

National statistics indicate that one percent of the American population is willing to go to distant lands and get killed for the defense of the homeland. Out of that one percent, a lot of military personnel have made it a choice of monetary convenience rather than a true willingness to get torn to pieces in a forgotten place thousands of miles away from the comforts of home. Without the need for official statistics, I am fairly sure that a much greater percentage of the US population would be willing to die in defense of their land once the enemy breaches our borders. If this attitude of the American people—this fighting spirit—is known around the world, with the history of the past 300 years bearing witness to the American inclination not to hold back punches when a fight takes place, it is also well known that the unwillingness to commit the "ultimate sacrifice" that other forces of the coalition have displayed in Afghanistan is closely correlated to their cultural background.

In the story of the encounter between the menacing crowd and the *Bersaglieri,* it was mentioned how the Italian soldiers were asked to watch the movie *El Alamein—The Line of Fire* directed by Enzo Monteleone, in their pre-deployment training. In the movie, a war story about one of the most valorous military engagements of World War II, there is a beautiful scene when a young Italian volunteer first encounters the brutality of combat. He had joined to fight a gallant fight, inebriated by the Fascist propaganda that war is won with heroism, faith and the natural superiority of the Italian fighter. After the onslaught of Indian and New Zealand's Maori troops, who had broken through the Italian lines during the night but had been dramatically pushed back, the young soldier keeps staring at the corpses of the soldiers from both sides, entangled in a brotherly embrace, now that their fight is over, and writes home: *Alla fine la guerra, quella vera, e' arrivata… Oggi ho visto in faccia l'orrore, a scuola ti insegnano 'fortunati quelli che muoiono da eroi' no ho visti un bel po' di questi eroi, I morti non sono ne' fortunati ne' sfortunati, sono morti e basta, marciscono in fondo ad una buca, senza un briciolo di poesia, la morte e' bella solo nei libri di scuola, nella vita reale fa pieta' e' orrenda e puzza.* (At the end, war, the real one, came to us. Today I stared in the face of horror; at school they taught us that men who die like heroes are the lucky ones, I have seen a bunch of these heroes; dead soldiers are neither lucky nor unlucky—they are just dead; they rot at the bottom of the bomb crater without a bit of poetry. Death is only beautiful in school's history books; in real life it is pitiful, it stinks of charred flesh.)

A movie like *El Alamein* does not inspire to die for whatever greater cause. Afghans have an easier time posturing against troops of nations who are not willing to engage in bluffs. An Afghan would not write about war in the way the young Italian volunteer did. I have yet to watch an Afghan movie that constitutes a total condemnation of war—there is always an abominable, unjust enemy who justifies the use of horror.

One day, I went to visit a remote village in a relatively safe area north of Kabul. I went there escorted by the driver and the interpreter. We had a nice visit with the local *Malik* (Village Head) and a bunch of *Mishr* (Elders) from the surrounding villages. I had even purchased a nice-looking *karakul*, the sheepskin cap for people of distinction like Ahmid Karzai. The young men of the village and surrounding areas, a lot more than I ever saw during a *shura* (meeting), squatted, forming a circle around us. In no circumstance, that day, did I feel threatened or ill treated. To the contrary, I felt very welcome and accorded the maximum courtesy by the villagers' traditional *melmestia* (hospitality). As it was getting late, we took up the *Malik*'s offer of shelter, again in a perfect show of traditional *nanawati* (asylum granting). We retired to the relative comfort of the assigned guest house on the outskirts of the village. I kept wondering how many times itinerant Taliban or Al-Qaeda fighters might have been granted the same courtesy and protection and how many of them might have rested their heads on the very *baalesht* (pillow) I was using for the night. I do not take for granted, or expect, the villagers' adoption of *Pashtunwali* (the code of the Pashtuns), as it really varies in its implementation from clan to clan or even from village to village within the same clan. The guest house was reasonably clean and warm.

At about four in the morning, all hell broke loose. The nearby New Zealander and Turkish FOB came under attack by increasing small-arms fire. Peeking through the few openings, we could see the same young men, who had entertained us so jovially a few hours before, run holding Kalashnikovs, some of them firing in the air and frantically whispering to each other. I expected our hut's door to burst open and to finally end my *quests* once and for all. For a few moments, I even longed to be a *bikram yoga* fan and, right there and then, I would have swapped the Afghan guest house with the stinking hot Scottsdale studio on the spot. I promised to myself—*if I make it alive out of here, no more needs for crazy quests and a bikram yoga studio life membership!* Even there, I might have been deceiving myself, for the hut door never burst open, nobody ever came in to shoot at us, and I never ended up getting a *bikram yoga* studio life membership.

The firefight outside was over in less than 30 minutes, and we did not manage to get any more sleep. We did, however, dare to leave the guest house, emotionally exhausted but still full of adrenaline, in the early hours of dawn. Dazed, we saw the same young men who had participated in the firefight, most of them smiling again just like the night before. They were bringing us *chai (tea)*, *naan* (bread) and hot *shirberenj* (porridge) for breakfast! Were we being served breakfast by the Taliban?

The interpreter must have realized how puzzled I was, my adrenaline still pumping because of the shootings of a few hours earlier. He spoke with the youngsters and started nodding his head in a gesture of understanding approval and then turned around and calmly explained that the young men were deeply apologetic for having disturbed our sleep, but a few of their itinerant *baradar* (brothers) had organized the execution of this elaborate *ejiraa* (battle plan) as a *show of force,* months before. The *ejiraa* had been debated at length by the local leaders and the religious students coming from Afghanistan during a number of *shura*, and it had been authorized by the majority of the chiefs and elders with some important limitations to the allowed bloodshed. For instance, the raiding party was to stop at a safe distance from the *koregee*'s military installations, and, if the sound of air support would be detected, the attackers had to immediately break off the engagement and go back home (that was not the drone age). The young villager assured us that it was one of the most exciting things that had happened in the area for the past seven years and that most of the local men, especially the young ones, did not feel like they wanted to be left out.

Naturally, these males had to pick between joining their *baradar* or the soldiers of the coalition, and they could not have possibly joined the *koregee*. It was an amazing night; most commented emphatically and *Inshallah* (God's willing) there had been no casualties on either side. This, for them, had been no more than medieval jousting. *What if one of them had gotten killed?*—I asked, floored by the absurdity of the explanation—*Then the village would have had his first Jahiid (martyr) in seven years*—the villager's reply came promptly.

I was wondering whether the coalition troops who came under the "jousting" attack knew of the real nature of the threat. I kept thinking if the sudden burst of uncontrollable fear would cause some of these foreign soldiers countless sleepless nights and lasting psychological issues. The questions I had about these young Afghan villagers were—*don't these guys get combat-related post traumatic stress disorder (PTSD) like ours do?—Is this all just a big game for them?*

Afghans, in general, seem so familiar with death. In big cities, young men are exposed to all the paraphernalia of modern society. But in the rural areas, which make up 90 percent of the country, they are nothing like our kids who play video-game virtual killers on *Call of Duty* or *Sniper Elite* on their *X-Box*. Our boys and girls learn about shooting others in video games, and, after they have heard the Marines or the Army calling to use their skills, they decide to join, *'cause they can do this shit for real!*

The Few, the Proud, the soldiers of the Army of One, go on to uphold the military posture of a great nation, one who will call any enemy's bluff if needed. But that night, north of Kabul, I started asking myself whether the American generations might have changed so much that the majority of our children, those who are taught to bluff by video games, might not be the best emotionally equipped, no matter how excellent their military training is, to call other fighters' bluff. I hope my son will never have to square off against a boy from *Shinkai* province. The boy from *Shinkai* has nothing to lose.

That night, I started worrying that a lot of our young *virtual killers*, as soon as they march in the dust of *Fallujah, Mogadishu* or *Khost* and get close enough to touch the headless guy they have just taken out from 1,000 yards away, will quickly lose their virtual bearings. We all understand that the first victim of war is innocence, but I started wondering whether that loss of innocence affects Afghans and Westerners differently. I keep thinking of my son, just after he has seen his best friend, Josh, bleed to death and asking for his mom or, even worse, when he has to collect from the blood-soaked dirt the little kid he has just shot by mistake while the kid's hysterical mother is cursing him forever. I am afraid our children might decide they want to die at their own hands to end the pain or they just stop functioning properly in their society of origin. In 2012, in the United States military, more personnel took their own life than we lost in combat-related incidents.

How many calls do our suicide-prevention centers receive from the latest virtual killer who is holed up in his dad's pickup truck, in the parking lot next to Camp Pendleton, and cannot coherently explain the fire that roars in his brain, why he feels so lonely and abandoned that this is burning his soul.

Does the same thing happen to those Afghan young men? Are there any suicide-prevention call centers in Kabul, Jalalabad or Kandahar for young Afghan men with PTSD? What is the suicide rate among Afghan fighters? These kids should be scared of us; for all intents and purposes we are the modern Roman war machine. The power of our weaponry is devastating. We have definitely gotten a lot more efficient at killing our opponents. Can one imagine our kids being on the receiving end of an *AC130 Specter Gunship's* barrage? We balance the downside of modernity—the mollification of the souls—with warfare technological advances. How much would the increase in the psychological malfunction be of our young warrior if our medieval enemy could field the same terrifying destructiveness of our weaponry?

To our kids and to the boys of the larger cities in Afghanistan, the image of death comes in a video game, a Hollywood blockbuster or a social media video. The rest of the Afghan's reality is one of immense natural beauty, but, for most of the fighters, it is a reality of dusty, bustling refugee camps turned into cities across a nonexistent border with Pakistan. It is a reality of dusty goat trails and natural impregnable fortresses. The dust these young fighters breathe reminds them of the millions of corpses that have been buried underneath. In Afghanistan, you can never fully bury the dead. The dead come alive in the glorious stories of the *Quissa Mar* so that the myth of war is allowed to continue and to give all of these youngsters, who have nothing else, meaning.

Drawing by Meranda Keller

On Sex and the Afghans

> "It is difficult to comprehend our attitude toward women. We cherish them. We love them. We protect them. And we dedicate most of our poetry to them. But we do not want them cluttering our life."
> — Shah Khan, the wealthy landowner in James Michener's *Caravans*

In Media Stat Virtus (virtue resides in the middle), extremes might never be good for societies, whether in food consumption or in sex, in passions or in aplomb, in any kind of overuse or underuse, extremes can produce very severe social malfunctions. There is plenty of literature about Afghanistan covering any possible subject in the land. I personally read five historical books covering the "graveyard of empires," eight titles about women's stories, two about drug proliferation, three about recent warfare, two regarding the Russian experience, two poetry books, one about Pashtun stories and countless other smaller publications, military reports, NGOs studies, et cetera. I have yet to find a book about sexuality in Afghanistan. I spent a full day rummaging the shelves of Sultan Khan's bookseller, the famous "Bookseller of Kabul," immortalized in a book by Asne Seierstad, searching for the forbidden subject. I could not even find a few pages of a study produced by an obscure NGO dedicated to women's subjects. The place is an overpriced treasure cove where one can find a lot of goodies. I found a few expensive social treaties on the mating habits of Asia's most common mammals, but nothing about the Afghans' relationship with sexuality. Buying Nancy Friday's *My Secret Garden* masterpiece on female sexuality in Kabul could get you pretty much stoned to death. Bringing it to Afghanistan, hidden in one's luggage, and gifting it to an English-speaking warlord makes you a hero, a welcome guest, a "Lion of the Region."

The very delicate subject of sex and the Afghans is not being documented. It is not even talked about. Most Afghans, I am sure, have very healthy sex lives and, rightfully so, talk very little about it in public settings. What is not being discussed with frankness is the plague of sexual deviancy in the land. It is not a popular subject because it hurts the susceptibilities of the devout and the outright bigot, but it is, without any doubt, the cause of a lot of trauma and strife.

One might argue that there is nothing about Afghanistan that conveys a sense of equilibrium. Definitely, it is not a land of middle grounds, particularly when it comes to sexuality. There is nothing balanced about the approach to sex, especially at the bottom and at the top of the Afghan social stratification. It would take an army of social scientists to accurately map the fabric of the land's *social capital* and their attitude toward gender issues and sexuality. A *Quissa Mar* has no ability to examine whether this complete lack of balance in sexuality is based on restrictive Islamic beliefs or on the demographic composition of urban and rural settlements. I had personally witnessed the same peculiar approach that young Afghan men have with women in Iraq in 2005 and 2006. In the pockets of orphaned kids or young captive insurgents, one would find rudimentary and childlike drawings of matchstick figures depicting, or trying to depict, females.

In Iraq some of these primitive drawings had stringy blond hair. In Afghanistan, one could also find a few pictures cut from the DVD covers of pirated Hollywood movies or images from the publicity material announcing the coming of the Afghanistan Star show into town. These little pieces of *sexual* literature, almost completely faded by use, accompany the everyday life of these young men. These are female images that, in the western world, would not cause arousal in the least. For an Afghan youngster, the sight of an uncovered shoulder or calf might be too much to bear.

Boys' lives are often subjected to *complete* apartheid from females of the same age group. Young men, growing up in larger urban concentrations or who are educated in *madrassas* or orphanages grow up confused as to how they should relate to the opposite sex. Those who go back home at night and have mothers often get spoiled into believing that they carry a lot more importance and status than their sisters or female cousins because it is the men who are the future sole breadwinners. A lot of them witness a very patriarchal approach to decision-making, in which the woman is no more than a supporting actor. Most of them are stuck into perennial teenager self-centrism and never grow up.

I have met a number of Afghan men in cities who have never emotionally grown up. They maintain their childlike posture to life. If they are sexually repressed, they tend to be more aggressive; if they are married and have a wife (or wives) and children, they tend to be domineering and narcissistic.

This incidence is less present in rural life, where women pick up a lot of the men's burden and work the land and domestic chores with no less strength than their male peers. In rural areas, however, both illiteracy and poverty are more rampant, and I met a few farmers who have no qualms selling their male and female children into slavery, at times sexual. More rarely, even wives have been known to be *seconded* to others to make up for financial losses, repay debts or merely to generate income.

Thankfully, the attitude of these men is balanced by a majority of Afghans who maintain self-respect and who abide by the *Pashtunwali* rules of protection. Even in most of the emotionally immature narcissists, the defense of personal, and, therefore, the family's honor comes as a priority. Male emotional immaturity is not a malady limited to feudal environments; even modern Western societies seem to display their shortcomings when it comes to men's emotional development. A study of the effect of inbreeding on the emotional development of the Afghans has been accepted as a very plausible source.

If one wishes to start a heated discussion among Westerners in Afghanistan, one might meet a number of journalists and humanitarian operators at a Mexican restaurant in central Kabul (a restaurant that I understand is now closed). There are a number of subjects that are guaranteed to start an argument—the emotional maturity of men, globally, is one of those subjects that can be considered the *slam dunk* of vociferous remonstrations. This very subject—of men's arrested emotional development—can be charged up with a general statement such as: *I have witnessed the same malady in the US, in Italy and here in Afghanistan. I blame the mothers for not educating their boys as to the value and the supreme importance of the feminine…* One might postulate this opinion loudly adding that, *If Afghan women could start enforcing their power and importance with their own male children, we would be able to change the status quo within two generations.* Then one might sit back and enjoy the debate that a few words like those can generate. Even the Norwegians, whom generally one can't get to react to anything meaningful, start behaving like a bunch of Latins and display feelings about the subject.

When the conversation gets going, this place ceases to be an ideal spot for romantic dates; restaurants like those are almost sanctuaries for geographical bachelors. A geographical bachelor or bachelorette is an individual who seems to be going through a divorce every time he/she gets deployed overseas. Geographical bachelors are *Quissa Mar*.

It is a very well known fact that, in war zones, some individuals feel exceptionally lonely and seek the companionship of a healing hand. In war zones, the acceptable threshold for attractiveness lowers dramatically. A plain-looking librarian looks like a *Playboy* centerfold after one month in Kabul. An average-looking accountant type or a security contractor with a 53 Intelligence Quotient, bulging biceps and a *six pack* might be considered the resident Brad Pitt. Plenty of deployed military personnel assure that romances and sexual escapades spark between female soldiers of the coalition and Slavic soldiers, who, in the words of a veteran Non Commissioned Officer—*back at home could only mate with small farm pets*.

It is now almost a tradition for the pilots of military transports taking personnel out of the war zone, to announce on the loudspeaker: *Ladies and gentlemen, you are just now flying over the Afghan border into Tajikistan; congratulations on making it back safely. Ladies, from this moment on, you are ugly again.*

The point is that if Westerners fail to uphold sexually ethical levels while deployed to a war zone, the Afghans have taken the practice of sexual deviancy completely into *gutter* standards.

On a typical Afghan side note—if one has never been to a restaurant like the Mexican one in central Kabul and wonders how much it would cost to take a date there, here is the answer: *If you work for an NGO, about $15 per person, plus tip. If you work for the American Embassy or for USAID, about $200 per person, plus tip. Cost of the actual meal $15 and $185 for the four shooters from the private security company who had to escort the dates to eat burritos.* This might be added to the Travelers Guide to Kabul.

Overall, the Afghans love beauty. Normally, their standards are high because there is plenty of beauty in Afghanistan, both natural and man-made. Afghan women are, on average, stunning but tend to age a lot quicker than our women, because of their lifestyles, the lack of gyms, beauty parlors and plastic surgeons.

Afghan men are, on average, also very good looking, but they tend to age or die very early, too.

Afghan kids are torn between the celebration of romantic love that can be found in songs and poetries of the land of *Rumi* and uncontrolled lust if they even witness clean ankles protruding under a *chadri*. These kids might exchange little innocent love notes with girls the same age and experience full-blown sex with other boys in their school dorms, sometimes with the complicity of adults.

One could debate whether the strict Islamic application of *Wahabist* social rules, applied by the Taliban movement, somewhat curtailed the onslaught of sexual deviancy across the country or created a time bomb of sensory repression. There are plenty of records that demonstrate that perpetrators of sexual crimes were severely punished under the Taliban, although it is said that not all members of the movement were in fact pure in their sexual practices. The book *The Kite Runner,* by Khaled Hosseini, published in 2003, describes two episodes of strong sexual theme—the rape of one of the boys by older kids and then a Taliban commander owning a *Bacha Bazi,* a boy dancer, whom the protagonist of the book eventually frees and takes to the United States.

One should spend time getting to understand the *Bacha Bazi* phenomenon. No matter how much I try to rationalize it, I personally find it disturbing, immoral and perverse.

Young boys are enlisted and, at times, literally enslaved to provide entertainment and sexual favors to powerful Afghans. Historically, *mujahidin* commanders, primarily from the North, would spend long periods of time fighting and away from female companionship; therefore, they would adopt a boy.

The *Bacha Bazi* practice goes a bit further. Poor children, as young as nine or ten years old, are purchased from their fathers or recruited from orphanages and trained to dance, sing and play a variety of musical instruments. Their ability to perform artistically might even become legendary, but the expected *clou* of the artistic performance is often the offering of sexual favors. These boys become the life of parties organized for the benefit of powerful men, former commanders and warlords. The owners of *Bacha Bazi* are generally rich men of limited education. The number, beauty or fame of the *Bacha Bazi* is a source of prestige for his owner. A powerful man might envy another just because he cannot own a *Bacha Bazi* who belongs to the other man's *stable*. *Bacha Bazi* are rented out for bachelor parties, just like exotic dancers or prostitutes in other cultures. Frequently, fights start between men who desire and claim sexual ownership for the night. Winning the right to possess the *Bacha Bazi* after a particularly admired performance confers status. The fights that might ensue sometimes claim the lives of these kids, victims of the perverse attraction of grown men who never grew up.

In Michener's *Caravans*, a book that describes a much-older Afghanistan, a similar episode of murderous consequence is narrated. An honor killing gets perpetrated because of the uncontrollable jealously, generated by a beautiful *Bacha Bazi*, between a young itinerant farmer and a policeman. Both of the young men are mesmerized by the *Bacha Bazi*'s irresistible beauty, but, incredibly, neither of the two is homosexual.

For a Westerner, it might be difficult to comprehend the dynamic of this kind of attraction, and this is not the kind of subject one might want to discuss with Afghan males to get more clarity. The few with whom I have been able to talk about this matter were married, well educated, had children and were clearly heterosexual. By *clearly heterosexual in Afghanistan* it is meant that there had been no overt sexual advances coming from these subjects. These men were declaredly against the *Bacha Bazi* practice.

The *Bacha Bazi* is not a recent phenomenon. It has ancient roots, and the indications are clear—its recent recrudescence is due to the fall of the Taliban, who had somewhat limited its practice. Religious extremism might be bad for society, but, in this case, it had temporarily worked for the right cause.

One of the most interesting studies about sexuality in Afghanistan is an unclassified eighteen-page study by a United States Army's Human Terrain Team (HTT) titled *Pashtun Sexuality*, in 2009. A great number of military personnel of the coalition, who are directly in contact with Afghan nationals over a protracted period of time, have read the report. Like other studies and stories I have elected to report, it is recounted almost *verbatim* in this book, courtesy of the US Army Human Terrain Program, so that its strength is not diluted. The only changes I have had to apply have to do with the explanation of military abbreviations and the adaptation of references by which the study is rigorously supported. The style of the report has been brought in line with the *Quissa Mar* narrative of the book. Also, the identity of the author, a female social scientist, to whom goes all my admiration, has been purposely omitted:

The Human Terrain Team AF-6, assigned to the Second Marine Expeditionary Battalion and collocated with British forces in Lashkar Gah, has been requested by these forces to provide insight on Pashtun cultural traditions regarding male sexuality for reasons of enhanced baseline cultural understanding for improved interaction as well as any Information Operations (a warfare tool) applicability.

Because of the extremely sensitive nature of this investigation, traditional HTT techniques involving a directed research plan and series of interviews executed to generate, test, and confirm hypotheses are not feasible. Direct questioning of Pashtun male interviewees on the subject is further hindered by the female gender of the social scientist writing. Instead, findings here will be based upon field observations and interview responses by Pashtun men which were revealing regarding the topic, although discovered through the lines of questioning of other investigations. As sexuality is an essential building block of all human interaction and culture, these incidences of insight have been abundant, even couched in other research goals. Secondary interviewees who have had extensive relevant interaction have been debriefed regarding their experiences. These include public health officers and medics who have treated a number of Pashtun men for sexual conditions, and other service-members involved, like HTT, in relationship-building and interpersonal interaction. Extensive open-source journalistic and academic writings on the subject have been additionally consulted, some involving directly quoted answers from Pashtun interviewees.

A culturally contrived homosexuality (significantly not termed as such by its practitioners) appears to affect a far-greater population base than some researchers would argue is attributable to natural inclination.

Some of its root causes lie in the severe segregation of women, the prohibitive cost of marriage within Pashtun tribal codes, and the depressed economic situation into which young Pashtun men are placed.

Other root causes include a long-standing cultural tradition in which boys are appreciated for physical beauty and apprenticed to older men for their sexual initiation. The fallout of this pattern of behavior over generations has a profound impact on Pashtun society and culture.

Homosexuality is strictly prohibited in Islam, but cultural interpretations of Islamic teaching prevalent in Pashtun areas of southern Afghanistan tacitly condone it in comparison to heterosexual relationships in several contexts. Pashtun men are freer with companionship, affection, emotional and artistic expression, and the trust bred of familiarity with other men. They often lack the experience of these aspects of life with women. This usurping of the female role may contribute to the alienation of women over generations and their eventual relegation to extreme segregation and abuse.

Military cultural-awareness training for Afghanistan often emphasizes that the effeminate characteristics of male Pashtun interaction are to be considered "normal" and no indicator of a prevalence of homosexuality. This training is intended to prevent service-members from reacting with typically Western shock or aversion to such displays. However, slightly more in-depth research points to the presence of a culturally dependent homosexuality appearing to affect a far-greater population base than some researchers would argue is attributable to natural inclination.

To dismiss the existence of this dynamic out of desire to avoid Western discomfort is to risk failing to comprehend an essential *social force underlying Pashtun culture—one with a variety of potential implications upon the efficacy and applicability of ISAF (International Security Assistance Force for Afghanistan) efforts and on the long-term future of Afghan society.*

HTT is often approached for advice by US and British service-members who report encounters with men displaying apparently homosexual tendencies. These service-members are frequently confused in the interpretation of this behavior. The British newspaper article below may be written with an attempt at humor, yet the Marines quoted typify the reaction often seen in service-members upon their initial encounters with Pashtun males. As HTT has observed with frequency while on patrols in Helmand and Kandahar provinces, these men are outwardly affectionate toward both one another and male ISAF members, are extremely gentle in their demeanor and touch, and have often taken great care in embellishing their personal appearance with fingernails dyed red, hair and beards hennaed in careful patterns, and eyes very occasionally subtly outlined.

The article titled "Startled Marines Find Afghan Men All Made Up to See Them," by Chris Stephen ran in the national newspaper The Scotsman *on May 24, 2002. Not even in reference to the more heavily Pashtun southern areas of Afghanistan, it read: In Baghram, British Marines returning from an operation deep in the Afghan mountains spoke last night of an alarming new threat—being propositioned by swarms of gay local farmers. An Arbroath Marine, James Fletcher, said: "They were more terrifying than the al-Qaeda. One bloke who had painted toenails was offering to paint ours. They go about hand in hand, mincing around the village." While the Marines failed to find any al-Qaeda during the seven-day Operation Condor, they were propositioned by dozens of men in villages the troops were ordered to search.*

Another interviewee in the article, a Marine in his 20s, stated, "It was hell… Every village we went into, we got a group of men wearing make-up coming up, stroking our hair and cheeks and making kissing noises." Beyond reacting to the unusual sight of made-up men, which one can readily accept as a style unique to a different culture, these Marines appear to have no doubt that they were being sexually propositioned.

One of the primary and obvious causes of this cultural tendency toward sexual expression between males is Pashtun society's extremely limited access to women. Heterosexual relationships are allowable only within the bounds of marriage, and Pashtun honor demands that a man be able to demonstrate his ability to support a wife and family, as well as produce abundant wedding-gifts for the bride and her parents, before he is allowed to marry. Therefore, given the economic situation of most young Pashtun men and the current state of employment and agriculture within the Pashtun regions of Afghanistan, marriage becomes a nearly unattainable possibility for many.

A controversial Los Angeles Times article highlighted this issue and featured an interview with a young Afghan man whose situation was typical of this circumstance: In his 29 years, Mohammed Daud has seen the faces of perhaps 200 women. A few dozen were family members. The rest were glimpses stolen when he should not have been looking, and the women were caught without their face-shrouding burkas. "How can you fall in love with a girl if you can't see her face?" he asks. Daud is unmarried and has sex only with men and boys. But he does not consider himself homosexual, at least not in the Western sense. "I like boys, but I like girls better," he says. "It's just that we can't see the women to see if they are beautiful.

"But we can see the boys, and so we can tell which of them is beautiful." Daud's insistence that his behavior should not label *him as homosexual is the next important point in understanding the nature of this dynamic, and opens the doors to a complex interrelationship between Islam and its cultural interpretations. Even men who practice homosexuality exclusively are not labeled by themselves or their counterparts as homosexual.*

To identify as such is to admit an enormous sin in Islam—one punishable by death under the Taliban and one that would result in severe tribal and familial ostracization today. However, it appears to be the label, not the action or the preference, that poses the greatest problem.

In the context of rural southern Afghanistan, the relationship between Islam (here defined as the teachings of Prophet Mohammed as expressed in the Qu'ran) and what is believed about Islam by the local faithful can contain vast differences. This is in great part due to a barrier in language and education. Not generally able to understand Arabic, the language of the Qu'ran, which is not to be translated, the Muslim faithful of southern Afghanistan rely on the teaching and interpretation of local Mullahs to inform them of what the Qu'ran says. The more rural the area, the far less likely it becomes that even the Mullah himself understands Arabic and the more likely that what is taught is based upon local cultural tradition, independent of Islam itself.

Homosexuality is strictly prohibited in Islam, but cultural interpretations of Islamic teachings prevalent in the area tacitly condone it in comparison to heterosexual relationships. A typical expression, echoed by a number of authors and interviewees, is that homosexuality is indeed prohibited within Islam, warranting great shame and condemnation. However, homosexuality is then narrowly and specifically defined as the love of another man.

Loving a man would, therefore, be unacceptable and a major sin within this cultural interpretation. A punishment of death for individuals publicly labeled as homosexuals remains a possibility even now, outside of Taliban rule, if enforced by an extremist family or tribe members. Familiar recent news highlighted the situation of the young Afghan actor who portrayed a victim of male-upon-male rape in the film The Kite Runner. He had to be removed from the country due to death threats.

Reading and understanding Koranic Arabic are two very different things. Muslims around the world, regardless of their linguistic background, are educated in religious schools to be able to read and recite the Arabic of the Koran. That is, they are taught to recognize, pronounce, and memorize the words in order. However, even this education does not teach students the meanings of the Arabic words they memorize. Students who do not natively speak Arabic, like those of Afghanistan, Pakistan, India, etc., remain dependent on teachers to interpret what is written for them, and these interpretations vary greatly depending on the culture and agenda of the teachers of Islam, but using another man for sexual gratification would be regarded as a foible and undesirable, but far preferable to sex with an ineligible woman, which in the context of Pashtun honor, would likely result in issues of revenge and honor killings.

These killings are a Pashtun, not Islamic requirement, although the two tend to become inexorably bound in the minds of rural villagers. Similarly, the social circumstance that has made women foreign and unavailable (excessive veiling, segregation, and exclusion from public life) is generally also attributed to Islam in Pashtun communities, but is in itself a cultural construct, passed and exaggerated through local tradition.

Another example of cultural misinterpretations of Islamic tenants, bent to support homosexuality over heterosexuality, comes from a US Army medic completing a year-long tour in a rural area of Kandahar province. She and her male colleagues were approached by a local gentleman seeking advice on how his wife could become pregnant. When it was explained to him what was necessary, he reacted with disgust and asked "How could one feel desire to be with a woman, who God has made unclean, when one could be with a man, who is clean? Surely this must be wrong." The religious basis for his statement lies in the Islamic regulation that women are ritually unclean for participation in prayer while on their monthly cycle. In the Qu'ran, the tenet does not extend to imply that women are unclean or unapproachable otherwise. However, local cultural interpretations have created the passionately, if erroneously, held belief that women are physically undesirable. Interestingly, the Qu'ran specifies a number of physical circumstances under which a man can be rendered ritually unclean, but none of these are extended to the belief that he is unclean or undesirable in general.

Therefore, it seems possible that such interpretations of Islam are at some point picked and chosen to support already-held beliefs or tendencies. Interestingly, the same medics treated an outbreak of gonorrhea among the local national interpreters in their camp. Approximately 12 of the nearly 20 young male interpreters present in the camp had contracted the disease, and most had done so anally. This is merely an anecdotal observation and far too small of a sample size to make any generalizations regarding the actual prevalence of homosexual activity region-wide. However, given the difficulty in procuring such data, it may serve as some indicator.

Of greatest interest here, however, is the way the men reacted to the education offered them so as to avoid the disease in the future. They insisted that they could not have caught the disease sexually because they were not homosexuals—important evidence of the rejection of the label regardless of the actual activities in which a man engages. Instead, they concluded that it was the result of mixing green and black tea, which became a running joke throughout the camp.

They also continued to return for treatment after re-contracting the condition, having not believed or heeded the instruction they received. These men were also openly observed to simultaneously share the same cots within their sleeping quarters, and did not appear to feel the need to hide or disguise this fact. Again, it appears to be only the label of homosexuality that causes them discomfort.

It's not only religious authorities who describe homosexual sex as common among the Pashtuns.

Dr. Mohammed Nasem Zafar, a professor at Kandahar Medical College, estimates that about 50% of the city's male residents have sex with men or boys at some point in their lives. He says the prime age at which boys are attractive to men is from 12 to 16—before their beards grow in. The adolescents sometimes develop medical problems, which he sees in his practice, such as sexually transmitted diseases and sphincter incontinence. So far, the doctor said, AIDS does not seem to be a problem in Afghanistan, probably because the country is so isolated.

However, beyond the issues of poverty, segregation, and tacit cultural approval which apparently contribute to the prevalence of consensual sex among adult men, there seem to be darker underlying dynamics additionally at play. To begin illustrating these, HTT turns to a field experience in which a principle interviewee was a boy in his very early teens. His circumstance, combined with the nonverbal reaction of his adult male companions to the women interviewers present, was revealing regarding the social and cultural factors underlying the exchange. The following is quoted directly from HTT field notes of the incident: "Upon arrival at Camp Leatherneck in Helmand province, HTT was initially limited in its ability to conduct research with foot patrols and therefore sought to engage Afghan truck drivers who came on to the base for general atmospheric information. For the most part, such drivers are *staunch allies who take enormous risks, as it is publicly evident that they assist American and Coalition Forces, and they frequently face reprisals from insurgent fighters. Also, to be noted, is the fact that truck drivers are highly cosmopolitan in comparison to most rural Afghan populations, as they have seen and traveled within many regions, including Western-influenced metropolitan areas. It should be anticipated that they would therefore be less likely to display local Pashtun resistance to the open and public presence of women."*

On day one, HTT met only a group of four or five truck drivers, all of whom were from Helmand, living approximately 50 miles away from the camp. The most striking interviewee was a boy, about 12–14 years old, traveling with a group of older men. He spoke English beautifully, Dari beautifully, Pashto with apparent fluency, and when asked about other languages he knew, said he also spoke Urdu. This was an absolutely brilliant child. Asked why he was traveling with the other men, they identified him as their "little mechanic" and said he could repair any problems they had on the road. This added greatly to the already very strong impression of the intelligence of this child. The boy told HTT that he was traveling with his brother, an older truck driver, and that their truck had been hit by an insurgent rocket on their way in. (He was proud to point out the location of impact.) The referenced brother was not present. The boy also explained that while their time on the road could be shortened, they take a circuitous route to the FOB, lasting about 10 days, in an attempt to throw off or avoid Taliban attacks.

I was deeply impressed with the boy, yet experienced a sense of wariness from the men who combined looks of distaste among themselves with slightly-too-slow requisite politeness toward the two female HTT members present. They had no such apparent problem with the male Human Terrain Analyst or Team Leader. The latter of the two approached in a US Military uniform. Nevertheless, I left the interview uplifted thinking that the future of Afghanistan was in the hands of brilliant, brave children like this.

This incident was later re-examined in conversation with a group of American interviewees who together and individually spoke with many, many years' experience working directly with the culture in country. They reminded me that one of the country's favorite sayings is "women are for children, boys are for pleasure." One of the interviewees shared stories of how groups of men, e.g., shepherding parties, would always travel with one boy "for fun." Sadly, the talented young mechanic came immediately to mind. HTT produced a picture of him with the group of drivers, and the interviewees were quite confident that their worst suspicions were correct. One interviewee then told the story of a time he found a 14-year-old boy quite literally in the hands of a group of Afghan security guards under his command. He physically fought the guards to free the boy and drove him back to Kabul, hours away, returning him home to his family, from whom he had apparently been forcibly taken in order to travel with the guards.

While in many areas of southern Afghanistan, such treatment of boys appears to be shrouded in some sense of secrecy, in Kandahar it constitutes an openly celebrated cultural tradition. Kandahar's long artistic and poetic tradition idolizes the pre-pubescent "beardless boy" as the icon of physical beauty. 19th-century British authors report their observations of Pashtun fighters singing poetic "odes of their longing for young boys." The Los Angeles Times author cited in earlier notes this tradition as alive and well in very recent literature: A popular poem by Syed Abdul Khaliq Agha, who died last year, notes Kandahar's special reputation. "Kandahar has beautiful halekon," the poem goes. They have black eyes and white cheeks.

Further, even the newly re-emerging musical nightlife of southern Afghan cities idolizes pre-pubescent boy performers, whose star status lasts only as long as their voices remain immature. While *these performers themselves may be quite innocent, the reputation of their availability to patrons of the establishments at which they perform is difficult to dispel.*

Known frequently as halekon, ashna, or bacha bereesh, "beautiful" beardless boys are coveted, almost as possessions, by men of status and position for sexual relationships. Further, the more attractive or talented the boy is deemed, the more his presence elevates the status of his patron. In the article "Afghan Boy Dancers Sexually Abused by Former Warlords," various interviewees state the following:

"Everyone tries to have the best, most handsome and good-looking boy," said a former mujahidin commander, who declined to be named. "Sometimes we gather and make our boys dance and whoever wins, his boy will be the best boy." Former mujahidin commanders hold such parties in and around Pul-e Khumri about once a week. "Having a boy has become a custom for us. Whoever wants to show off, should have a boy," said Enayatullah, a 42-year-old landowner in Baghlan province.

A key feature of this relationship, slightly different from the homosexuality practiced by men with other grown men who have limited access to women as addressed earlier, is its more coercive nature rooted in an imbalance of power (economic, rank-associated, status/age-associated, etc.) between the parties involved. According to one observer: An apparent distinction seems evident in this particular Kandahar variation… The dating and courtship appears more coercive, more opportunistic and seems to take advantage of younger guys who almost have no other choice than to accept the money or gifts from bigger and more powerful "commanders" whose bit of authority is bestowed by their gang-member status, their guns and the shattered legal/police system.

Even where the halekon tradition is not "celebrated" per se, it appears to underlie a number of Pashtun social structures, most notably the recruitment of very young "soldiers" by commanders of paramilitary groups. (This is so much true even today, that current law prohibits "beardless boys" living in Afghan military and police stations.) This in turn fits under the traditional warrior ethos which defines the role of men within Pashtun culture. This dynamic played a major role in the functioning of the warlord culture that preceded the rise of the Taliban in Afghanistan.

By some accounts, the first incident that brought Mullah Omar and the Taliban to prominence in the eyes of the Pashtun people actually involved a dispute between two warlords over a particularly attractive *halekon*. This dispute took the pedophilia of the warlords to such an extreme that the locals themselves were repulsed and happy to embrace a force of reform.

Tim Reid wrote in The Times of London, "In the summer of 1994, a few months before the Taliban took control of the city, two commanders confronted each other over a young boy whom they both wanted to sodomize. In the ensuing fight civilians were killed. Omar's group freed the boy and appeals began flooding in for Omar to help in other disputes. By November, Omar and his Taliban were Kandahar's new rulers. Despite the Taliban's disdain for women, and the bizarre penchant of many for eyeliner, Omar immediately suppressed homosexuality."

Perhaps "repressed" homosexuality would be a more apt statement, as the cultural tendency has not disappeared. However, open displays of homosexuality, in which the label of homosexuality could not be denied, became publicly punishable by crude executions under the Taliban. Now, in the absence of this possibility, the underlying cultural traditions appear to be returning to visible life with greater freedom.

Now that Taliban rule is over in Mullah Omar's former southern stronghold, it is not only televisions, kites and razors which have begun to emerge. Visible again, too, are men with their "ashna," or beloveds: young boys they have groomed for sex.

Kandahar's Pashtuns have been notorious for their homosexuality for centuries, particularly their fondness for naïve young boys. Before the Taliban arrived in 1994, the streets were filled with teenagers and their sugar daddies, flaunting their relationships. It is called the homosexual capital of south Asia.

Such is the Pashtun obsession with sodomy—locals tell you that birds fly over the city using only one wing, the other covering their posterior—that the rape of young boys by warlords was one of the key factors in Mullah Omar mobilizing the Taliban.

However, the Taliban should not be viewed as free of the culture and tradition of homosexuality of the Pashtun world of which it is a part. Writers have argued that even within the Taliban, the tradition of halekon and the isolation of boys from the influence of family while they are assimilated into the identity of a fighting group in which they are also sexually objectified and abused, is precisely what occurred with prevalence behind the walls of the madrassas. The now-iconic Los Angeles Times article on the issue states: "…many accuse the Taliban of hypocrisy on the issue of homosexuality. 'The Taliban had halekon, but they kept it secret,' says one anti-Taliban commander, who is rumored to keep two halekon. 'They hid their halekon in their madrassas,' or religious schools."

Whatever the source, there is frequently the risk that Pashtun boys will face a set of experiences that mold their beliefs regarding sexuality as adults in ways that are ultimately damaging, both to themselves and to Afghan society. It appears that this set of experiences becomes cyclical, affecting generations, and that this cycle has existed long enough to affect the underpinnings of Afghan culture itself.

From these findings, a model of this cycle might be ventured. It seems the cycle begins in isolation from the experience of women's companionship and the replacement of such companionship with men. Significantly, in the case of Taliban madrassas, many boys spend their formative years without even the influence of motherhood in their lives. Women are foreign, and categorized by religious teachers as, at best, unclean or undesirable. It is then probable that the male companionship that a boy has known takes a sinister turn, in the form of the expression of pedophilia from the men that surround him. Such abuse would most likely result in a sense of outrage or anger, but anger that cannot possibly be directed at the only source of companionship over the years, emphasizing Eve's role in man's downfall and emotional support a boy knows, and on which he remains dependent.

This anger may very well be then directed at the foreign object—women—resulting in the misogyny typical of Pashtun Islamism. Men and boys therefore remain the object of affection and security for these boys as they grow into men themselves, and the cycle is repeated.

The fallout from this cycle affects both genders, and could possibly be a part of what leads to violence against women and women's suppression in Pashtun culture. If women are no longer the source of companionship or sexual desire, they become increasingly and threateningly foreign.

Two initial findings add to the cycle of male isolation from women. One, put forward by the Provincial Reconstruction Team in Farah Province, who conducted regular round-table discussions with local women, is that boys, even when raised in the home, are separated from their mothers' care around the age of seven and are considered the charge of their fathers.

Another, more complex phenomenon, highlighted in the Los Angeles Times article as well as the Reuters article and others, is that men who take on a halekon often attempt to integrate the boy into their families by marrying him to a daughter when the boy is no longer young enough to play the "beardless" role. This maintains the love relationship between the father and son-in-law which inevitably makes difficult the establishment of a normal relationship with the wife.

The once-halekon becomes a father with his new wife, and then begins to seek a teenage boy with whom he can play the "bearded" role. The children born to this father inevitably register the nature of their mother's marginalized role. When to this is added the further isolation that occurs when boys are groomed for the halekon role by fighting groups or madrassas, it becomes almost unimaginable that boys would learn to form a normal and familiar attachment to a woman.

Talibs and halekon of fighters and other powerful men, when kept from the one universally nurturing experience of women—their mothers—are left with no way to relate to females whatsoever, and therefore no way to counter the negative labels assigned to women. While these men are excessively mild toward each other, the opposite side to the coin is a tendency to aggression toward women.

HTT can again cite anecdotal, but personal, field experience which typified the way in which the behavior patterns of men, gentle toward one another, can turn quite opposite toward women, and the way these behaviors are imitated and transmitted to the next generation of men. The following took place on patrol in the Maywand district of Kandahar province:

Upon exiting the Mullah's compound, I was confronted with an irate neighbor—a man in middle-age, clean and apparently relatively wealthy in appearance... He expressed his horror that I, a woman, was present with the patrol. He would not make eye contact with me or shake my hand, but instead only referred to me with angry gestures. I maintained a respectful distance while he sat nearby to engage the men of the patrol. When formally addressing the men, his demeanor changed. He shook hands with each, with every display of gentleness and respect. The traditional first handshake between Pashtun men grips only the first joints of the fingers, and he used this with each, along with much bowing. It was explained to him that I was present in order that men would not enter a compound where women might be seen, and he was significantly appeased…

After this conversation, as the group said their goodbyes and began to move away, the neighbor approached me and extended his hand. I took this to be an invitation to a handshake, offered now that he understood that I was there out of respect for the traditions of his culture rather than in an attempt to disrupt them. When I offered my hand, he took it in a crushing grip and with unexpected strength bent my wrist back into a painful joint lock.

I ultimately wrenched myself from his grip, and as I sought to rejoin my patrol, I was mobbed by the village boys, who I had previously showered with gifts of candy and school necessities, led by the neighbor's oldest son. This boy appeared to be approximately 11 years old. Grabbing my arm, he attempted to practice the same maneuver his father had demonstrated, to the delight and cheers of the younger boys. The noise of the children caught the attention of our American interpreter, who returned and scolded them for their behavior. He attempted to shame them by asking "is this the way you would behave at home?" The oldest boy proudly answered that it was, indicating that his mother and sisters were treated with the same violence and disdain. While the encounter with the father hurt my wrist, the encounter with his sons broke my heart.

In conclusion, due to both cultural restrictions and generational cycles of certain experiences, Pashtun men are freer with companionship, affection, emotional expression, and the trust bred of familiarity with other men. They often lack the experience of these aspects of life with women. This usurping of the female role *may contribute to the alienation of women over generations, and their eventual relegation to extreme segregation and abuse. If ever the cycle of abuse is to be broken and the Pashtun culture heal itself from its wounds, which continue to fester in patterns of violence and conflict, the role of women as mothers and companions may be key.*

Why would one insert such a disturbing chapter into a book about story making and understanding of a country we have waged war in for the past 12 years? A narrative of this kind, although off-putting, highlights the profound challenges posed by practices that have been accepted over hundreds of years. The disenfranchisement of the man-woman relationship promotes violence and instability. It is not by chance that Pashtun happen to be the most aggressive ethnicity in Afghanistan. However, the problem is not limited to Pashtun areas, nor it is just a calamity brought about by Afghans.

In orphanages, male prostitution can be found in structures where the supervising personnel connives with clients for monetary gains. Older men are allowed into those orphanages that have poor security measures. In other instances, kids are permitted to exit without supervision or literally released temporarily in the care of escorts who come and meet them outside the gates of the compounds. In every case, the children trafficking takes place with the staff's acquiescence and full knowledge.

As mentioned in the HTT study of Pashtun sexuality, in the Afghan armed forces, homosexuality is by far more frequent than in the ranks of foreign armed forces operating in the same area. There are constant stories of Western soldiers being sexually propositioned by their Afghan colleagues.

Some of these Afghan service-members try to look desperately feminine, despite their camouflage battle dress uniforms, to vie for the attention of the *koregee* boys. Rajiv Srinivasan, a young US Army First Lieutenant, who served as a platoon leader in Afghanistan, wrote in his 14 October 2010 personal blog: … *I was recently solicited by a clearly gay ANA (Afghan National Army) soldier when I visited the ANA eastern outpost. It was actually one of the most bizarre things I had ever experienced. The soldier knew I spoke Urdu. Word has apparently gotten around the ANA battalion of my Indian descent, so he automatically started flirting with me in a foreign tongue. He desperately tried to appear feminine and attractive in his BDU blouse and flip-flops, though failing miserably. Unfortunately for him, sporadic facial hair and body odor aren't really my thing, nor are men for that matter.*

It should be accepted by now that the average Afghan boy and young man might well be sexually confused and repressed. When there is no healthy outlet, he might end up using his inner energy fighting because he has no way to channel his masculinity into something constructive other than labor. The same could be said of older men who have grown up in complete isolation from females. Indeed, most Afghan men seem to struggle with their sexual identities in a country where, at least on paper, homosexuality and cross-dressing are considered a serious crime.

As in most Afghan paradoxes, homosexuality is condoned, embraced and ridiculed at the same time. In 2011, Afghan news reporters questioned men who had placed rainbow flags stickers of the *Lesbian, Gay, Bisexual and Transgender Movement* on their vehicles. The reporters became quickly aware that the men were unaware of the meaning of the rainbow flags, thinking that it was just another Western fashion. When told of the meaning of the symbol, they quickly began removing the stickers to avoid being seen as homosexuals or supporters of the movement.

While most reported episodes of harassment are just brushed off as a nuisance, there have been instances when Western military personnel have felt increasingly threatened and found it difficult to complete their missions. In other cases, the actions of grown-up, sexually confused males can really fall into the realm of ridicule.

On a hot August morning, I was touring a remote village on a CIMIC (Civil Military Cooperation) Functional Specialty assessment. As a Civil Affairs (CA) economics functional specialist, I have to assess the economic conditions of a particular area and identify projects that can be sustainable and impactful in aiding normalization and stability. It is my preference to go on these assessments lightly armed or not armed at all. I have a number of reasons for that posture and, knowing the terrain, I do not believe it is the martial skills of a middle-aged banker that are going to save the day in case of an insurgents' attack.

On this particular assessment, my armed escort was manned by two burly ISAF's Highlanders, the battle-tried Scottish royal infantry regiment. Highlanders are a dive into the past. They are no-nonsense, carry the dry humor and dignity of the old British Empire, and they are definitely stuck in their glorious past.

We passed in front of one of these primitive, dirt-floored buildings that dot the landscape of many isolated Afghan villages. Outside the door, which was a simple dusty curtain, sat an old *mujahidin*. His toothless smile opened wide in the middle of a henna-dyed wild beard. He literally stared at me, gawked at my buttocks and swirled his tongue in a clear sexual innuendo. I don't get embarrassed too easily, but this was sudden and too much to take.

Should I have been flattered or flabbergasted? Most men wish women would pay those kinds of attention to them. Occasionally Western men find themselves the object of open sexual advances. They are so rare that one might even have to take some time to decide whether these advances are wanted or unwanted. The majority of these rare cases happen with women propositioning men. So, for a heterosexual man being propositioned overtly by a male *Klingon* look-alike can definitely be unsettling. I mean, being middle-aged, without the muscles of a twenty-something Special Forces operator and balding, I really do not look like *Bacha Bazi* potential. I consider myself a *WALRUS*, in the US Navy, *WALRUSES* are like SEALS—just fatter and slower, and I am definitely no Adonis.

SEALS are trained to kill the enemy. We are trained to eat the enemy's food, so that they can starve to death.

The toothless gay *mujahidin* scene had already become hilarious, but it eventually got even more comical. The young soldier from East Kilbridge, who had been escorting me, a fanatic *Celtics* supporter, asked me, matter of fact, if I wanted him to shoot the bearded tongue swirler. I was still recovering from the shock and amusement and, to make light of the embarrassment, I jokingly replied: *Yah man, take out the old perv!* My blood froze when I heard the typical metallic sound of a no-nonsense Scot clocking his weapon. Fate and an inability to resist urges were going to end forever the old *mujahidin's* tongue-swirling-attraction technique. I promptly barked the order to stand down, more out of terror than authority. Being dementedly horny does not warrant a death sentence, maybe just a solid beating. The amazing thing was that the old guy did not even budge and went on with his attempt to lure me until we disappeared from his field of vision. After we had a dinner conversation about the whole matter and the shock had somewhat dissipated, I recalled an interesting detail. The old man's dirty feet sported a brightly colored toenail polish. I appreciated the effort to look presentable.

Phone sex and phone mating are now global phenomena. Afghans are taking phone mating to creative heights. Afghanistan went from quasi-medieval communication grids in 2001 to almost 18 million GSM users in 2012. In 2007, I spent one week at an NGO's headquarters in Kabul, coaching the NGO staff on administration and not-for-profit management procedures. I sat down for a reasonable time with the local personnel, mostly women, who had been issued cellular phones for the purpose of the organization's business. During the course of a five-hour training session, one of them received eighteen random phone calls from males who were just *fishing*.

Every single time the woman took the calls, I would stop the training and stare at her, amused, while she would answer in a monotonous tone and hang up every single call within a minute. After eighteen interruptions, I felt compelled to ask her why she kept taking these calls. The lengthy explanation that came with her answer was startling to the point that I asked the woman to keep answering the phone so that I could keep observing the craziness. The story was that a horny and hopeful male would dial a random number and, if, *inshallah*, the voice on the other side was that of a woman, he would try to start a conversation. The exchanges would be truly comical: *Hello, May the Peace be with you, who is this?—May the Peace be with you too, It is Ahmid, who are you?—Well, Ahmid you called. Who are you looking for?—You have a really nice voice. Where do you reside?—*The woman would not reply to that, so the male would say something sweet like—*I have been looking for you all my life!* At this point the poor, horny and hopeful male does not stand a further chance; this kind of communication ends there. The woman who hung up the phone does not even look upset, bored or annoyed. She actually looks flattered and somewhat proud of herself. Then, I could picture the man giving the cellular phone number, the one he just dialed, to a friend of his in a sort of competition about who could get the farthest. He has found a *fish*, a big one indeed, sounding from the lovely voice, another *fisherman* might be luckier. So, another man dials in, 20 minutes later—*Hello, May the Peace be with you, who is this?*—*May the Peace be with you too, It is Yousef, who are you? Well, Yousef-jan you called. Who are you looking for?*—*I heard you are the most beautiful woman in Mazar. But nobody knows your name* (the *fisherman* is getting romantic)—*Vale, tashakur* (yes, thank you), *Yousef-jan you have just called Peshawar* (although we really are in Kabul)—comes the witty answer of the NGO female staff member and another poor, horny and hopeful male bites the dust. The woman now looks even prouder. I wish there was a study on the *pick-up* success rate of the Afghan cell phone *fishermen*. In the meanwhile, Roshan, the most popular cell phone network provider in Afghanistan, is the country's single most profitable corporation behind the opium traders.

    The cell phone *fishing* game might be a romantic and endearing avenue to the normalization of relationships between the two sexes. During the NGO management training, the game clearly disrupted productivity, but, in a country where relationships, even between grown adults, assume the tone of Western middle schools' romances, one must be flexible and accepting without expecting too much responsibility in return. This game allows a female to be able to reject a male without the risk of getting physically abused. However, it is not rare that a number of spurned hopefuls, when their optimistic dreams get crushed by a woman's wits, start whispering or shouting obscenities.

    Even without understanding Dari or Pashto one can easily identify the subject of the conversation between Afghan women during their *segregated* lunches because of the rolling of eyes and the laughing. Recounting to each other the *gallantries* of the young Afghan *Casanovas* is these women's favorite pastime.

In 2006, I was staying at the guest house of an NGO in *Karta Se,* Kabul. *Karta Se* is a decent area of the capital and, while staying at this nice compound, I was sharing it with an American couple who were humanitarian volunteers, a German couple who were tourists (yes tourists!) and a Turkish engineer who was working on a water-development site in northern Kabul.

I used to meet the man during the morning *chaa-ye-sowb* (breakfast) and have pleasant conversations with him. His English was not good at all, but the language of football is international. We would delight each other and somewhat lessen our homesickness recounting legendary games between *Juventus* and *Galatasaray* or *AC Milan* and *Fenerbache.*

At the end of our breakfast and just before heading out to his work site, the Turkish gentleman would always lean closer, look at me in the eyes in an all-knowing complicit manner, and promise to me that he would take me to a Chinese restaurant. I found it odd that he would insist about this invitation every single time we met for breakfast, and I finally accepted, setting up a date and a time. This was, after all, a good way to break off the monotony of *Qaabeli pilau* or *kechriqorut* (both traditional Afghan dishes).

I mentioned the invitation and the insistence to a female NGO worker who promptly, but discreetly, advised me to excuse myself out of it, without explaining the reason. When I tried to do what my colleague advised, the good Turkish man seemed crushed. *What the heck, a good serving of chow mein and a fresh Tsingtao can't be that bad!*—I convinced myself. We also had a good compromise, he would pay for dinner, and I would use my driver. I felt that with my loyal Najibullah at hand during the evening, I could excuse myself and get back to *Karta Se* whenever I wished.

The genuine expression of pleasure in Najibullah's eyes when I announced where he was taking me that evening should have warned me even more about the place we were going to have dinner. I had never seen my driver so excited to take me anywhere. When he first was assigned to me, I could not decipher his feelings about things. It took me almost a week to see him smiling for the first time. It was when I gave him my sunglasses as a present, he promptly invited me to dinner with his family. Also in that case, I was told by my NGO friend to decline politely the invitation. This time an explanation was offered—everybody knew that Najibullah had barely enough food for his wife and kids. He would take food badly needed by his family to feed me, and that would not be fair. That time I had heeded her advice.

Najibullah is a man of my kind, a man of passions. When, one day, our white Toyota minivan was hit from behind by one of the few Kabul BMWs, he proceeded to leave his driver seat and pummel the BMW driver without even pausing a millisecond to assess the damage to the vehicle or the people inside it. After the evening at the Chinese restaurant, he considered me a brother.

A travel advisory for the tourist guide to Kabul should state—*if you want a good serving of chow mein and a fresh Tsingtao in Kabul, you do not go to one of Kabul's Chinese restaurants. Go over the northern border with China and cross it.*

Within the first ten minutes after entering a Chinese joint in Kabul, one definitely feels like *Indiana Jones* in a *casbah*'s brothel. Even the characters one typically encounters in there seem to be straight out of a fantasy movie. The demographics of the typical Afghan brothel are composed of:

    a. Females of Mongolian complexion, some middle-aged and a few of them outright senile (10 percent of the brothel's fauna). Some say—*You can't really tell age in Asian people*. In a Kabul brothel, one can.

b. American results of three centuries of in-breeding. Rednecks who could be considered *le crème de la crème* of places like West Virginia, Kentucky and the Carolinas, men who generally work for Private Security Companies or logistical support contractors. They either drive trucks or are generally putting their cowboys' skills to use acting like soldiers of fortune. They tend to be the ones who add up to the taxpayers' $185 burrito. These faithful NRA members and their *muji-killer*'s t-shirts amount to roughly 10 percent of the brothel's population.

c. Turks, Armenians, Macedonians, Georgians, Slovaks and, united for once in desire, Indians and Pakistanis; all of these are roughly 15 percent.

d. The rest is composed mostly of Afghans, some of them coming from rural areas like on a pilgrimage. They wear their best clothes for the important occasion. Incredible-looking multi-colored leather jackets and tight jeans seem to be the trend in the land. Big medallions are included.

The health standards of places such as this one put any sane individual definitively off food. So, I ended up drinking 15 *Tsingtao*, one after the other, hoping to drown the embarrassment forever. I kept rejecting the invitations to go to the rooms in the back of the restaurant while pulling the excuse that I cannot possibly function like a real man while so heavily intoxicated. I decided it is good custom to keep congratulating my Turkish friend's strength in being able to perform while inebriated at the same time ordering the very disappointed

Najibullah to rush us back to safety. The last thing I remembered was the pain in Najibullah's eyes before he disappeared somewhere in the back of the establishment and then getting us lost while driving the white Toyota minivan on the way back to the guest house.

An old television advertisement for credit cards would have mentioned—*total duration of the Indiana Jones Kabul's brothel adventure: 89 minutes. Cost: $45 worth of Tsingtaos charged to the Turks' tab. Value of the entire experience: Priceless…*

In life, one never ceases to learn. We often assume things that end up contradicting our expectations. In the Chinese restaurant/brothel, one would have thought to find a number of sex-deprived coalition troops, but those military personnel one does not meet in Kabul's establishments of ill repute.

In this extreme case, despite lengthy periods in the Afghan war zone, ISAF's members' attraction standards seem to have held to a higher level of decency. Curiously, one finds plenty of Italian, French and Spanish military personnel getting facials, manicures, pedicures and innocent massages at the famous Beauty School of Kabul. Nourishing the body nourishes the soul. In 2012, I witnessed a courageous US Army enlisted soldier entering the barber shop of a southeastern Afghanistan base and asking the resident Filipino lady if pedicure and manicure service were available. He did so right in front of a number of American military personnel waiting for their buzz haircuts. If he noticed the awkward stares of all present, he did not show it. When it was confirmed that the services were available, he booked an appointment and moved on. This is, in my opinion, healthy, but it requires courage because the traditionally chauvinist stance of armed forces worldwide does not promote a public personal statement of these kinds of preferences.

With regard to the Afghan establishment of ill repute, they get blown up every once in a while. When one hears that the Taliban have destroyed one of the Chinese *restaurants* or a perfectly legitimate Indian food joint they should question whether the responsible parties are really ethically motivated or whether there are underlying financial interests, and it is just a *Mafia* hit.

One might start trusting in the moralistic motivation behind the insurgent struggle if the signs of clan wars over commercial interests linked to illicit trades were not all over Afghanistan. My driver confirmed two years later that the place had been blown up by the Taliban because it served alcohol. But, then, I got the accurate details of the bombing, there was no suicide, no martyr. The bomb was placed at the establishment during the night, and the owners had been warned that it might soon happen. For someone who was born in the South of Italy, this technique feels strangely familiar. It looks like the *restaurant* owners might have refused to pay protection money. These Taliban are starting to look a lot less like the protectors of *wahabi* morality and more like a bunch of *picciotti* (Cosa Nostra's foot soldiers).

Pornography is starting to saturate Afghanistan. The Internet might be connecting the world, but in a lot of Afghan places of work, it is just a tool to access free pornography. Middle-aged bureaucrats might be useless at creating and managing databases or rationalizing processes via web-based applications, but they are proficient in porn search. In any Afghan *okumat* (government) office, one will witness a familiar story: mountains of papers are slowly being replaced by computer servers and centralized archives. The effective users of the new systems are the youngsters and they tend to be less than 20 percent of the office-bound civil administration of the country. Even if computers are starting to fill the working spaces, it is always them, the younger generations, who seem to be the most familiar with technology and the only ones at ease with it.

Older civil servants, those who have been brought up with black-and-white *televeesur* (televisions—a Russian word that dates the coming of this appliance into Afghanistan) and radios, keep looking at these computers, these diabolical machines with distrust and a feeling of inferiority and hopelessness.

These bureaucrats all act very similarly. In the presence of the guest, who has to comfortably sit on the plush couch facing the important desk, they take *nonchalant* pride in clapping their hands to order the office *boy*, generally a man in his late 50s, to serve *chai* and candies. Their computers sit idle on the important desks, most often turned off. They are the ones who clap their hands again to instruct the office *boy* to find the younger member of their staff when the damn thing needs to be started or operated.

To be fair, this phenomenon is not only an Afghan trait. It might be global and generational. My father, who is in his 70s, still goes to work every day. He is not a civil servant but runs his own business, or, according to my younger sister—*he thinks he runs his own business*. He has a love/hate relationship with the computer—love, because his assistant manages to get most things done with this thing—hate, because he cannot use it. He gets intimidated by it and reminds him that he is getting old. When he comes into work in the morning, he daily reminds his assistant while pointing at her laptop, to *appicia' a machinette!* (which literally translates as "*start the machinery!*"). He is definitely a product of his generation, and I am sure he would love to clap his hands and order an *espresso,* but he knows better because he values his life too much. Women in Italy are a lot more combative than their Afghan sisters. Clapping to order coffee gets you an *espresso* thrown at you in any Italian setting.

One of my father's salesmen fondly remembers when, during the hiring process, my father, in the middle of his final interview, wanting to know if the candidate was computer literate, asked him: "*O sai usa' u' centre elettroniche?*"—*(can you operate the electronic center?)*. The poor young man, then in his 20s, wondered if, by mistake, he had been sent to interview at the European Atomic Agency or NASA rather than to the toiletries distributorship he had applied for.

In any case, these middle-aged Afghan civil servants might have no understanding of how these diabolical machines operate, but they suddenly become computer savvy when in need of surfing Internet porn. It is both funny and embarrassing to witness the sheer amount of pornography they are able to download on these machines, gigabyte after gigabyte of filth, which they then struggle to erase when they get caught with their hands in the cookie jar and manage to look like guilty pubescent kids.

Hand-clapping bureaucrats, who rely on the constant presence of computer-literate youths, display Steve Jobs' inventiveness and exploratory skills on the subject of Internet pornography. When assistants get called upon to fix the bureaucrats' frozen PCs or to get rid of the usual malevolent virus, they get the full lowdown of their bosses' curiosity. It spans from pictures of straight heterosexual nature to graphic homosexual videos, from stories of midget love to lurid literature of human intercourse with animals. The weirdest one we experienced was the man searching for explicit pictures or videos of the Queen of England, yes the 86-years-old monarch! How sick is that? In April 2011, Libyan rebels raided *Bab-Al-Aziziya*, Muhammad Qaddafi's compound, and found pictures and notes about the Libyan leader's secret lust for Condoleeza Rice, the former US Secretary of State. The dictator was said to be turned on by her display of power and her proud African roots. Do middle-aged Muslims have a fascination with the sexual lives of powerful women? Is there a psychological implication to power and sexual dominance?

Even young Afghan administration staffers, working for International Organizations or for NGOs, cannot resist the temptation to explore their sexual curiosity within the *intimate* setting of their work computers. Mark M. Lowenthal is one of the visiting lecturers on *intelligence* at the Armed Forces Communications and Electronics Association in Fairfax, Virginia. Dr. Lowenthal served as the Assistant Director of Central Intelligence for Analysis and Production, as the Vice Chairman for Evaluation on the National Intelligence Council and as Counselor to the Director of Central Intelligence. One of the most memorable of his quotes is: *it is amazing how much of their privacy ordinary citizens are willing to give up in exchange for the comfort of easy access through Internet or other technological means.*

One should never forget that lesson. What happened to US Army General David Petraus is a confirmation that nobody is above scrutiny, not even the Director of Central Intelligence. One wishes young Afghan staffers had more common sense, but they keep leaving permanent records of their sexual explorations. Their computers and emails become public diaries of their sexual preferences. Like in the case of the older civil servants, when something goes wrong with their computers and a technician has to be called in, their private life gets thrown out in the open. Their sexual interests become conversation material for a year's worth of lunch breaks. In the case of the government bureaucrats, they try to dump responsibility to a willing underling ready to take the fall in exchange for favoritism. The same would not work for the young NGO staffer, whose power is very limited and operates in a work environment where the majority is made up of women. It is known that even if interested in sex, women are not big consumers of porn. The majority of porn is very degrading to women.

One wonders if our biggest accomplishment in Afghanistan has been exporting vast quantities of San Fernando Valley's finest product. Without going to the extremes of pornography, scantily clad women become *desktop wallpapers* in offices where the only workers are men. Once, I was called over by one of the young men working for a charitable foundation; he wanted to show his personal computer's screen wallpaper—a high-resolution, stunning picture of a half-naked Pamela Anderson. He was truly proud of the prized possession, turned around to look at me and exclaimed: *I love America!*

In Kabul, I met with Said Mohseni and with Abdul Wahid Nazari for different reasons.

The Mohsenis are an Afghan family that emigrated to Australia, became investment bankers and then came back to found the Moby Group, the first Afghan media conglomerate. Moby Group owns Tolo TV.

Abdul Wahid Nazari is the very capable managing director of RTA, the government-owned National Radio and Television of Afghanistan.

In 2007, when I visited Said Mohseni in the family's heavily guarded television studios, Tolo TV was starting to give an audience-rating beating to both RTA and Ariana TV, Afghanistan's original television enterprises. We discussed at length the reasons for the sudden popularity of Tolo TV, and Mohseni came up with a number of different factors, such as transparency, modernity, higher production value and variety. I felt the points that Said made were all valid, but I left Moby's office with the certainty that the steep increase in audience was related to something more popular. Tolo TV was the first Afghan broadcaster willing to finally show *some skin* to mass viewers.

Whether through news reading, Indian soap operas or talent shows, Afghan audiences could finally see beautifully refined women and could dream and appreciate that in the intimacy of their homes. Even girls could dream of emancipation and imitate American female rappers while protected by the sanctuary of their bedrooms.

The Taliban had banned, among a number of things, filmed entertainment, music, dancing and kite running. The thirst for music and television was great by the time the repressive regime fell. After the coming of the Westerners and the routing of the religious zealots, Afghans had been very ready for liberating their consumption of entertainment. The religious lobby behind RTA tried to pull a few morality hurdles to slow Tolo's audience growth but to no avail. The typical line was that Tolo's programming was corrupting the masses. With time and a few inevitable incidents, a typical Afghan compromise was achieved with desirable consequences. Both RTA and Ariana realized they had to keep up with Tolo's production quality and therefore started broadcasting appropriate products to satisfy their audience's needs. Gone were the interminable military parades and imam's prayers, and in came good-quality news reporting, political commentary, social debate and sports. Tolo, on its part, somewhat *toned down* its more controversial programming and its aggressive investigative journalism.

With the advent of technology, sped up by the *occupation*, Westerners might have unwittingly increased the risk of sexual proclivities unbalance in Afghanistan. A few humanitarian operators are left with the worrying afterthought that in pre-9/11

Afghanistan, although women were considered second-class citizens, they were, in the majority of cases, protected and cherished. Now that the ready availability of pornographic material is a *fait accompli*, the tendency to objectify women and boys might become even more pronounced.

The inevitability of technological globalization transcends the *polluting* presence of foreign troops. Even if military hordes are going, as usual, to leave, technology is in Afghanistan to stay. What will happen when we will have left for good? Will the Afghan people be able to self-regulate, or will there be a clear risk of fundamentalist restoration in order to counteract the social damage caused by excessive liberalization in a very short time? In my opinion, especially with regard to sexual balance, things are bound to get worse before they improve. I mean it. The place is already a difficult one to deal with. When one adds the danger of getting shot or blown up with having to watch out for a 73-year-old female volunteer so that she does not get groped in the aviary section of the Kabul *bazaar* or personally have to undergo the invasiveness of a 200-pound border patrolman who pats you where he should not, a little longer than he should, while staring sensually (or so he thinks), that difficulty will increase.

On Afghan Courage

The person who is cornered will fight.
— Afghan proverb

While Napoleon Bonaparte, Anais Nin and Robin Williams were born in different regions (Aiaccio, Corsica; Neully, France; and Chicago, USA), they have one thing in common. They possess a vision that many Afghans share.

The French emperor used to affirm that humankind should aim to possess two great virtues. He believed that these two primary virtues should be held by every society in order to thrive—*the courage of men* and *the virtuous purity of women*.

The Cuban author, born Angela Anais Juana Antolina Rosa Edelmina Nin y Culmell, stated that life shrinks or expands in proportion to one's courage.

The American comedian, in his unromantic, but no less philosophical, style believes that *one should never pick up a fight with an ugly individual because ugly people have really nothing to lose*.

In these three different beliefs lay the essence of Afghan behavior when it comes to courage.

Stereotypes tell us that courage varies depending on one's heritage. Jokes abound about the inability of Italians and

French to stay in the fight. It was because of these stereotypes that Medal of Honor recipient Salvatore Giunta was heralded by Italians and Italian-Americans as the symbol of an *Italianess* that is not about *La Dolce Vita*. As an American service-member of Italian descent, he proved that, contrary to popular perception, a few Italians know that there are a few things in life worth dying for. The boy might have Italian DNA in his blood, but he is from Clinton, Iowa. He is, after all, one of those who believe in a nation that is not afraid, a nation that fights back with a vengeance.

On November 16, 2010, President Obama mentioned the following words while conferring the Medal of Honor to Salvatore:

…During the first of his two tours of duty in Afghanistan, Staff Sergeant Giunta was forced early on to come to terms with the loss of comrades and friends. His team leader at the time gave him a piece of advice: "You just try—you just got to try to do everything you can when it's your time to do it."

Salvatore Giunta's time came on October 25, 2007. He was a Specialist then, just 22 years old.

Sal and his platoon were several days into a mission in the Korengal Valley—the most dangerous valley in northeast Afghanistan. The moon was full. The light it cast was enough to travel by without using their night-vision goggles. With heavy gear on their backs and air support overhead, they made their way single file down a rocky ridge crest, along terrain so steep that sliding was sometimes easier than walking.

They hadn't traveled a quarter mile before the silence was shattered. It was an ambush, so close that the cracks of the guns and the whizz of the bullets were simultaneous. Tracer fire hammered the ridge at hundreds of rounds per minute—"more," Sal said later, *"than the stars in the sky."*

The Apache gunships above saw it all, but couldn't engage with the enemy so close to our soldiers. The next platoon heard the shooting but were too far away to join the fight in time.

And the two lead men were hit by enemy fire and knocked down instantly. When the third was struck in the helmet and fell to the ground, Sal charged headlong into the wall of bullets to pull him to safety behind what little cover there was. As he did, Sal was hit twice—one round slamming into his body armor, the other shattering a weapon slung across his back.

They were pinned down, and two wounded Americans still lay up ahead. So Sal and his comrades regrouped and counterattacked. They threw grenades, using the explosions as cover to run forward, shooting at the muzzle flashes still erupting from the trees. Then they did it again. And again. Throwing grenades, charging ahead. Finally, they reached one of their men. He'd been shot twice in the leg, but he had kept returning fire until his gun jammed.

As another soldier tended to his wounds, Sal sprinted ahead, at every step meeting relentless enemy fire with his own. He crested a hill alone, with no cover but the dust kicked up by the storm of bullets still biting into the ground. There, he saw a chilling sight: the silhouettes of two insurgents carrying the other wounded American away—who happened to be one of Sal's best friends. Sal never broke stride. He leapt forward. He took aim. He killed one of the insurgents and wounded the other, who ran off.

Sal found his friend alive, but badly wounded. Sal had saved him from the enemy—now he had to try to save his life. Even as bullets impacted all around him, Sal grabbed his friend by the vest and dragged him to cover. For nearly half an hour, Sal worked to stop the bleeding and help his friend breathe until the MEDEVAC arrived to lift the wounded from the ridge. American gunships worked to clear the enemy from the hills. And with the battle over,

First Platoon picked up their gear and resumed their march through the valley. They continued their mission.

It had been as intense and violent a firefight as any soldier will experience. By the time it was finished, every member of First Platoon had shrapnel or a bullet hole in their gear. Five were wounded. And two gave their lives: Sal's friend, Sergeant Joshua C. Brennan, and the platoon medic, Specialist Hugo V. Mendoza."

Heroic acts are the result of courageous actions undertaken by ordinary men and women reacting with exceptional measures in extraordinary circumstances.

Salvatore's story is an amazing one. Afghanistan has plenty of Salvatores. In Afghanistan, it is the poor children who go and fight because they have nothing to lose. They are not like their middle-class, educated *Al-Qaeda* colleagues. These kids are provided shelter and the promise of a better future by imams who run *madrassas* for children who have no hope. Then they are recruited by warlords and insurgents with narratives of honor, courage and brotherhood.

We have often read books about Western military episodes. We have watched war movies about amazing victories and tragic deaths. We have tried to put ourselves in the shoes of a US Marine ready to storm the beach of Iwo Jima. Now, let's do something different—Let's imagine being a Taliban fighter.

You are waiting to attack, and you are wondering if your cover is good enough. You have slept in the open and ate very little for the past three days while your commander is planning this show of force. Everything has been planned carefully. You have a cellular telephone and a walkie-talkie, but communication is being kept to a minimum because the Americans have a diabolical ability to intercept your conversations, and you are in constant fear of these invisible birds the Americans call drones.

You have been told that, two days ago, Abu Rahid's compound was completely evaporated in a cloud of flames and smoke without a simple warning sign. Ahmed and his brothers couldn't find anything left of the seven members of the family and the three guards who were sleeping in the place. It was Abu Rahid's third safe house. He never felt safe but was fearing much more for his children's lives than for his own. He believed in the inevitability of death and often talked about it.

He had mentioned during the last supper, when he had said goodbye to his fighters going back into Afghanistan, that he was tired of moving from place to place and was ready to die in his own home. He was a true martyr, and he was always thankful to Allah for giving him, in this lifetime, a chance to be martyred by the best of the best, a lifetime chance to fight against Americans' accurate and superior firepower. The Russians—he recounted—were fierce and ruthless, but the Americans were truly a better and more worthy opponent. He did not hate the Americans. He had worked with them to defeat the Russians.

Abu Rahid was rarely wrong, and you are fully aware that you are fighting against the best soldiers in the world. They are professional killers, with superior training, weaponry and air support. You have already personally witnessed the devastating effect of American firepower on your comrades. You have seen M16 rounds slice through Gulbiddin's brain, and you remember your black turban, your sandals and your hands soiled with Gulbiddin's cerebral matter and blood. You had cursed the fantastic aim of those foreign soldiers whom you loathed and loved at the same time, because they give you meaning as the glorious fighter you are. The stronger the opponent, the more valorous the *mujahidin;* you are the pride of your clan. You truly miss Gulbiddin, his jokes, his willingness to help you carry the MH-250B, the heavy machine gun. It is time to avenge Gulbiddin or join him.

You had wished you could help your friend when he got hit; his pleading eyes can't be easily forgotten. You wish you knew what to do with Gulbiddin's injuries, but you were never taught combat first aid in the *madrassa,* nor would you know where to take your friend with such horrible injuries. You wish you had that miraculous backpack with the big Red Cross painted on it, the one that one of the enemies always carries, with all its healing goods. You have been instructed to take out these insolent healers first. These crusaders have no shame portraying their cross in battle; they use it as an amulet for good luck and healing.

You have your own battle amulet. You carry the holy words in your vest, which is not thick and heavy like that of the infidels. Bullets tear through it easily, but it does not matter because, like this, you can run much faster. You pat the holy verses neatly folded in the pocket right on top of your heart. Your *madrassa*'s teacher, the holy man Imam Mohammad Musa, the good and pious man of God, rescued you, clothed you and fed you for the past eight years. He even took the time to write those words just for you. He used his own elegant penmanship to bless you and protect you when you were called to face the most formidable opponent of all. He told you that you were finally ready, he had soothed your fears and filled your heart with purpose and courage.

Imam Musa always had good, fatherly words for you. He treated you with the utmost respect, and your only job was to memorize the holy words in a strange language, do *namaaz* (praying) a few times every day and behave in a pure and disciplined manner. It was a very fair deal, little work in exchange for clean clothes, respect, protection and a full belly.

Imam Musa's elegantly written words are now protecting your heart:

> *And slay them wherever ye find them, and drive them out of the places whence they drove you out, for persecution of Muslims is worse than slaughter of non-believers… but if they desist, then lo! Allah is forgiving and merciful. And fight them until persecution is no more, and religion is for Allah.*
>
> Holy Quran 2:191–193

You hold your breath, hoping that the American won't hear a sound. These *koregee* devils are quick in reacting and very murderously accurate. You know that your only good chance is in the first ten seconds of the fight and in the chaos that ensues.

The first shadow approaches; he is walking slowly, slightly bent. He is making almost no noise at all, and he is wearing his expensive night vision. Your eyes have had hours to adapt to the lack of light. He is so close that you can smell him and his silhouette so massive that you cannot miss.

Has he seen you? You pray Allah to give you two more seconds to properly take aim. Your mind is racing as much as your heart. *Can he hear my heart? Can he hear me breathing?* Why so many questions crowding your mind again? You are asking yourself whether you have even released the safety lever this time. It should be coming natural by now, but it seems that the closeness of these devils impairs your will. You do not want to repeat the fiasco of last week, when you had a clear shot but, in the excitement, you had forgotten the damned safety lever. *Am I going to look like a fool again?*

You, most possibly, are going to die tonight, but one of your last thoughts is about the risk of looking again like a fool to your comrades. You take the shot, the enemy warrior goes down and you feel suddenly elated, but the devil gets up, you take the shot one more time, and down he goes again—Are these devils immortal?—Everybody is shouting and the noise is deafening. You are now shooting uncontrollably with your eyes closed. Even keeping them open does not help, as your vision is now blurred. You are giving it everything you have, and you are fully aware the enemy warriors know where you are, and your position is compromised. The noise is deafening, and the cordite smell fills your nostrils. *Allahu Akbar* (Allah is the Greatest)! *A'uzu billahi minashaitanir rajim* (I seek refuge in Allah from the outcast Satan)! *Al-hamdu lillhahi rabbil 'alamin* (Praise be to Allah, the Lord of the Worlds)!—you are shouting with all your strength, you feel no fear.

Almost blind, you grab the loaded magazine you have placed next to you. Then, all of a sudden, everything goes black and you are having problems breathing. You think of your friend Qari Abdullah, the one with the beautiful voice who used to be always chosen to sing the holy verses. He was positioned just a few yards behind you, and you wonder whether he, too, will be a *shayid* (martyr), just like you, tonight. You wonder whether he will survive and be proud of your fight and will recount stories of your valor to your family and to the other students, back in your village.

You are feeling much calmer but cannot lift your arms. They are suddenly heavy like rocks. Your mind wanders away from the fight, and you remember when you had found American writings on the wall of that abandoned crusader outpost.

You had asked Qari Abdullah what they meant, as he could read English well. He was raised in Saudi Arabia because his dad, who was working in an oil refinery, had taken him there. He translated for you—*Even though I walk through the valley of the shadow of death, I will fear no evil, for you are with me; your rod and your staff, they comfort me.*—Qari, the boy with the beautiful voice, had confirmed that the crusaders have their holy words, too.

In your dying moments, you realize that becoming a *shayid* was not so bad, that the courage you displayed did not imply the absence of fear; to the contrary, it thrived in the presence of the fear caused by the approaching American warriors because it blossomed from your powerful will to go on. Maybe your amulet ended up working after all—*Paradise, here I am. Bismillahir Rahmanir Rahim* (in the name of Allah, the Most Beneficent, the Most Merciful), *I am coming home.*

Personally, I was always jealous of my comrades who, at basic parachutist-qualification airborne school, would jump out of the aircraft savoring the thrill and the adrenaline. I was terrorized before every single one of my jumps. I kept imagining a slow inexorable plunge to my death. Yet I jumped every single time. I did it because I did not wish to look like a fool to the others. I did not want to be any less than them. Now, I can't really remember the fear but only the feeling of elation when hearing the *swoosh* of the canopy opening in the immense silence of the sky. I cannot even think to compare that primordial fear of death with the emotions that can arise when waiting to kill a fighting machine who has mastered the ability to fight back. The fear I experienced must not even come close to the last moment of a young *Talib* fighter. Therefore, I have respect for him. I respect my enemy as I respect my comrades.

Afghans do not like to pick fights with someone stronger than themselves. With the exception of a few fanatics, they are abundantly clear on who carries the bigger stick in this recent fight. So the majority of the Afghans, if they could choose between fighting against us or just seeing us going home, would choose to see our backs going safely back to Miami, Rome, Paris, Budapest or Birmingham.

Also the majority of them fight for ideology, for monetary benefit or because our welcome has been overstayed. Afghans are either consummate idealists, mercenaries or both. But overall, when they start fighting a much stronger enemy, it is because they have decided they have very little to lose.

It is common knowledge that life in Afghanistan and *Pashtunistan* is hard. What is not common knowledge is that defining anyone who takes a shot at us as an insurgent and any insurgent a *Talib* is erroneous and misleading. There are times when we get plainly shot at because one of our colleagues cannot hold his physiological needs any longer and ends up urinating in an otherwise peaceful farmer's property. Go and relieve yourself in the garden of a Texan or an Ozark mountaineer and you get a Talib out of each one of the two.

More frequently, we are militarily engaging clans, warlords, smugglers and petty criminals who are defending their turf and their economic interest. We are in the middle of a traditional mafia economy.

Afghans who do not fight for pure ideology—they are approximately 85 percent of the *insurgents*—tend to fight close to their homes. Theirs is one of the most ancient professions, and, within their tribal and clan allegiance, they will side with the highest payer or with the party that can guarantee the most reliable medium to long-term security. The reason that these fighters rarely choose the side of the *crusaders* is that, even if the *crusaders* could pay more, it is only for a limited period. They all know that, despite their assurances to the contrary, the *crusaders* will eventually leave. Therefore, a medium- to long-term view versus a short-term gain with the added risk of violent retribution weighs heavily when deciding which side to take. In some instances, fighters have decided to *reconcile* with the central government after an understanding had been reached with hardliners. This understanding implied that the fighters who would accept the government's handouts would do so only with monetary gain in mind and no effective intention to change sides—just a neutral posture for a limited time period.

Afghanistan's fighting professionals negotiate more than shoot. A great number of confrontations are decided by defections and power shifts rather than massacres. Massacres do happen, but their numbers pale in comparison to countries like Mexico, Syria or Nigeria. Killings generate so many revenge actions that short-term armistices are preferred to save face and resolve controversies.

The majority of insurgents decline to lay down their weapons and embrace the Kabul government-sponsored reintegration programs for two primary reasons. The first one is that the majority of rural Afghanistan still has difficulties accepting the authority of a central government that is seen as very removed from local issues and is considered a puppet of foreign interests. The second is that most fighters believe the attractive option of subsidized neutrality to be pricey because it does not always imply a neutral position. Some fighters who sign up to the government options are not only required to cease fighting Kabul but also to report infiltrations and pressures by those who have chosen the opposition's side. Fighters fear that, by choosing the reintegration programs, they will always be seen as working for the Kabul government.

The choice is often of a practical nature. It is not a function of courage or lack of it.

Reconciliation schemes, allegiance negotiations and bartering power are nothing new in the region. Thousands of years of warfare and reconciliations have become a way of life for people who have become very pragmatic about lifestyle, possessions and ideals.

All over the world, people who have very little fear death less than those who have a lot. With these individuals, the threat of retaliation or death is not the most ideal bargaining chip. Often, dying a glorious, quick death becomes an attractive alternative to years of boredom, subjugation and financial struggle.

If centuries of practical wisdom constitute a hard scenario to tackle, ideology is an even harder turf to negotiate on. A kid from a displaced family, with a poor, difficult past and no vision for the future, finds easy refuge in the enlarged Islamic family that offers everything. He feels finally identified within a global brotherhood that celebrates the sweetness of the afterlife and the heroism of those who accept martyrdom in the name of the struggle. Had we been born in a refugee camp in Pakistan to witness hunger, epidemics and little hope of improvement, we might be making a similar choice.

Affiliating with something bigger than us has been the defining factor in our teenage years. Affiliation provides a quick alternative to the identity needs that any human being wants satisfied. If the identity comes associated with the honorable quest to better the life of others, it becomes an easier choice. Teenagers might be described as fundamentally selfish, but those who participate in team sports, charitable endeavors and religious affiliations seem to thrive and grow happier.

In conversations with true *believers,* a few interesting matters came to light. Mercenaries, even the few who hate and despise the enemy, kidnap, plant improvised explosive devices and kill, matter of factly. They recount having little feelings or no feelings with regard to their actions as if what they do is all they know. Some of them might hold grudges because of family members who have been killed by the enemy, but most of them are just conflict professionals. These fighters have respect for the enemy fighter, because they know that, without the enemy, they cease to have meaning and a job. Most fighters caught as prisoners after a firefight show respect and curiosity toward their coalition captors. Few remain despondent and hateful. The majority act mellow and agreeable. They enjoy Western food, soda and clothing until they are released and go back to fighting. These fighters are very curious about the military prowess of the opponents and, after they get captured or injured in the fight, they often hold no hard feelings against the people who shot at them. One can see plenty of injured captive "insurgents" being nursed to health in coalition medical facilities. They might have been hit while planting IEDs, and, while they are recovering, they can be seen helping the kitchen staff, sweeping floors or chatting with nurses and injured coalition soldiers. Then, when they get released, they go back to planting IEDs for 15 dollars a blast.

The fighting style of Afghanistan professional mercenaries seems to adhere to a more ritualistic style that doesn't always have to result in killings. It is often marked with bombastic shows of courage, like in the case of the *show of force* narrated earlier. British author Patrick Hennessey wrote a book titled *Kandak: Fighting with the Afghans*, which was published by Allen Lane in 2012. In the book, Hennessey tells of his experience training and fighting alongside the *askar* (the Afghan soldier). From initial contempt toward the apparent Afghan rabble comes an appreciation of their courage and resolve. In one case, he describes Quiam, one of the *kandak*'s (battalion) leaders, scolding an Afghan National Police (ANP) officer for his lack of courage.

Quiam is a member of the Afghan National Army (ANA), a much better trained and equipped force than the ANP. When the policeman argues that things are easier for the ANA because of their better equipment, Quiam strips off his uniform and gear to show that he can fight the Taliban naked and he proceeds to run naked out of his covered position.

In Afghan warfare, surrenders are often negotiated without a single casualty being inflicted, and the enemy is often afforded an escape route so that he can be fought against one more time. Different aggressive posture stances and threat techniques are widely used before punitive action is undertaken.

True believers, fundamentalists and xenophobes, are difficult to gauge. A consummate negotiator might assume that if a fundamentalist had to choose between laying by a sun-soaked pool with a *piña colada* (little umbrella included) and getting shot at by a bunch of jarheads, he would chose the *piña colada*. Any reasonable civil affairs officer might believe that if he could show the *teeth behind the smile* to a potential *jihadist*, the latter would chose the smile rather than the bite of the United States' military might. To most operators in Afghanistan, when giving the choice to a potential enemy, it should be just about common sense—*Your pick: Either you personally get a nice new motorbike, a security job protecting your village, and your village gets a new mosque—or you get shot. With the risk that other members of your family might get shot, too. What do you prefer?*

With time, all of us ground operators and professional negotiators get humbled by our mistaken definition of common sense. It is astonishing to witness the amount of believers who prefer to be shot. Dealing with Western values, one would erroneously assume that any man has his price. The world of Wall Street, Hollywood and consumerism is light years away from the world of radical *Umma (*the Nation of Islam). Thankfully, the majority of Afghans are radically religious only to the point of personal interest. Most Afghans have a price.

With regard to those few hardliners that cannot be persuaded, one could assert that *Guantanamo, Abu Ghraib, Quala-i-Jangi*, the *Extraordinary Renditions* program and *Enhanced Interrogation* techniques have proven that motivated hard men are just too hard to break.

Even if a terrorist, one can admire a man's resiliency and commitment to the cause even when torn apart by very sophisticated interrogation techniques. We all have reasons for going to war. September 11, 2001, was, for most of those in the Western world who decided to go to war, the origin of a belief that our families were not safe from those who hated our way of life, who despised our beliefs.

I am not a man of war, but my decision was prompted by the stories of two people who had lost their lives as a consequence of that day. Robert Talhami was a Pakistani-born equity derivatives broker at Cantor Fitzgerald and one of the funniest and sweetest men I knew. A father and a husband like me, one who would worry about paying his mortgage on time, his children's education, Robert dissolved in a ball of fire on the 104th floor of One World Trade Center. Massimo Ficuciello, a graduate of the London School of Economics, was an Italian banker, who had the passion and the initiative to contribute. His choice was to serve on a deployment as an Italian Army Reserve Public Affairs Officer in *Nassirihya*, Iraq. Another *Islamist* ball of fire took his life.

We all believe that our beliefs have better ethical grounding and that we will eventually prevail. In the US Armed Forces, we are certain of where ideologies stand, and we want to believe that we will always act better than those who called us into a fight. But most of us cannot fail to admire the stamina and determination of enemies like Khalid Shaikh Mohamad, the Al-Qaeda operative, who was *water-boarded* 118 times in March 2003 and refused to cave in. Warriors admire valor and resilience when presented with them. We admire colleagues like John McCain or Louie Zamparini for their heroic resistance to North Vietnamese and Japanese torture, but even enemy combatants can gain our respect.

For a warrior, admiring Khalid Shaikh Mohamad for his ability to summon the strength of his beliefs every time he got tested to the extreme does not imply that the warrior would hesitate a single second to kill Khalid in battle. I have discussed this very subject with many Afghans, and they all shared the belief that, when faced with a foe of this kind, the only course of action is killing him. Afghans spare only those enemy prisoners whom they consider threats. Those whom they do not consider threats are considered undeserving of respect.

When dealing with radical *Integralism*, one could even come to understand the social need behind the basic purism of the *salafist* teachings, but when these beliefs translate into unconditional hate for anybody who thinks differently, negotiating is useless.

A great warrior, German Field Marshal Erwin Johannes Eugen Rommel, Der Wüstenfuchs (the Desert Fox), wrote about the need to fight wars without hating the enemy. He hoped for conflicts where honor and gentlemen's culture could balance the inevitable horror of death. The title of his North African campaigns, which were posthumously published in 1950, is *Krieg ohne Hass* (War without Hate).

In 2006, during my last tour as an Italian Civil Affairs reservist in *An Nasiriyah*, Iraq, with Italy wrapping up its war there, I ended up becoming the *de facto* liaison officer to a much-larger American medical unit. Most times it felt like we were reliving *MASH*, the popular 1970s TV show about a Korean War field hospital, all over again. I will keep the names of all involved anonymous because of the story I am going to recount. Despite the war, the atmosphere was relaxed, and we were going about our duties in a professional manner, which allowed for routine and even some spare time.

By the end of 2006, the security situation in our *Shia*-dominated area of operations had become relatively stable. The relationship with the locals was well managed; however, a few final infiltrations from *Al Qaeda* hardliners kept forcing segments of the population to take sides. On a particularly rough day, a number of US casualties were *MEDEVAC'd* to the US Army Role 3 Hospital at the nearby Tallil Air Force base. Expectant casualties define personnel who are so critically injured that only complicated and prolonged treatment offers any hope of improving life expectancy. Despite the amazing abilities and professional actions of the US medical personnel, a few soldiers lost their lives. I was amazed at how feverishly the entire hospital staff worked and how all of their coordinated actions resulted in perfectly timed clockwork procedures. It was clear that these brave doctors and medics worked on the fallen long after they had risen to heaven. One of the medics later confirmed my impression, adding that, at times, the extra effort is for the benefit of the fallen soldier's comrades who are witnessing the inevitable. The mood around the *MASH* quickly turned somber to the point of depression.

The Italian military canteen at Camp Mittica was very popular among coalition troops because it carried free wine during dinnertime and weekends. It was somewhat refreshing and representative of the value of history to see British *Desert Rats* and Italian *Ariete Armored Brigade* personnel eating and drinking together. Men who only sixty-four years before would have been slaughtering each other on the hot sands of North Africa under the command of the *Desert Fox*.

I did not have to ponder too much. The application of the Italian Uniform Code of Military Justice is somewhat more lenient than the American, so I took matters into my own hands, loaded a Military Red Cross ambulance with wine, parmesan cheese and salami and passed through the Tallil Air Force base checkpoint sporting the friendliest of smiles. I drove the familiar route to the containers-turned-bedrooms where I knew the US medical officers were housed and we had a *serata romana* (Roman evening) with American country music in the land of the Ziggurat.

Soon enough, everybody's mood was definitely turning merrier, either because of the overpowering taste of seasoned Parmesan cheese and *salame di Felino*, because of the fabulous wine or because of Vince Gill's lyrics: *It is hard to kiss the lips at night that chew your ass out all day long...*

Suddenly I realized that the gentleman I had been talking to for the past 45 minutes had three Stars on his DCU (Desert Camouflage Uniform). We had been lost in conversation about the idyllic scenery of *Amalfi*. For some time we had truly forgotten where we were. I had never seen the officer before, and I had been hanging around the American compound for the past two months. So I guessed he was just visiting the hospital. Three Stars in the Italian army indicate a captain. Three Stars in the US Armed Forces indicate someone with a lot more military clout. He either thought I was a Lieutenant General myself, or he was just a very nice and accommodating gentleman.

The subject had moved from the splendor of the *Amalfi* coast to how Civil Military Cooperation (CIMIC) had to deal with the disruptive elements created by fundamentalists who would not settle for a new pickup truck, a job and a new mosque for their community. Those who preferred to keep fighting to the point of killing moderate Iraqis or who took the time to film themselves decapitating hostages.

He asked me how I thought we should deal with those hardliners that we had no ability to sway to the negotiating table. He was told of the amount of time I'd spent dealing with villagers and their *sheiks*.

He might have expected the typical cautious response that most Italian military personnel offered when asked a similar question. Maybe he expected a response right out of a *Captain Corelli's Mandolin* scene, a movie about the Italian occupation of Greece in the Second World War. After all, the setting was the same: good music, good food, good wine and great company of fellow warriors. In the movie, a *Puccini lover* Italian officer philosophizes, with a *Wehrmacht* (German Army) colleague, over a good glass of Greek *ouzo* about the inherent injustice of war and the fruitless act of killing.

The setting might have been similar, but this time the answer coming from a peace-loving Italian Civil Affairs officer might have surprised the Vice Admiral—*Kill them all*—I answered with little hesitation.

142 • *The Afghan Paradox*

*Afghan National Army (ANA) soldier
(image courtesy of the Australian Army)*

Laughter (courtesy of Penelope Price)

Afghans' Use of Humor

> *Here is a desperate appeal!*
> *The terrorists have kidnapped our beloved President*
> *Karzai and are demanding ten million dollars or*
> *they will burn him with petrol. Please donate*
> *what you can! I have donated five gallons.*
> — Afghan joke

Zalmai is a fierce-looking former *Panshiri mujahidin* who heads the security detail of the Kabul *Marastoon* for the Afghan Red Crescent. The man is a man of few words, dignified posture and kind acts. He served under Ahmad Shah *Massoud*, the beloved anti-Taliban warlord who was killed by Al Qaeda operatives posing as a French television crew, just before the attack on the twin towers.

One day, *Zalmai* asked me to remove my *pakul* and hand it to him. He proceeded to "treat" it by wetting it, stretching it and patiently rolling it to make it look more like one belonging to a real *Panshiri* rather than to a nerdy foreigner. He took his time, carefully focusing on each single movement of his hands. It felt like a ritual, and, in the course of the process, he did not say a single word. His methodic movement was the story. Then he handed me the hat, and his serious gaze finally broke into a smile, he muttered something in Dari that made all present laugh. *Here is your hat. At least you will stop looking like a mushroom.*

Zalmai may be a man of very few words, but he has the gift of a handsome, all-knowing face with piercing black eyes. His mouth might be frozen in a constant frown, but his eyes are always smiling. One day I commented on his eyes to an Afghan friend who confirmed that Zalmai had a refined sense of humor for a man of his education and *he knows a lot of things*. Zalmai has eyes that look at one and, in a heartbeat, seem to know everything about the person. One has no secrets when looked at by Zalmai. He is one of those people who can read right through an individual and somehow, in the middle of a tense situation, they seem to see the person's light side, the side that does not dramatize things, the one that appeals to calm, that does not overreact, the side that does not compel to fight because it perceives no threats.

Zalmai is legendary at the *Marastoon* because he has been told he has the exceptional ability to connect all of his life experiences into a woven quilt of lightheartedness that allows him to see a smiling kid in almost everyone he meets. The few stories that Zalmai recounts are entertaining, and he manages to get everybody's mood turned for the better. The few times he speaks, he uses humor.

Often, his humorous stories defuse edgy situations. Always, they teach something appropriate.

Laughter is a great medicine. In the words of one who "has read a book," it is "*scientifically proven*" that laughter promotes the multiplication of "natural killer" cells in the body. These cells attack and neutralize rogue cancerous renegades. The laughter cells are the powerful ones. Laughter cures many ills.

The more one laughs, the more a bunch of *Delta Force / Navy SEALs* cells enter the fray and beat the crap out of the insurgent cells that cause our bodies harm. Imagine the adrenaline rush at thinking about this cavalry charge of heroic cells right inside our bodies while we are laughing uncontrollably at our friend John, who, yet again, has managed to make a fool of himself with his pickup lines for the girls he desperately wants to get to know. The Afghan females laughing at the poor telephone *Guidos* live longer, healthier lives. Their daily routine of laughter at the expense of the romantic hopefuls is their antidote to a life of stressors.

I met Yasin Mohammed Farid when he was in charge of the physiotherapy department of PARSA Afghanistan in 2006. The first day we got acquainted, he accompanied me on a tour of the clinic in *Karta Se* and proceeded to explain how a lot of the ailments had psychosomatic origins. The trauma of continuously witnessing violence and death but, above all, the absence of levity were making people's bodies stiff, inflexible and prone to breaking down.

I have fond memories of laughter and even greater memories of the merry existence during my childhood with my aunt Adriana, who liked taking me to the movies every single day of the week. My Neapolitan relatives live longer because they laugh a lot; more importantly, they find the strength to *ridere per le follie del mondo* (laugh at the world's craziness). Sure, there are plenty of tragedies in life, but the laughing part is overwhelming; it dwarfs the sadness.

Thinking of the good laughing cells charging brings back a memory. Here is how a story about the benefit of laughter would be described by an Afghan *Quissa Mar*.

Every time Zia Adriana and I watched something bad happening to a character playing, let's say a doctor or a sailor, my auntie would beg me to never undertake the medical or mariner profession. This went on for about six years. A few hundred movies later, with the same thing happening every single time,

I was running out of jobs. Auntie Adriana would leverage the love I felt for her to extort a promise that would preclude me yet another career. By the sixth year of watching movies, I knew that the only profession that remained open to me was to become a nun. I ultimately blame my aunt if, according to my football coach at university, Frank Siegmund, I decided to waste my education and became an investment banker. There were no investment bankers' deaths in the movies I watched with Zia. The hyperbole of an Afghan-styled storytelling would move to a related story line:

    The memory of my childhood's crowded cinemas is sweet and overwhelming. There were a few adults who smoked and filled the air with the acrid fog of the cheap *Nazionale* cigarettes. The kids were the real show stealer, tens of them sitting, squatting or standing everywhere—in the corridors, two to a seat, with their backs against the wall, every inch of the theatre was filled with humanity. Boisterous, loud, all of us loved to participate with the action of the movie. It is when the cowboys are defending their families and the precarious position of their encircled wagons against the scary *Sioux* warriors that all the Neapolitan kids are frozen in a fearful state. All of us kids are waiting anxiously. Waiting for what? To hear something familiar, something we have heard many times already—that distant trumpet sound of the charge that tells us the cavalry is coming to the rescue. I am not exaggerating when stating that some of the kids were watching the film for the third consecutive time but still managed to forget that, sooner rather than later, the charge always comes. All the children in the audience grow restless and impatient. All they can hear are the *Sioux's* terrifying battle cries. Finally we can all hear it, even before the cowboys in the movie—the sound of the rescuers' charge. The cinema explodes. The wave of the cavalry provokes a flurry of frenzy. *Scugnizzi* (street urchins) and middle-class kids are running everywhere. Children are hugging each other, shouting cries of relief. Some adults have to restrain kids who want to burst through the screen to get in the fight. I loved it. I loved the charge. Now, imagine that every time we laugh heartily, a similar scene unfolds in our livers, kidneys, lungs, spine, etc.

This is an Afghan-styled story about the health benefits of laughter. The typical American listener would have stopped his active listening at the lack-of-suitable-employment paragraph. Being able to read the above story, to enjoy it and to grasp its concept enables one to communicate suitably with Afghans.

Being humorous is about being able to bring hilarious childhood memories into the daily occurrence of adulthood.

Afghan life, as an adult, can be very grim. Afghan kids always seem to find a way to the lighter side. This ability helps their resiliency. The common denominator between Afghan adults and kids is their willingness to dream. We should keep the Afghan dreaming because, when they cease doing that, they start fighting. They not only dream of real things like wealth or safety, they dream about kings and queens, dragons, jewels and fantastic animals. Their coping mechanisms are common—the more they witness war, death, violence and poverty, the more they dream of a better life, one that is mixed with romance and fantasy. Afghan fantasy is their most valuable natural resource.

A great fantasy is a necessary ingredient to good humor. There were two very funny guys in my first workplace—a trading room. A trading room is a very stressful environment. Millions are made or lost within minutes. Careers are made or lost with it. In the tense atmosphere of the place, laughter would explode as a needed relief when two of my former colleagues would perform their hilarious antics. One of these brokers was Irish. The other was English. They were from different backgrounds, similar cultures, but had the same abilities.

They both had the great ability to correlate the reality they were experiencing with a fantastic alternative, often a childish one. They were both keen observers. They could remember the most detailed minutiae and attach them to humorous alternatives. Afghans might not be as sophisticated, but they have a great memory, intense attention to details and an amazing fantasy. These are all necessary ingredients to be humorous individuals.

Afghan memory is legendary. They rarely forget wrongdoings over the course of centuries, and they put the average Westerner to shame. During a meeting with the 60-year-old *Pashtun* Deputy Director of Education Services for the province of Uruzgan, when asked how he could speak such good English, he answered that he had learned it 40 years before from a visiting Peace Corps volunteer and then proceeded to mention the volunteer's name and his 40-year-old full address in a small Ohio town.

If it is true that Afghans can be very funny, some other nationalities, for arcane reasons, are just not. Everybody should just be funny. Anybody should fulfill his God-given duty to keep the child who resides inside each one of us alive and kicking.

When one gets deployed to an unforgiving war zone, terribly missing home and unable to *Skype* loved ones because the Internet access is, at a minimum, spotty or completely nonexistent, the cheapest relief is laughter. It is common to participate in get-togethers where military personnel can share cigars or NGO operators have cookouts and time seems to stop and lift all present out of a war zone and transport them to a better place in the soul. Memories are shared and good food enjoyed but, most importantly, laughter fills the conversations. Even if the grim realities of war can make levity a tough thing to achieve, the solution is to *ridere per le follie del mondo* (to laugh about the world's craziness).

The International Security Assistance Force (ISAF) for Afghanistan provides the human material for great socio-anthropological studies on humor. A number of nations coming together to fight provide us with the best opportunity to analyze cultural predisposition to humor. Common experience in Afghanistan dictates that most members of the ISAF can come up with pretty good jokes. Laughter abounds around joint bases whether intentionally caused or the result of a cultural misunderstanding.

The Brits have a fantastic "black humor" that serves them well in the most atrocious of events. If the Space Shuttle blows up and kills a number of astronauts, one can rely on the good Englishman to come up with a number of jokes about the accident within two hours following the tragedy. Lady Diana dies in a freakish accident, and some sort of tongue-in-cheek joke is guaranteed to be promptly created. The jokes are relayed with traditional British aplomb, cut-and-dried effectiveness and accuracy. Black humor is theirs, sometimes outright macabre but definitely very witty.

Americans tend to think that the Brits' jokes are not very politically correct, but they secretly laugh at the amusing ability that the more reserved Anglos possess to test the boundaries of decency.

The American military can be pretty funny too but very often without intending to do so. Americans, who have been in a hurry since 1492, in their effort to maximize speed and efficiency, tend to abbreviate everything and end up with acronyms that either sound crazily funny or that in other languages might have the most embarrassing meanings. Americans are also fond of titles to define the inherent importance of duties or professions. They come up with the most fancy and elaborate ones.

On this tendency, Afghans and Americans are cut from the same cloth. For example, one cannot just simply be a *Civil Affairs Officer*. That definition might appear too limiting or confusing so they come up with titles that demand a perverse creativity.

Here is one example of American creativity—One day, Navy Lieutenant Junior Grade Martin Fellow is approached by a Macedonian officer just outside Camp Eggers in Kabul. A few days earlier, these two very officers had been discussing the usefulness of storymaking in the context of warfare in Afghanistan. This time, the Macedonian reopened the conversation by showing the naval officer an ISAF press release with the quote from Air Force Major John Matthews. The two officers both agreed that the quote represented a perfect example of effective storymaking for both foreign and Afghan readers. The quote stated—*A lot of them [insurgents] are sick of fighting, they are sick of listening to Pakistan, because that is where all their orders are coming from. They are sick of fighting Afghans.*

This quote is a great example of a locally impactful message. Like many good stories crafted by Afghans, plenty within this statement cannot be corroborated, but the essence of the message is impactful for readers as it asserts that the insurgency might be turning because of the realization that Afghans are being killed by Afghans and that foreigners are calling the shots. So far so good, but then comes the anti-climax. Major Matthews' title is defined as an *Afghan Hand*—a title that should have required some internationally savvy public relations. The *Afghan Hand* program might be extremely successful, but its name is a source of countless international jokes. It was a name that, while well meant, in the jargon of *Skopjie's* blue collar classes means *one who masturbates Afghans*. When the Macedonian officer had mentioned the issue to the coalition Reintegration public affairs specialist, the American service member explained that *Afghan Hand* indicates a Cultural Immersion Specialist, which for the Macedonian promptly translated into *one who is specialized in diving agriculture*. So Lieutenant Colonel Pandev finished his tour of joint coalition duty bringing home to *Skopjie* a number of *Afghan Hand* stories.

Germans always think they are very funny, but they are definitely not. However, they do make every non-German around crack up because of the way they laugh uncontrollably at jokes that do not qualify as such. Germans are generally the creators and beneficiaries of these pseudo-jokes.

One day, French Foreign Legion Staff Sergeant Antoine DuPre' came to a group of *Bundeswehr* (German Army) and Dutch personnel chatting amicably. They formed a little crowd, oblivious that they were in a war zone, a scene more suited to a corner of Frankfurt's *Jurgen Ponto Platz*. In the middle of the assembly, a German Non-Commissioned Officer (NCO) was recounting, in heavily accented English, a joke that he had just read on the web:

To prove that the recent drone attack has not hit him, Bin Laden decides to write a letter to British Prime Minister Cameron—the *Bundeswehr* still cannot emotionally get over World War II, so the butt of German military jokes are still the Allies—*he does so in his own writing, to affirm that he is still alive and very much in the fight. Cameron opens the letter which, in the tradition of the best Grisham's novels, contains a coded message:* **370HSSV-0773H**— The NCO promptly displays Bin Laden's coded message to all present. *Cameron cannot figure it out, so he sends it to William Hague, the British Foreign Secretary, who summons all of his aides* but still cannot figure out the riddle. Scotland Yard gets called in and, with them also failing to decipher the important message, MI5 intervenes. After a week in which MI5 keeps butting heads with the unbreakable code, it is decided to finally consult the great minds of the *Bundesnachrichtendiest* (the German intelligence agency). *Hauptmann* (Captain) *Sigfried Stocker, of the Bundeswehr,* takes one look at the message and replies, "Tell the Prime Minister he is looking at the message upside down."

The joke is pathetic but the scene becomes really brilliant. All around the NCO, people are laughing so hard that they are falling over each other. Some are crying hysterically. Antoine suddenly feels that Germany might have shut down all of its insane asylums and transferred the patients to its armed forces. The Frenchman witnesses these guys being incapable of stopping the laughter for about 30 minutes. Non-stop eye-watering laughter, 30 minutes long to be precise, with just one bad joke. The French now knows the meaning of *Deutsche militärische effizienz* (German military efficiency).

The Dutch, *me-ole-tulips*, are truly hilarious. Like their German cousins, they also tend to think they are very funny, and they also are not. However, differently from their German colleagues, they cannot make anybody laugh because they just cannot properly laugh themselves unless they are completely drunk, which is a frequent occurrence while cruising bars in *Amsterdam* or *The Hague,* but a difficult feat to accomplish in *Tarin Kowt* or *Zabul*. Not that they did not try.

When, after a four-year involvement, the Netherlands ended their military mission to Afghanistan, the US administration was somewhat disappointed, but most of the coalition breathed a sigh of relief, confident that the replacing nation, as long as it wasn't Switzerland, could outperform the Dutch in the humor department.

The same American psychotherapist whose definition of truth I addressed in a previous chapter, states that in life all you need is not love but laughter. This is certainly valid in a war zone. The Dutch might have accomplished good things in southeastern Afghanistan, but their humor is a lasting legacy.

Afghans' love of laughter makes them prefer foreigners who have a sense of humor. That ability breaks down language barriers and rarely needs interpreters. Smiles are infectious. One's smile is rarely met by a look of hatred. It does happen, but the majority of Afghans responds with smiles to smiles.

Harvard University Divinity School graduate Zackary Warren, while serving in Afghanistan in 2009, put together a compendium of Afghan jokes that depict some interesting social traits. The jokes span a number of social subjects and issues such as politics, the military and romance.

On the political front, the easy target is and always will be the President. Hamid Karzai, considered by most just an American puppet, has the very difficult job of appeasing numerous parties with completely different interests. He is a professional juggler and, contrary to the belief of many, he is an outstanding politician. I am one of the few who seems to believe that he is the right man, in the right place, at the right time. History, as George W. Bush—a controversial president himself—frequently mentioned, will judge. Karzai is known as a very intelligent individual but described as somewhat too passionate.

Afghans like to express their dissent and disappointment with funny jokes about him, such as—*to commemorate the ascension to the Presidency, the Afghan Post has officially launched a new* stamp with the effigy of our beloved President. But the people of Afghanistan are confused which side of the stamp to spit on.

The way they express their feelings about corruption and the security might be told in a joke:

Robber—*Give me all your money!*—Karzai: *Don't you know who I am? I am your President, your brother and Commander-in-Chief of all the Nation's glorious troops!*—Robber: *OK, in that case, give me back all my money!*

Among those who have known President Karzai intimately, he has been recognized as an individual with a propensity to see the bright side of things despite continuous challenges that would have made a Western statesman, serving in a similar environment, break down. His job, while perched at the top of a powder keg, is a constant chess game, where pieces can change color at a moment's notice.

He is known to give in to outbursts of intolerance toward the West's lack of understanding of his precarious role. The way I see it, when willingly taking on a position of responsibility that has all of the expectations ending in failure, one is either crazy or a natural optimist.

One might compare statesmen's positions in relation to what they face when they take office. Presidents like Barack Obama, Spain's Prime Minister Mariano Rajoy or Greece's Antonis Samaras, who are willing to take the reins of their countries when they are close to financial meltdown or plagued by crippling political impasse do not face the personal risks that someone like Karzai has to live with daily.

Karzai's decision implies a willingness to put his life at risk just as his predecessors. Karzai has plenty of history to learn from. One definitely needs a great of sense of humor and a willingness to belittle danger when the majority of his political predecessors have died prematurely. I wonder what keeps Rajoy or Samaras up at night—the thought of their national financial system failing or being castrated, hanged from a lamp post and then dragged behind a car in the streets of Madrid and Athens?

There is a story about Karzai's humor that was recounted by a reliable source. How can a Kabul-based source be considered reliable? The storyteller, a humanitarian operator who has worked in Afghanistan for many years, is a woman, and she is of Scandinavian descent. These are two factors that help define truthfulness in Afghanistan: gender and ethnicity. Women lie less than men, Scandinavians are said to lie a lot less than other nationalities because they have very little fantasy. It is agreed by many that, to be a decent liar, one needs to possess a decent fantasy. It is a matter of DNA. Scandinavians also have little or no sense of humor, again because they are unable to summon fantasy when it is needed. So, even if there is very little chance that she invented the story, the entire theory of truthfulness would be thrown into disarray if the woman had heard the story from a Gulf Arab. In that case, the story would be surely invented. This is because Gulf Arabs have a great fantasy. She assured me that she did not hear it from a Gulf Arab, so the story is Kosher, as this is the cycle of truthfulness in Afghanistan. Everything could be true, and, at the same time, it could be completely fabricated.

Here goes the story—*A former Northern Alliance commander, now a warlord and a member of the government cabinet, had been stopped, with his large entourage, by a colossal traffic jam in the proximity of the Salang tunnel. With a strong display of authority, he enquired about the logjam with Afghan National policemen who were standing nearby. The poor guys confirmed that the Presidency had ordered the tunnel shut for security reasons as US Vice President Biden had just landed at Bagram and was traveling in the area.*

Angered by Karzai's unilateral act of arrogance and in order to impress his entourage, the minister/warlord dials the President on his cellular phone and, after listening to Karzai's excuses, starts delivering a barrage of insults. Karzai keeps silent while the pleased warlord unleashes his repertoire of profanities. The President's silent posture encourages the minister/warlord to increase the level of lewdness of his rant until Karzai's wife is mentioned with a clear reference to what the man would do to her if he ever got his hands on her. By now the warlord has the conversation on his cellphone's loudspeaker so that his entourage can hear the beating he is giving the President.

At this point, Karzai interrupts the man with: "Wait a minute! This might be the only intelligent thing you have mentioned in the past ten minutes. I see two great benefits here. The first one is that you and my wife will stop nagging me and let me do my job in peace. The second one is that you will be finally able to prove to our brothers that you do not copulate only with men…"

The story goes that everybody, including the offending warlord, started laughing in unison. A more dangerous confrontation was therefore avoided, to the President's credit.

There are a few reports about Karzai's lack of emotional balance, but many believe that his ability to defuse difficult situations with good humor has helped him stay alive as the President of an Islamic Republic that includes a lot of inflated egos and hotheads in its government and social ranks.

He is an emotional man, not in the negative sense, and he fully represents the passions that most Afghans possess. We have witnessed him crying when describing civilian casualties and smiling warmly when negotiating with individuals critical of his management of the nation who do not understand how perilous his job is. Humor in Afghanistan is an instrument for survival.

When it comes to the butt of jokes in the Afghan military, soldiers and policemen from *Wardak* are the chosen ones. *Wardak* is primarily *Pashtun*, rural and illiterate. These ingredients make *Wardakis* easy targets. This is similar to the militaries of other nations. Geographical provenance and belonging to different armed forces has always been the source for competitive attitudes and mutual bantering.

US President George W. Bush approached a wounded American soldier in his hospital bed to award him a Purple Heart. The President pinned the medal to the soldier's hospital gown and told him: *Good job, Ranger!* The soldier, who was just starting his recovery, promptly replied: *Mr. President, I am a Special Forces Operator; they would not let me into the Rangers—my IQ was too high!*

A soldier from *Hazara-jat* recounts that once there was a *Wardaki* soldier who had been working in one of the remote provinces for a long time, so he asked one of his *Kandahari* friends who had gone to school to write a letter to his family on his behalf in which he included a photo of himself on top of a donkey. His father received the envelope and saw the letter and a photo inside it. In the letter, the *Wardaki* son started: *Dear father, I hope you are having a good time. Here is a picture of me—I am the one on top.*

The same soldier from *Hazara-jat* tells of a *Wardaki* who had recently become a soldier and was on patrol one night in one of the provinces. On his shift, he saw a shadow move, and, being nervous, he shot it. There was no cry or answer. The next day, he went to the place where he'd fired his AK-47 the night before. There lay a donkey, dead with a single bullet wound. The soldier immediately went to his commander and said: *I don't want to do this jihad anymore.—But why?* his commander asked. *Because, Sir, this isn't a holy war anymore. This is killing our brothers.*

Two young soldiers from a small village, a one-hour drive from *Maidan Shar*, are posted to the 201st Corps in Kabul. They are extremely happy for the adventure because they have been told that the city offers them the mirage of easy women and crazy escapades. When, after a month, they are given a 24-hour leave from duty, they decide to visit a Chinese restaurant so that they can finally know what a woman looks like. The senior NCO of their *kandak* calls them over before they leave the base and proceeds to distribute to them condoms that the International Committee of the Red Cross has donated in order to stifle the rampant epidemic of sexually transmitted diseases among young recruits in Kabul. The NCO does not counsel them on the risk of sexually transmitted diseases because he knows they would not mind if they caught one but prefers to order them to use the condoms so that the woman will not get pregnant and a forced marriage could ensue. The two *Wardakis* acknowledge the order and promptly go into town and visit an aging Chinese prostitute. Three weeks later they meet on the roof of their barracks looking at the beautiful starred night sky and start reminiscing about the magical night with the enchanting mermaid. They laugh and slap each other's backs with a deep sense of pride and male bravado. Soon, the older of the two boys asks his friend: *Hey, Zahir, do you care if she gets pregnant? Not at all*—answers the younger man. *Well in that case I will remove this thing at once.*

American military personnel, like their Red Army predecessors, are also the butt of Afghans' jokes. A number of young

Afghan soldiers believe Americans have really bad habits, are arrogant and rude.

An Afghan story goes that an American soldier had unzipped his pants by the roadside and was about to urinate on a mud wall when all of a sudden the Afghan National Army (ANA) arrived. The ANA noticed what he was about to do, seized him, threw him in their vehicle, and drove him to a place where the security was better and the walls very high. *You are safe to piss here,* they told the American. The American was very impressed and told the ANA men: *You have truly shown me just how hospitable Afghans are.*—*Oh, it's nothing,*—said the Afghans, *you're an American, and this is the U.S. Embassy. You will feel more at home now relieving yourself.*

Courtship, marriage and sexual jokes are rarely charged with strong erotic innuendos. Despite the weird dynamics of Afghan sexuality, one would be hard pressed to hear an Afghan tell a *dirty joke*. They prefer clean, respectful jokes that have a tint of malice in the dialogue.

An example could be a girl was walking down the street, chatting away on her mobile phone. A young man, romantic hopeful, whistled at her and said, *I wish I were that phone of yours, so your mouth would touch mine. If you were my phone,* she promptly said, *then you'd know how much I charge you every night.*

There is the story of the young woman who went to the bazaar with her grandmother. When she entered a shop to buy some vegetables, the young shopkeeper winked at her. The girl picked up some vegetables and asked the price. The shopkeeper said, *"Just one kiss from you would be enough."* The girl smiled and said. "Vale, then just charge it to my grandmother."

There is also a story about a university student, a girl, who once arrived late to class at her university. The professor asked her, *"Why did you come late?"* *"A boy was following me,"* she replied. *"If that was the case, you would have walked faster,"*—the teacher said. *"I was walking fast,"*—she said, *"but the boy was walking too slowly."*

One morning a Kabuli's neighbor asked him a question, *"Last night we heard noises coming from your house. It sounded like someone falling down the stairs. What happened?"* *"Don't worry,"* the Kabuli replied, *"my wife threw my robe down the stairs."* *"Come on Kabuli,"*—the neighbor said, *"A robe doesn't make that much noise."* *"It did,"* the Kabuli replied, *"I should know, I was wearing it."*

Once, two young women were sitting together in a beauty parlor, talking about men. *"What's your fiancé like?"*—one asked. *"Fast as a lion and smart as a deer,"* the other said, *"He really belongs in the zoo."*

These typical Afghan jokes can be found in Zackary Warren's compendium of quick Afghan funny narratives. In the same booklet, Warren mentions that the Dari language, the word *bill* means *shovel*. He observes that, although this poses no significant cross-cultural misunderstandings, it can often create funny jokes when an American named Bill and Afghans interact. There was once an Afghan woman who was married to an American man. The couple had lived happily overseas for many years. One day, the woman's mother called her from Afghanistan. "*What are you doing right now?*" the mother asked. "*I'm eating dinner with Bill,*" the daughter replied. "*Ya Allah,*" the mother cried, "*they don't have spoons in America?*"

In Afghanistan, it's customary for a wife to move into the house of her husband's family as soon as they are married. One wife moved in with her husband's family but refused to do her share of the chores for months. Her husband complained to his mother, and the two thought of a plan—they would quarrel over a broom, and the wife, seeing their argument, would get so fed up that she would take the broom and sweep the floors herself. The very next day, the husband and his mother staged their argument. The wife walked in and shook her head—"*Oh husband, oh mother-in-law, please don't quarrel. Take turns.*"

Kim Barker, the AFPAK correspondent for the *Chicago Tribune,* could see the dark humor and dysfunction in many of the absurd events of daily life in both Afghanistan and Pakistan and wrote a book about them: *The Taliban Shuffle—Strange days in Afghanistan and Pakistan.* The book might make very interesting reading for anybody wishing to learn more about Afghanistan's humorous idiosyncrasies.

A very interesting article in the *Christian Science Monitor,* authored by Lane Hartill, and published February 23, 2005, addresses, among many things, two very important social trends. The first one is the Afghan use of humor as a coping mechanism for extraordinary situations that create psychological stressors. The second is the use of humor as a powerful tool for civic education and finally for political promotion. I liked the article so much that I decided to neither summarize nor edit it. I report the article verbatim, as it is a story worth telling on its own:

> Mubariz Bidar would give Robin Williams a run for his money. He's an Afghan comic who has this city—once ruled by severe Taliban—howling at their former oppressors. His spot-on impressions of everyone from a Taliban soldier to an Afghan drug addict would have even Mullah Omar giggling into his turban. At a recent impromptu performance, Mubariz wraps on a long black turban—a favorite Taliban accessory—and twists his face into a scowl. He grabs a Kalashnikov to complete the look. Then he screams at the men to go to the mosque, physically prodding them with his rifle. He grabs one long-haired man and berates him for letting his locks grow—a Taliban pet peeve. His imitation is so precise that the audience can't stop laughing. It's a disturbing sight for outsiders, but for Afghans who remember the hard-line regime and can finally laugh at it, it's a welcome release.
>
> In a country that had been stung by successive violent regimes, humor has long been a trusted coping mechanism. Even when in power, the Taliban were the butt of jokes, behind closed doors—that targeted everything from their spot checks for shaved armpits (a rule in Islam) to the radio call-in show where people dedicated songs by mullahs (minus the music, of course). Like others, Afghans have used humor to channel dissent, avoid aggression, and let people separate themselves from the ruling group, experts say. From youth using humor to cope with, and eventually bring down, Serbian leader Slobodan Milosevic, to comedian Jay Leno's post 9/11

monologues of Osama bin Laden jokes, comedy is gaining legitimacy as a post-conflict healer. In fact, stand-up comedians from the Arab world, Israel, and the Palestinian territories plan to travel to both Palestinian and Israeli locations this year to give comedy performances promoting peace. "Humor is especially important in conflict and post-conflict countries, because it is a way of transcending or disengaging from the difficulties," says Don Nilsen, a member of the International Society for Humor Studies and a historian at Arizona State University, who used to work in Afghanistan. "The humor used by the Jews in Nazi concentration camps allowed the Jews to take a little bit of control of their own lives," he says. "Humor is a way of inverting the power system."

Back in Khost, Mubariz continues to thrill the crowd with impressions—this time with the fake, but flawless, twitter of a Chinese bride. Mubariz is one of the lead actors in Khost Theater, a small band of dedicated actors in this conservative eastern city that is taking comedy to the masses.

Comedy as civic education. Before last October's presidential elections, a Kabul-based nongovernmental organization hired the actors to promote voting in some of the country's most remote southern villages. Hundreds of people saw each show; the message stuck. Women's turnout in Paktia province, which borders Khost and is so traditional that women are rarely seen in public, was among the highest in the country.

The success of the shows, Afghan observers say, illustrates how effective humor and theater is for educating a public with a low literacy rate (only 64 percent of Afghans can read). It may be, they say, the best way to unify the country's four major ethnic groups that are still quietly split along ethnic lines—one of the major obstacles to lasting peace.

"Theater has a big role in unifying the people in the country," says Mohammad Azim Hussain Zadah, the head of the theater and cinema department in the Fine Arts Faculty at Kabul University. "It's like a guide for the people."

In fact, says Mr. Zadah, "If officials want reconciliation and rehabilitation in the country and want to bring peace and stop ethnic tensions … they should strengthen cinema and theater in the country. Reading about unity in a book is one thing," he says, "but, we see it in theater. We reflect what unity means. We get better results when we see it." Comedy in Afghanistan thrived from the 1800s until the 1960s, when Afghans held actors in high esteem, and Kabul's royal family frequented theaters.

But after the Soviet invasion of 1979, actors slipped out of the country, and comedy declined. During the factional fighting in the early 1990s, mujahidin literally blew the roof off the once-stately theater that used to show Molière and Chekhov adaptations. And when the Taliban arrived in 1996, comedy came to a standstill. Now, with more than $8 billion worth of reconstruction aid estimated to flow into the country during the next 3 years, comedy is finding its footing once again. In fact, one of the most popular shows on Tolo TV, a private cable station in Kabul, is "Lahza Ha," (Moments). It's the Afghan equivalent of Candid Camera, where pranksters stop Kabulis on the street and con them with gags.

The show is so well liked that some Afghans pray early so they don't miss it, and jokes are rehashed the next day.

Mubariz and his fellow unemployed actors in Khost City stick with comedy even though they aren't paid. They make do with fraying stick-on mustaches and ingenuity. Indeed, the Afghan version of "Desperate Housewives" requires Mubariz to be the only forced drag queen in the country. Because women are stowed behind walls in this staunchly conservative city, he's left to don a scarf and screech the falsetto whine of a desperate Afghan housewife.

Getting into character—To study women, he cooks at home—a job strictly reserved for women here—and grills his 10 sisters-in-law for material. "I learned a lot of acting from them," he says. He also watches Mr. Bean, Jackie Chan, and Charlie Chaplin films and then practices in front of a mirror.

Mubariz's muses help him and the other actors perfect their delivery to communicate educational messages to audiences—such as the dangers of opium and the benefits of voting. Mubariz speaks fluently both official Afghan languages, Dari and Pashtu, and uses both in performances, a subtle way of reaching across the ethnic divide. This is a challenge for many actors in the country.

"The problem is the people aren't educated," says Mohammad Sharif, one of the actors at Kabul Theater, as he huddles around a tiny wood stove in the dank bowels of the complex. "They just think, 'this is a Pashtun. He's against me. I'm a Tajik. I'm against him.' The theater explains for the people that we are all brothers and can work together."

But ethnic reconciliation after years of war isn't always easy. During the presidential election, Gulmaki Shah Ghiasi, the head of Kabul Theater, put on plays encouraging people to vote. People flocked. She estimates that more than 1,000 people came to each of their 200 shows. But in Jalalabad, a majority Pashtun city two hours from Kabul, angry locals attacked the actors during a performance, possibly because women were part of the cast. "They're not going to kill me," Shah Ghiasi says, her nose ring winking in the afternoon light. "They just want to scare me. But I'm not afraid."

Recently, the confirmation of the use of humor as a powerful tool for civic education and for political promotion comes by the style adopted by the Italian comedian turned political activist Beppe Grillo, which is bringing him a growing number of followers in a country dominated by the old party system. Heading his *Five Star Movement,* the comedian is using a style that the *New York Times* defines as *a deft mixture of mordant humor, righteous anger and grass-roots organization to tear apart the Italian political establishment which has no more appeal amongst the younger generations.* He verbally *slaughters* the traditional politicians with his modern and sarcastic lingo, against which the old-style politicians have failed to calibrate their rhetorical oratory. The parliamentarians, whom he attacks with refreshing humor full of anecdotes and sarcasm, reply with obsolete hyperbole and baroque phrases that have become too common on the political scene of the past 70 years. Humor can be a winning instrument when it comes to politics as long as it is backed by solid programs. Irony about the opponents would defuse the vitriolic attacks that are now populating almost any Western and, in particular, American elections. Vitriolic attacks in Afghanistan could not be sustained over the long term—the bullets would start flying.

On February 22, 2012, the press office of the US Marines Corps reported the endearing story of a Lance Corporal Edgar Lima, who made a lot of friends among the young population of an Afghan village by contorting his face, sticking his tongue out and generally acting in a very funny, non-ordinary manner for a patrolman. All of this in order to entertain the kids. The first kids started laughing wholeheartedly and called for more of the others to join. Soon enough the laughter became infectious, and Lima left a trail of laughing young villagers behind.

Personally, I was always against wearing full body armor, kevlar, goggles and weaponry when deployed for Civil Affairs missions. I understand the validity of security measures but could not see the point when I had to go to the signing of a healthcare memorandum of understanding in the *Dhi Qar* province, and the Iraqis would all be elegantly dressed in a jacket and tie and I would be looking like I was ready for a fight. Dressing in full battle gear might be instrumental as an intimidating posture to avoid escalation of force or to protect from small-arms fire, but it is an obstacle to relating for effective communication.

This is why when intimidated kids realize there is a smile, a jovial soul, a funny joker underneath the killing apparatus, their trepidation gives way to a willingness to relate to the visitor with the first things than can be found in common—taste buds and smiles. When Afghans greet foreigners or one another, they tend to pat their heart as a show that they are emotionally present. The salute is often accompanied by a friendly smile. The Afghans greet saying, "I am here, and I am emotionally ready to tell you that you are welcome and that you are accepted in peace. *Salaam Aleikum* [literally May the Peace be with you]." Then they go into this greeting *dance* where they enquire about the other's well-being and health all the while wishing the other person a great and fulfilling life. They *dance* while smiling all the way through. I have met hardnosed mullahs who, when confronted with a continuous smile of appreciation and peace or with the stroking of their beard in a sign of respect, have broken down in big happy grins of friendship and hospitality. Once you have sipped the compulsory cups of *chai*, you will be told that they were initially suspicious of the motives of your visit, especially if the visit had come unannounced.

Father and son courtesy of the Australian Armed Forces

Combat Narratives

"Taliban fighters claim they have forced NATO troops to retreat from one of their bases in Afghanistan's Wardak. But NATO says the claims of success are Taliban propaganda."
— Al Jazeera's Jennifer Glasse reporting from Kabul,
7 September 2012

THE BATTLE BETWEEN NATO and the Taliban for *The Story* in Afghanistan is a very important source of material for future information on warfare planning. In asymmetric wars, such as Afghanistan, the lines between public information or public affairs (PA), Military Deception (MILDEC) and Military Information Support Operations (MISO) is often blurred.

Public information is defined as information of a military nature, the dissemination of which, through public news media, is not inconsistent with security, and the release of which is considered desirable or nonobjectionable to the responsible releasing agency.

Military Deception is defined as actions executed to deliberately mislead adversary military decision-makers as to friendly military capabilities, intentions and operations, thereby causing the adversary to take specific actions (or inactions) that will contribute to the accomplishment of the friendly mission.

Military Information Support Operations is defined as a force able to provide combatant commanders, US Ambassadors and other agencies the necessary tools to execute *inform and influence activities* across the range of military operations.

In order to write a comprehensive overview of communication in Afghanistan, I have commissioned different stories or reports from different sources. Some of the material I plucked from the wealth of available Afghan information. Some others were crafted just for the purpose of the book.

For *combat narratives* I enlisted the help of the Civil Military Fusion Center (CFC), an organization that facilitates the sharing of open-source unclassified information between civilian and military stakeholders operating in complex crises. The former head of the Afghanistan desk, a pragmatic man with a fine mind, assigned the study to Miss Raj Salooja, an Assistant Desk Officer with a background in civil-military coordination and post-conflict reconstruction.

She had worked previously with the World Bank and Canadian Government, and she is a Master of Science graduate in the Foreign Service program at Georgetown University in Washington, DC. Salooja and CFC compiled the following study about how the portrayal and perception of events is critical to the development of success for either side.

The brief begins with an overview of how ideas and values are shaped by both insurgents as well as ISAF. The second section looks in closer detail at the strategies employed by both sides in terms of narrative themes and methodologies. Upon comparison, we find that the capacity and effectiveness of information operations of the Taliban and ISAF is asymmetrical in the three main components of the information battlefield: *Time, Access and Impact*.

Time: Without the need for verification or approval, the Taliban is able to respond in real time and gain an upper hand in how events are perceived.

Access and Impact: While ISAF are engaging with local populations, there still remain areas where neither they nor the Government of the Islamic Republic of Afghanistan (GIRoA) are present. The Taliban is able to hold particular sway over narratives in such locations. The longstanding rule of the Taliban prior to 2001 has allowed the group to become a part of the many facets of Afghan society, particularly in Pashtun areas and in parts of the country that they formerly ruled. The Taliban are not viewed as an entirely "outside" force in certain parts of the country compared to ISAF and, as such, the civilian population views their actions differently. While the Pashtun areas are not monolithic in their receptivity to Taliban actions, the Taliban is more effective in face-to-face communication and are able to access areas otherwise difficult for ISAF forces to reach.

Why is Narrative Important? The war in Afghanistan is based on a difference in values, policies and ideology between the Afghan Taliban and ISAF since 2001. Both parties require the support of Afghan civilians to achieve their missions, for popular support to fall into line with their view on how the country should be governed. As Thomas Elkjer Nissen notes on a paper addressing the Taliban's information warfare, "the Taliban must keep local audiences on their side, or at the very least keep them neutral, until [the] IC [international community] runs out of political time."

A 2011 study by Jason Lyall, Kosuke Imai and Grame Blair attempts to measure civilian attitudes toward the Taliban and ISAF using a sample of 204 villages in 21 districts of five Pashtun-dominated provinces. They were asked the following question: "In your view, how often do foreign forces (or the Taliban) take precautions to avoid killing or injuring innocent civilians during their operations?" Possible answers were: always (3), sometimes (2), rarely (1), and never (0). A higher score (such as 2 or 3) is positive and suggests that the group in question is highly concerned about civilian casualties; a low score would mean the opposite. The study found that the mean response for ISAF was 0.56 versus the Taliban's average score of 1.92. The Taliban was seen as much more concerned about civilian casualties, and Afghans perceived ISAF as having little concern for Afghan civilians. The authors conclude that "these findings are stunning when we consider that the Taliban killed an estimated 2,080 Afghan civilians in 2010 alone while ISAF was deemed responsible for 440. Yet the perception remains that ISAF, rather than the Taliban, is wielding violence indiscriminately, suggesting that individuals in our sample area do not believe that ISAF is protecting them."

While the study recognizes that "it is neither the case that Pashtun attitudes are monolithic toward the combatants, nor are these attitudes uniformly affected by combatant actions," the research is useful as it begins to shed light on the ways in which civilian attitudes could be impacted by efforts on behalf of ISAF and Taliban insurgents to shape the perception of events.

In a March 2009 press briefing, then US Ambassador Richard Holbrooke recognized that "the information issue" had become a "major, major gap to be filled." The following sections look more closely at that gap.

Yes, the Taliban use Twitter! In the fall of 2011, the Twitter account used by ISAF media (@ISAFmedia) responded to a comment made by Taliban spokesman Abdulqahar Balk (@ABalkhi) regarding an assault by Taliban insurgents in Kabul. What ensued was a back-and-forth debate on Twitter that covered issues such as civilian casualties, responsibility and the larger ISAF mission. As with all Twitter content, each message was limited to 140 characters (*see Box 1, below*).

> The exchange began when @ISAFmedia addressed comments from @ABalkhi by tweeting, "Re: Taliban spox on #Kabul attack: the outcome is inevitable. Question is how much longer will terrorist put innocent Afghans in harm's way?"
>
> @ABalkhi) wrote: "@ISAFmedia i dnt knw.u hve bn pttng thm n 'harm's way' fr da pst 10 yrs.Razd whole vllgs n mrkts.n stil hv da nrve to tlk bout 'harm's way'"
>
> @ISAFmedia responded: "Really, @abalkhi? Unama reported 80% of civilians causalities are caused by insurgent (your) activities http://goo.gl/FylwU"
>
> @ABalkhi tweeted in response "@ISAFmedia Unama is an entity of whom? mine or yours?"
>
> The back and forth between @ISAFmedia and @ABalkhi is ongoing. @ISAFmedia later tweeted to @ABalkhi a YouTube video of the commander of NATO-led forces, General John Allen as he checked on troops after the attacks: "Hey @alemarahweb, does your boss do this? http://goo.gl/9XpYn #Kabulattacks #ISAF #COMISAF"

Box 1. Twitter Exchange Regarding Taliban Assault on Kabul

The embrace of technology by the Taliban began in the early 1990s, when the Taliban began renovating presses, launched new publications and maintained the Voice of Sharia, a radio station for Taliban ideas and statements. Since 2001, the Taliban has focused their use of information technology on discrediting the ISAF mission. As Greg Bruno of the Council on Foreign Relations (CFR) notes, within days of coalition forces entering Kabul, Taliban leader Mullah Omar stated that, "The military intervention was not about terrorism or capturing Osama bin Laden, but rather about hijacking Afghanistan's religious traditions." Such a theme has remained consistent through the Taliban's approach toward shaping the narrative of the war. Nissen cites three additional, recurring themes:

The Taliban will be here when ISAF is gone: As Nissen notes, "This has a cognitive effect creating a reluctance on part of the local audiences to support ISAF; they will have to live with the Taliban when ISAF withdraws—either from the area or, eventually, from Afghanistan."

The Taliban is strong and the enemy (ISAF) is weak: This perception is exploited by pointing out that ISAF cannot maintain a presence throughout the entire country whereas the Taliban is in places that neither GIRoA nor ISAF is able to control or govern.

GIRoA is a puppet of ISAF: According to Nissen, this is, "a message that resonates with the general Afghan resentment of all foreigners."

Utilizing the narrative of past struggles with the Soviets and British, the Taliban also play on previous instances of foreign occupation to color the present-day international mission in Afghanistan. While such narratives have a powerful influence, the issue goes beyond themes and into the use of rhetoric.

According to Nissen, "The Taliban often refer to themselves as mujahidin, or freedom fighters, a simple and effective technique that plays on the collective memory of the Soviet occupation and expulsion, with the intent of portraying ISAF as the same as the Soviet regime." The use of metaphors such as "crusaders" and "infidels" also plays to a collective memory. This is because the Taliban "understand their local audiences, their culture and their situation much better than ISAF does, and they legitimize their actions and propaganda claims with reference to The Qu'ran and Islam in a way that ISAF is precluded from doing."

Messages that fall within these narratives are generally delivered through the following methods: chants *(tarana)*, magazines/newsletters, night letters *(shabnamah)*, poetry, video, websites (Facebook, YouTube, Twitter) and sermons/radio broadcasts. A number of key Taliban means of communication are:

Night Letters: Taliban "night letters" are usually handwritten messages sent to a specific person to intimidate him or her. In 2011, Spencer Ackerman of *Wired Magazine* notes that the Taliban began sending out "night letters" via SMS that include "interviews of suicide bombers intercut with their attacks."

Face-to-Face Interaction: As Nissen notes, most Taliban information is dispersed through face-to-face communications, "with local leaders and elders to persuade them not to support ISAF or (GIRoA)."

Video: It was noted that, in 2009, the Taliban established an official YouTube channel titled "Istiqlal Media" that was discovered by terrorist media expert Evan Kohlman, who notes that bandwith may have had something to do with the launch.

"Recent efforts to distribute high-resolution jihadi media in standard formats RMVB, AVI, MPEG—have simply overloaded their web servers and exhausted their bandwidth. Now, it appears that the Taliban webmasters have finally come around and recognized the merits of YouTube, using the US-based service to test out, directly embedding video into their sites. By turning to YouTube, the Taliban gain a free, highly-reliable video broadcast service with the potential to reel in a vast, viral audience."

As Stephen Biddle notes, the insurgent attacks are often planned for "the biggest public relations punch." If the Taliban aims to portray that the Afghan government is unable to protect the population, insurgents may plan an attack and arrange for it to be photographed and distribute the footage online. "The whole purpose of the military activity," Biddle says, "is to create video."

Creative Counter Insurgency is required in approaching the Afghan warfare scenario. In a 2009 paper, authors Thomas Johnson and Chris Mason note that US and NATO officials "continue to misread the fundamental narrative of the enemy they are fighting, determined in this case to wage a secular campaign against an enemy who is fighting a religious war." The narrative of religious war or resistance resonates with many in Afghanistan. However, the study by Lyall, Imai and Blair shows that, despite the difficulties, it may be possible for ISAF to mitigate the negative impact of violence on civilian attitudes through restitution efforts. While the authors acknowledge that this finding is based on a small subset of individuals, it shows one way in which the shaping of the narrative by ISAF has the potential for positive outcomes. As Tim Foxley notes, "the Afghan Government could be doing a lot more to undermine the insurgency—in particular, the recruiting base of young, poor, mainly Pashtun men in southern Afghanistan and north western Pakistan—with a media campaign that challenges and exploits the often confused and uncoordinated Taliban communiqués."

ISAF's primary narrative in Afghanistan appears to focus on democracy. As Nissen notes, "ISAF's master narrative does not exploit cultural differences as the Taliban do." One difference, and major challenge for ISAF, he highlights, "is that ISAF's narrative has to address both Afghan and global audiences, whereas the Taliban's narrative really only has to resonate with local or Afghan audiences."

In general, ISAF information efforts fall into three categories according to Tim Foxley of the Stockholm International Peace Research Institute: (i) routine "good news" stories (bridges built, hospitals repaired, money spent); (ii) defending against its own mistakes (e.g., ISAF forces kill civilians); and (iii) reacting to Taliban information operations initiatives (e.g., Taliban claims that ISAF airstrikes have killed civilians).

While ISAF forces have employed a variety of techniques, they continue to develop new ones. For instance, Rajiv Chandrasekaran of *The Washington Post* describes what he labels the "Mullahpalooza Tour" in a 2010 article—*Then there's what Marines call the "mullahpalooza tour." Although most US military units have avoided direct engagement with religious leaders in Afghanistan, Nicholson has brought over Lt. Cmdr. Abuhena Saifulislam, one of only two imams in the US Navy, to spend a month meeting—and praying with—local mullahs, reasoning that the failure to interact with them made it easier for them to be swayed by the Taliban. At his first session with religious leaders in Helmand, the participants initially thought the clean-shaven Saifulislam was* an impostor. Then he led the group in noontime prayers. By the end, everyone wanted to take a picture with him. "The mullahs of Afghanistan are the core of society," he said. "Bypassing them is counterproductive."

A similar program was implemented by the US Marine Corps and its coalition partners in Regional Command-Southwest in 2009. Lt. Col. Patrick Carroll and Patricio Asfura-Heim outline their experiences in reaching out to religious leaders and the lessons learned while doing so. They note that mullahs represent a critical access point for influencing opinion because of their influential role in Afghan society. They find that the "most credible voices to counter the Taliban's rhetoric were moderate mullahs themselves; i.e., Islamic religious leaders who did not believe in the Taliban's extremist interpretations of the Qu'ran, who would support GIRoA and who were at least neutral—possibly even positive—to the presence of ISAF." A British-led delegation of the Helmand Provincial Reconstruction Team also carried out an engagement program in 2009 with religious leaders. While identifying who is considered a "moderate" is difficult, much can be learned and shaped through engagement. For example, in a report by Philip Pelikan on the "Mullah Engagement Program" that brought a group of Afghan religious leaders to Great Britain, one religious leader noted that, "The Taliban tell everyone that Britain is an infidel nation hostile to Muslims, but the mullahs were able to see for themselves that in fact Britain is a tolerant country in which Muslims can build mosques and practice their religion peacefully."

In addition to religious figures, units also began reaching out to avenues of society otherwise left unnoticed: women. In his article, Chandrasekaran notes that the Marines have established Female Engagement Teams (FETs) made up of female Marines who accompany combat patrols that meet with the women in villages, dispense medical assistance and identify reconstruction needs. He quotes MSgt. Julia Watson: "Men have really opened up after they see us helping their wives and sisters." The shaping of narrative requires an engagement with Afghan civilians across the spectrum of society and from many different angles as the US Marines and FETs demonstrate. Understanding the role of religious figures and women within Afghan society allows ISAF forces to engage these actors in a way that is conducive to counter the narrative of the Taliban.

Semantic infiltration is at the core of Afghan insurgency strategy. In October 2010, the World Policy Institute and EastWest Institute hosted two experts to talk about new strategies in terrorism. Tom Parker of Amnesty International stated that at "the heart of the conflict against terrorism is an issue of competing ideas and narratives. Muslims susceptible to radicalization must be educated in order to mitigate the *information asymmetry* that fosters terrorism." He proposes that, "if these adherents are exposed to new ways of thinking, particularly from credible religious leaders who emphasize the atrocities committed by terrorists upon Muslims and the Qu'ran's strict ban on suicide, there is potential to reverse or prevent the radicalization process." For Parker, this idea of "information asymmetry" is based on the notion that adherents are often provided incomplete information and how they come to understand events is often extremely limited to the one perspective offered by extremists.

Parker argues for a strategy of counter-narrative that achieves "semantic infiltration" that he defines as being a system where "Al Qaeda and other terrorist groups are pressured to acknowledge positive values in their public statements, such as concern for human rights" that forces them to speak within a "value system that they can't adhere to," further undermining their popular support. He cites the example of the release of two recorded messages by Osama bin Laden calling for humanitarian aid to flood victims in Pakistan, as well as action to combat famine and climate change.

A number of forms of asymmetry are discussed below. These primarily concern time and impact.

With regard to *Time*, one of the major differences between the capacity of ISAF versus the Taliban to reach their audience is time. In a speech in February 2008, Michael Doran notes that US forces carry out an operation and "within 26 minutes—we've timed it—the Taliban comes out with its version of what took place in the operation, which immediately finds its way on the tickers in the BBC at the bottom of the screen." The Taliban's ability to comment and report on ISAF operations in real time contributes to their success. NATO messaging meanwhile requires verification and approval that takes time. This can lead to the perception that ISAF forces are slow to either respond or react.

For example, Nissen notes that in a February 2007 visit to Bagram Airbase by then-US Vice President Dick Cheney, a coincidental suicide attack was "exploited by the Taliban because the Vice President's presence ensured that the attack was headline news on all international media." The asymmetry emerges when US officials who tried to play it down, "the Taliban quickly claimed that they had planned the attack, portraying the Taliban to local audiences as more capable and dangerous than they really were."

With regard to *Access and Impact*, one of the Taliban's most effective means of communication is at the local level, from face-to-face interaction. As Tim Foxley notes, insurgents often belong to the same tribes as the local population and share the same language and culture. As such, they are also able to gain access to populations that are otherwise more difficult to access for ISAF forces.

The limited extent to which ISAF forces are able to reach, both literally and metaphorically, the Afghan people rest on what the 2011 study by Lyall, Imai and Blair describes as the "intergroup bias" dynamic. Defined as the "systemic tendency by individuals to evaluate one's own membership group (the 'in-group') or its members more favorably than a non-membership group (the 'out-group') or its members." The implication is that "negative actions by an in-group, by contrast, are understood as situational in nature ('forced to be bad'), while negative actions by the out-group confirm prior biases that the out-group and its members are inherently 'bad' actors." All this is to say that actions carried out by the Taliban have a different implication toward civilian population perceptions than those carried out by ISAF. In particular, the Taliban is generally "let off the hook" more easily, and populations tend to be "more forgiving, since such acts are justified to appeal to extenuating circumstance." This is part of the explanation for why ISAF forces are "often blamed by victimized individuals for harm that was actually inflicted by the rebels themselves."

In conclusion, the difficulty that ISAF faces in addressing narrative is tied inherently to the nature of its role as an outside force. Part of the asymmetry is a product of issues, such as time, access and impact, as noted above. Differences also emerge through the portrayal of the battle as either religious or secular, which impacts the types of methodologies employed by each actor in their attempts to reach civilian populations, which as Nissen notes, remains as the "centre of gravity for both sides."

The military definition of centre of gravity in a conflict is the source of power that provides moral or physical strength, freedom of action, or will to act in a conflict.

Drawing by Meranda Keller

Afghan ancient compound (courtesy of Penelope Price)

The Lost Afghan Diary

"Italian Priest in Kabul Flirts With Fate"
— John Pomfret, Associated Press
Los Angeles Times, March 18, 1990

There is a significant group of expatriates forever "chained" to Afghanistan. One meets members of this group in almost every segment of Afghan society. They are the alumni of the American International School of Kabul (AISK). The school was an elementary through high school on Darulaman Avenue in Kabul, land that was made available by the Afghan Crown in 1965.

AISK ceased to exist in 1979, when the Soviet Union invaded Afghanistan, and 14 years worth of academic legacy have managed to create a hardcore nucleus of faithful alumni who keep the memory alive by heralding their *Scorpion* (that is what they call themselves) affiliation. They were the children of foreign area officers, embassies' employees, humanitarian workers, development advisors and wealthy Afghans.

It was a *Scorpion* who approached me in 2007 and gave me Father Angelo Panigati's diary. The *Barnabite* priest had served in Afghanistan more than 25 years and had taught French at the American International School of Kabul. Father Panigati traveled extensively around Afghanistan and officiated Roman

Catholic mass in a number of posts, including a tenure at the Italian Embassy's chapel.

The *Scorpion* begged me to publish it so that the priest's story would not get lost. The American alumnus believed that Father Angelo's stories contained useful information about the Afghans that would have helped with bridging the gap in communication that the military visitors were experiencing after toppling the Taliban.

Father Panigati's little-known memories were initially preserved by a young man who was the son of one of the Italian diplomats serving in Kabul, and they were eventually translated from Italian into English by Sister Mary Crucifix Buttaci, a nun who had served with Father Angelo in Chile. Sister Crucifix had entrusted the translation to the *Scorpions* who had stayed behind in Afghanistan to pass the story to the newly arrived expatriates.

Father Angelo returned to Italy to die in 1999. His memories, unpublished until now, are the property of the world. The following is the entire diary as it was given to me:

Shah Rukh, the youngest son of Tamerlane, who commissioned the building of the sanctuary Gazargah, could not have foreseen six centuries ago what a profound psychological effect that place of prayer would have on the only Catholic priest in Afghanistan. During my visit in 1966, this artistic jewel and former center of Muslim learning near *Herat* was still an asylum for criminals seeking refuge from the law. I was visiting the tomb and rendering honor to the great Muslim poet and mystic, Khwaja Abdullah Ansari, when a laborer approached me with the question, "And you, of whom are you a slave?"

I did not know the person well enough to answer him properly, but Rahim, who helped in my house and accompanied me on long trips to visit my parishioners, asked him, "What do you mean, slave of whom? He is a creature of God, like us!"

I understood, then, there was also a place for me, a priest of Christians, a foreign minority in a solid Muslim country. Of course, I had to keep within the limits of rendering services only to the Christians who were in the country temporarily. I was forbidden to proselytize or do mission work outside of my recognized obligations. The country was at my disposal—to learn of its beauty, its customs and, finally, to share the religious spirit in those points that were similar to mine.

At the beginning of my stay, I was first greeted as *mullah sahib* and also *priest sahib*.

A *mullah* is generally recognized as being a man of religion. A *sahib* is the English equivalent of "mister" but also connotes respect. Little by little, after having shared bread and salt with some Afghan friends—friendships made slowly but to last forever—within the family, they definitely called me *Padar-jan (Dear Father)*.

In the bazaar, they continued to call me *priest sahib*, but on my ID card that permitted me to visit my parishioners who were working as technicians and volunteers away from Kabul and often in remote areas of the country or who were even detained as prisoners, the official title with which I traveled was *Prayer Guide*. This is what a Muslim is called who, when facing Mecca, directs the prayer meeting. Naturally, they knew I was not one of them but recognized that I was a man of *The Book,* one who prayed to a God who, without being called *Allah*, was the same God of *Abraham*, great and merciful, of their adoration.

My parish, geographically, was large, twice the size of Italy. The number of parishioners was small, but the religious assistance I was able to provide was appreciated everywhere. Long journeys took me to every corner of the country: crossing the long chain of the *Hindu Kush* mountains; to the desert of *Registan*; up to the steppe along the *Amu Darya* River, and to the corridor of the *Paropamisus* and *Elburz* mountains.

I always carried a first-aid kit for those nomads I met along the way, especially in the isolated places where there were few inhabitants. Their thanks for any help was expressed traditionally by the kissing of the palms of the hands of the giver.

Always, the question directed to Rahim was: "Who is he?" His reply was always the same: "a Christian prayer guide." In one house, Rahim was explaining the title "Prayer Guide" using the title *muallim*, which means teacher. He explained that it was my obligation not only to accompany my people in social prayer, but that I had also to advise, direct and to teach The Book — The Gospel.

Convinced of the truth of my religious mission, the charming way the Afghans treated me showed them to be wise, tolerant, and serene; this was especially evident in areas where the isolation and under-development were the greatest. I am not a romantic type. Many years in difficult, rough places have made me even more rustic by nature. Therefore, you cannot call me naïve or a dreamer if I say that ecumenism is not experienced only in discussing or dialoguing but to a greater extent in personal contact with people who have integrity and tolerance. A tribal chieftain actually called me "brother."

"Do you not know that I am not a Muslim?" I asked him. "Of course I know that," he replied.

"I understand, however, that from morning to night, wherever you are, whomever you are with, or whatever you are doing, you are exactly like myself, that is, one who is aware of and living with God."

As a teacher, I could not have received a better response from somebody who did not ask for any hierarchical title. I, in turn, addressed him as *Dear Father*.

If people ask me about the Islamic religion, I never give didactic information. Twenty-five years in the land of the Aryans were not enough to give me a profound and exhaustive understanding of Islam. Nevertheless, I am able to formulate answers based on my many rich experiences and personal contacts while living among Muslims. I saw, heard, admired, tolerated, and understood a religion lived.

Can I add that I often had to compare my life with theirs? Well, a comparison never led me to add praise to nor detract from different religions. The integrity I have seen expressed by Muslims in the practice of their faith has been good for me. The simplicity of their faith has separated me from formal analysis of Christianity that creates confusion and obscures the essentials and the true spirit of the Christian faith.

Rather, the Muslims have helped me to better know Christ and His Church, of which I was the only official ecclesiastical representative among them in Afghanistan. He, who was recognized by the tribal chieftain as "always with God," had to place himself at the service of the small international Christian community. He had to overcome the limits of his own intellect, his temperament, his likes and dislikes, his own tastes, even his own culture, in order to be a true guide. He needed to be a man of prayer, teacher and, above all, a Dear Father.

Submission or Fatalism?

I have learned that Islam means submission to the inscrutable *Will of God*. Defined thus, it might seem that man, in his dealings with God, must only obey Him blindly. The Islamic religion that I observed in daily living in Afghanistan, offered me a view of a rich interior that a superficial knowledge of the Muslim religion would want to exclude. My memory will help me, if only feebly, to recall significant episodes where that rich interior was manifested in a convincing way. Both fatalism and submission present many negatives. It is enough to list their synonyms: subjection, subordination, resignation, inevitability, intimidation and suppression. The daily reality presented me with manifestations of acceptance that involved the whole individuality of my Afghan friends; they showed intelligence, heart, and sensitivity. My memory guides me to episodes that left lasting impressions.

The Monday After Easter

One of my duties as Pastor was to visit my little flock in Kandahar to celebrate Easter, the feast of joy. The weather seemed quite good when I started out, but soon, only a few miles from Kabul, I was faced with a snowstorm. There was little I could do with my little car and was forced to turn back. Upon returning home, I sent word to my parishioners at the camp in Kandahar that I would come the next day. It was necessary for Rahim, my traveling companion, to accompany me because the trip in the snow would be slow going and would take more than twelve hours. But the next day, Rahim came late.

We finally started out facing a trip of 500 kilometers in thick whiteness on slippery roads but, with prudent driving, finally managed to arrive in Kandahar, a weary 14 hours later.

The group awaiting us received us cheerfully, as they always did, but would not let me forget that the tardy riser, Rahim, made me arrive late.

In Asia, it is customary for chiding, because of a fault, to follow a polite greeting or even a diplomatic introduction. "See, Rahim," I exclaimed, "thank God we have arrived, but had you come earlier, we would not have been so late." Usually, during long trips, I sang while I drove, and he, Rahim, slept.

We did not speak at all on that trip, even during the breaks while taking tea and participating in individual conversations with other travelers. Up to the moment of my mild rebuke, I had said nothing about his tardiness, but the time had arrived, I thought, for me to do that.

"Excuse me, Father," he replied softly, "around four this morning, my son died."

Rahim's answer left me stunned. I could have told him that he had the right to stay home, but I already knew the reaction of Muslims in this circumstance. This is what God wants.

"This is what God wants," we told each other. I knew Rahim well and understood his profound sensitivity and his attachment to his numerous family members. He cried, but he accepted.

"May God strengthen you," I prayed. It was impossible for me to stop comparing his acceptance with my own dealings with the Lord, whom Jesus has taught me to call "Father." I would not have been capable, as was Rahim, of such a painful, though human, acceptance.

Some of the individual cases I mention may make us think that they were exceptional, but they were not. Difficult circumstances were routine in the lives of the many people with whom I was in contact, and the acceptance they showed was equally convincing.

Lashkargah, in the desert region of Registan (Desert of Death), was among my monthly trips.

To get there, one had to leave the cement roads of Kandahar, and hunt and pursue the rocky and red, sandy roads that flanked the Helmand River. Normally, we arrived in late afternoon, giving me time to meditate among the ruins of Kala-i Bost, a tenth-century city and said to have been one of the most architecturally remarkable of its era. It was demolished by Genghis Khan, but in a later reconstruction, many forts were added to the site. However, the beautifully decorated Arch of Bost is the lone survivor of this once powerful citadel.

When the technicians and the specialized laborers were ready, I would join them and celebrate Mass. The return trip was always early the next morning. During one return trip, as I was driving by an embankment, a very large rock broke loose and struck my oil sump, crushing it.

Trying to fix it 40 kilometers from Lashkargah was impossible. I waited about ten hours for a passing car that could give me a ride back. Finally, a large Volvo that served as a taxi from Kandahar to Kala-i Bost added me to its ten passengers. I managed to find a small seat in the open-roof car. The taxi returned to Kandahar every night from the desert. About ten people assembled each evening to wait for the taxi. This time was the same as always, except for me. I told the people there that my car had broken down, so I needed to tow it to the first repair station, 100 kilometers down the national highway. The discourse was neither heated nor quarrelsome. Some smiled and wished God to accompany me. They would have tried to leave the next day; but the ruins of Kala-i Bost taught that the value of time in history is indeed relative. One of the group, who had waited longer than I, stepped forward and insisted that I take his place. He had made this decision because for him, it was the Will of God.

One of the finest examples of the Muslim attitude of acceptance was demonstrated to me in the behavior and words of the chief of a clan of nomads. This exceptional man knew 14 languages and spent the winter months in the West, while his clan spent time in the plains of the river Indus during its seating, or gentle, period.

"In Europe, they speak of us as a Third World," he began his discourse over tea, "It is true, as far as progress goes. It is not true, as far as existential reality goes. The Westerners are a bit like the peasant—they know not why the seed grows. A sense of life is truly missing. The rhythm of life is heavy, simply because the necessary dependence on God is forgotten. The vital problems are frequently exasperating, and one's own limits are attributed to circumstances or to other human beings. We, from birth to death, and during all the phases of our development, feel that God is guiding us. Joys, sorrows, success, sickness, health, old age, and death are not products of a blind destiny, but are willed by God. Great and Merciful. We know the Biblical words of Job: *The Lord gives and the Lord takes away. Blessed be the name of the Lord.*"

How can we not think of Jesus' teaching that helps us to pray: *"May Your Will be done"*?

What difference is there between the Islamic acceptance of the Will of God and St. Paul's meaning:

"It is the Lord that gives us the desire and the will to do according to what He designs." Wisdom from a nomad chieftain at its best.

The patience of nomads during their daily 30-kilometer treks, or during their pauses, is rather an example of true serenity and calm than of simple resignation. The natural catastrophes, war and plunder, crimes, famine, thievery and all manner of havoc that nature or man can inflict are part of the nomad's all-inclusive submission to God and represent a balance of life of which we, also, become aware at our age of reason. Anything that might better a situation is welcomed, even by the Afghans, but without illusions. The four generations of people who wanted to guide the country never had the trust of the people. The propaganda spread by loudspeaker in the central park in Kabul was scorned by the passers-by; women, old people, and also children would continue to talk in groups or sing to themselves. The response to the blaring rhetoric was always the same, "Lies!" The Afghans did not believe in a *heaven on earth* promised by the politicians.

But the drama of war demonstrated that their acceptance of a tragedy permitted by God is not fatalism. Assad, an Embassy driver, lost his two sons. The Regime captured one in the city; the Resistance drafted another. The brothers were obliged to fight on opposite sides. They both died fighting. Assad's sorrow was immense and, even for a Muslim, beyond consolation. Can fatalism be in accord with a sorrow so great?

He Lives!

For the Afghan, Jesus is a penultimate prophet, yet they never pronounced Jesus name without first placing the word "Holy" before it. Even when they, with timidity and displeasure, offered objections to Christianity, their respect and veneration for Jesus never wavered. It is known that the Qu'ran gives a lot of space to the Lord of Christians, even if it presents Him with pronouncements very different from those of the Gospels. My daily contacts with the Afghans, even though I was prohibited from proselytizing, were quite amiable, vast and profound. They extended to all walks of life: to the personnel of the Italian Embassy, to the employees of various offices of social services, to the people of the bazaar, to the merchants, and even to the police. The latter, thanks, one could say, to the hippies and foreign drug addicts! I was always treated with respect rather than with tolerance.

Two events of Christian life, Christmas and Easter, rendered my rapport stronger with the Afghans, especially the personnel of the Italian Embassy and of the International School where I taught in order to earn a living. (The little Chapel on the Italian Embassy grounds—extraterritorial—was the property of the government and was not a source of income for me.)

Christmas, in Dari, the language of Kabul, was called Feast of the Birth.

Before the Soviet invasion, even the Afghan market was beginning to be invaded by the Christmas consumerism typical of the West. The foreigners who were Christians could find Christmas trees and decorations, greeting cards, and sweets and other special foods for holiday celebrations.

In the embassy and at the International School, the Afghans were involved in the construction of the Christmas scenes. The one at the Chapel was visited with interest because the nativity was presented in an Afghan setting. First of all, the figures in the panoramic scene were placed against a background of the Hindu Kush mountains (created from papier-mâché), and they were dressed in a variety of Afghan costumes, the nomads in their colorful apparel, and the people from the bazaar in their everyday attire, but shown conducting their various trades as bread *(naan)* carriers, water and cheese porters, laborers pushing carts, and the merchants with their commissioned goods. Those who helped with the scenes used to bring their families to the Chapel. It was quite moving to hear the children say: "That's Mary… That's baby Jesus and that one is Joseph." Playfully, some would point to the little animals, to a donkey, an ox, or one of the camels and would attach to the animal the name of a little brother or sister standing nearby, creating a jolly camaraderie around the *crèche*.

It was a sort of unconscious ecumenical dialogue that went on with the visiting Afghans when my parishioners were celebrating a baptism, a wedding, or a funeral. Sometimes the Afghan helpers took part in the events. However, a great theological contrast occurred during a Holy Week service at the Chapel. One of the guards at the Embassy door was a leader in prayer and a sort of *mullah* in his neighborhood. In his Qu'ran, it was written: "*They did not kill Jesus, but instead Allah has taken Him to Himself. He will return on the Day of Judgment.*"

According to Islam, God hid Jesus from the Jews, as they wanted to kill him, and substituted another man for him. You must know that, in Asia, the greeting is the highest form of civility, even to the extent that one greets his enemy before killing him. Well, my mullah of the embassy door did not greet me on Good Friday. To venerate the dead Jesus was an insult to the Qu'ran. Passing him, I greeted him saying: "Don't worry! On Sunday we will believe in the same life!" On Easter Sunday, I said to him: "Jesus is alive." "Really, Father?"—he asked. Peace was made later between the door man and me, thanks to the war.

The Soviet troops had finally retreated, and my parish was left with only some soldiers of the United Nations and Red Cross volunteers. The Protestant community decided to remain in Kabul in spite of the dangers that existed, since the communists were still in charge. Many of the group remaining were doctors and nurses. The Afghan communists were divided into two groups and had begun fighting each other. One day the Minister of Defense decided to intimidate the president, who belonged to the opposing group, with a *coup d'état*. The minister had at his disposal bombs and arms. At about 1 p.m., the attack began.

There were three objectives of the destruction: the Presidential Palace, Radio Afghanistan, and the political prisoners. My house was in the middle of the triangle. For one hour, all the targets were hit. But at a certain moment, the opposing military planes took off. I knew then that the real danger had begun. I had left my house, where I was reciting my breviary and was almost safe. It occurred to me that my *mullah* of the door might be in danger, so I had gone to grab him and quickly push him under the strong cement steps of the ambassador's residence.

While I was returning, a bomb hit the embassy wall and catapulted me some meters toward the little Chapel. I hit my head, not against the door that was no longer there, but against the quilted leather curtain that hung in its place in order to protect me from the 18 degrees below-zero temperature. I was safe, along with the two dogs that always followed me. Only the cement walls were left of the Chapel, the house, the offices, and the residence.

A few days later, it was Easter Sunday. It had long been the custom of the Catholics and Protestants of the Kabul international community to celebrate Easter together. We always assembled at 6 a.m. for the Service at Dawn, in the Mogul Gardens of the British Embassy.

A cross was erected and, in the pale light of early morning, we joined in prayer, meditation and singing the joyful Easter hymns. However, after the Soviets left, this ceremony was transferred to the grounds of the Italian Embassy. In 1990, and my last Easter in Kabul, instead of being held in the snow-covered Embassy garden, the ceremony was held in the residence.

Unfortunately, the recent missile strike had severely damaged the building, and the floor was still covered with shattered glass, smashed windows and blinds, detached doorknobs, broken tables, and fragments of porcelain. The most presentable table became our altar, and the cross, placed against the east window of the room, was fashioned from two iron rods salvaged from a destroyed garage. It is difficult, I believe, to sense what Easter is amid so much destruction. It is the feast of triumph of life over death, of the new over the old, from the beginning to the end.

I sought out my *mullah* of the door friend, who now called me the savior of his life, to make him understand that he, the Qu'ran and I that day believed the same reality: Jesus was alive!

The Name

In Luke's Gospel we read*: "Now on the eighth day they came to circumcise the child; they were going to call him Zechariah after his father, but his mother spoke up. 'No,'—she said, 'he is to be called John.'*

"They said to her, 'But no one in your family has that name, and made signs to his father to find out what he wanted him to be called. The father asked for a writing tablet and wrote: 'His name is John.'"

The Qu'ran notes the birth of John and says that Allah, himself, announced to the father what his name should be.

I wanted to write this passage from the Gospel because therein lies much affinity to the traditional Afghan ceremony of the name. Three days after the birth of an Afghan child, the family calls the *mullah* to introduce the newborn into the Muslim community. I was invited once to such a ceremony. The ritual impressed me because of its similarity to the Gospel narrative of Luke. The grandfather of the child interpreted for us. He honored me, not only by having me assist at the ceremony but also by asking me to suggest a name for the child. (Of course, I asked for his suggestion first.) I was with about twenty family members, but they made me feel completely at ease, such was their thoughtfulness and lack of prejudice. We began to speak in a lighthearted way, as was the custom in their tradition. No, this name is not good. Not even this one. The motive was to say little but in a picturesque way. The conclusion had to be arrived at. At a certain point, the grandfather suggested, "Let's leave the choice of the name to our guest." I gave my choice, and the climate of the house changed. The *mullah* approached the child and sang in its ear the invitation to prayer.

One who is accustomed to the loud call to prayer by a *muezzin* from a tall minaret cannot imagine the emotion that is felt hearing that commanding call reduced to a gentle melody whispered into the ear of a newborn. This all lasted only a short time, but it invited me to think about this new life and what it meant and suggested to me the answer: Life is an invitation to prayer. There is nothing over-reaching about this affirmation. The religious man is always with God and, even when not in formal prayer, is still praying because he is conscious that God is with him.

As for the ceremony of circumcision, it is not administered to infants in Afghanistan, but rather at a later age, usually between three to ten years.

If one reflects on the importance of a name in Afghanistan, one sees that, as a nation, it may lag behind others with respect to infrastructure and material wealth, but in reality it enjoys a high degree of culture honed over centuries and a civilization remarkable in many respects. Before all, names are always spoken with great deference. Of course, there may be secret names used in the intimacy of family. In my twenty-five years in Afghanistan, I never heard anyone make fun of a name. Yes, they judge people. They say: he is making a mistake, he's lying, he does not understand, he's prejudiced, but whatever he is or does, he is always called by his name. If he is a friend, the word *jan*, a term of endearment, is often added to his name.

But another point of reference for a name is the person's connection with God. The majority of Afghan male names express an attribute of the divinity of God and finish with God's name: Gift of God, Mercy of God, Lion of God, Justice of God, and other similar appellations. If one can say that the religiosity of a country is in the air, everywhere, in Afghanistan this is especially true in the names. It is the line from Isaiah that makes us understand what life is all about to those who believe in God: "*This is what the Lord who has created you says: 'I have called you by name, you are mine . Because you are precious in my eyes, because you are honored and I love you.'*" (Is. 43)

He who is convinced of this reality, spends his life without fear. A type of detachment, erroneously called fatalism, which is a trust in Him who has called us to life. How many times I have witnessed this trust and this tranquility, even in those moments of horrible suffering during the wars when my Afghan friends were tested so severely. Many of them had attached to their names words that reminded them that they belonged to God. In our Baptism, we receive, with the name, the same call that mysteriously renders the Sacrament more spiritual. We should feel every day the Voice of God calling us by name to an active intimacy with Him in prayer.

God's human creation, over millennia and up to today and beyond, is inestimable, but the Gospel assures us that God does, in fact, occupy Himself with each of us. He knows our names very well. We can add that the name, in the language of each culture, is more descriptive and offers more information about the person. The sister, for example, is called thus because she was fed with the same milk as another—the neighbor who shares the same shadow. The name, then, in this way comes to have a profound social dimension. The moving ceremony during which the newborn is gifted with his name gives the name life and real value.

Called to Prayer

Seeing ten thousand persons perfectly aligned and making the same ritualistic gestures in prayer with extraordinary precision is a moving spectacle. This is exactly the number of seats signed on the pavement of the great mosques in Kandahar, Mazar-i Sharif, and Herat. Islam is sincerely practiced by the vast majority of Muslims at these mosques. The first impression given is of a united community. The impression may be true. But the Christian view, that community is similar to communion, remains perplexing. In Islam, the centrality of God is so strong that the ten thousand who are praying are thinking solely of God. All pronounce the same formula of praise and thanksgiving. Even when asking God for help for others, they ask God to guide those others toward good, that is, toward submission to God's Will. He who is sitting in front or in back or at his side does not enter into the suppliant's awareness, only God. The fraternal community is, in a certain way, limited even by its very profession of faith. No one pleads for himself because God always knows what we need.

The 12 years of war that I lived through in Afghanistan produced in me a more profound understanding of the outlook of my Muslim friends. Prayers of intercession are very important.

You pray for us! How many times I heard this plea from families that suffered a tragedy during the war. And yet, especially among the Shiites, they have deep feelings toward their dead who, because of their goodness and martyrdom, are considered saints.

Deep in the desert and in the center of cities, tombs are erected to these saints. These are of great importance to them, and they would never remove them. The bond between the people and saints is not based on prayer. The multicolored stripes that create a flag for the place of interment of the saints attract the passers-by. They touch the earth, the door of the sanctuary, or the sarcophagus of stone only to share the power of the good and strong man that proves he was holy. The colored flags record the petitions of those who visit the tomb. They say to me: "You pray for us!" Yet, they never see Christians praying in the streets. Bells in the church were forbidden. Their *muezzin* instead…

If there's something monotonous in weather conditions in Kabul, it is the mornings. They are always calm, even though it may have rained or snowed during the night. Every *muezzin* from each minaret of the big cities looks toward the Suleiman Mountain waiting for the first white clouds from the sky. The *muezzin* lifts his hands to the level of his eye and when feeling the eyebrow, intones the invitation to prayer. It is repeated another four times during the day. The hands rise to the sky with open palms and a hand curves around a listening ear. (Is it not man speaking or listening to the proclamation of God?)

The Christian who hears the call to prayer from the minaret cannot help but remember his prayer.

You pray for us! In the silence of your room. In secret. And your Father who sees you in secret will reward you. And in this setting, we understand this reward to be our belief in the love of God for each of us and therefore receive a gift of filial trust in Him, Our Father. It is always an inspiration to watch the Afghan pray. Even when beyond the range of the *muezzin*'s call, everyone knew, just by being in contact with nature, when it was time to pray.

The place didn't matter. It is precisely this that made them offer such pleasing spectacles that were always moving. Some prayed kneeling on top of a bus. A choice place was against a wall of a bridge. Once I saw a man praying, kneeling facing Mecca, on a small board suspended across an abyss while the hundreds of sheep crossed the board.

But the faithful who prayed in Kabul were called to prayer in a resounding way. At dusk, when the sun disappeared behind the Paghman Mountains, the cannon on Sher Darwaza Hill, overlooking Babur's Tomb, gave a thundering boom at the end of every day of Ramadan. This resounding blast signaled the end of the daily fast that Muslims observe during the holy month.

Hundreds of children could then be seen running through the streets, thinking of the hunger of the adults, shouting: "Let's eat!" The desired meal was offered only after the penultimate prayer of the day. Given the formalism of Muslim prayer, one would think that every day would be the same. Instead, Friday's prayers and those of the feasts had a special religious choreography with civic tones that inspired fervor and reverence. The turbans of the men were impeccable and sometimes had gold or silver decorations. The gestures during prayer on that day in the great Id Gah Mosque were more solemn than usual, having a symphony of colors. There was an opening for male vanity, but the call was always to prayer.

The Village Visits

The streets are none larger than the palm of your hand. Guests: The first impression when you are invited to share an Afghan home is that you are going to share only the walls, the sky over the little courtyard, and God. Again, God comes up. But you cannot separate yourself from this atmosphere. It is in the nature of the people. A little at a time, you realize that, even in the poorest courtyards, you will note that there are birds and flowers. You sit on the pavement, but it is always covered with a rug. For guests from the West there will be two cushions—one, against a wall, will serve as the back of a chair. The greeting in the language of each place means welcome, but also "your visit makes me happy."

It is not easy to be invited by the Afghan. The many years of isolation have made them slow in mixing with strangers. Slow, but not ill-disposed, they need time to get to know people and to be able to speak and to be understood. They invite others to their homes, especially on feast days: the feast of the Breaking of the Fast; the Feast of the Sacrifice; the Feast of Nawroz, the New Year (March 21), when each family plants a tree in the garden or in the courtyard. They also invite others on the feast of the Birth of Jesus.

There is a strict protocol to be followed when inviting guests. The best and characteristic dishes of the Afghan table are served in abundance. The teapots are the only single serving implements. The rest of the food is served on large platters in the middle of the floor rug. Those who will partake of the meal sit around the platters on the rug. Naturally, a prayer of thanksgiving is said before the meal. The length of the meal may be long, unless someone says, "I must go."

I would like to relate some episodes of hospitality that remind me so much of the parable of the Good Samaritan, even if the times past were so very different from the present.

On a cold, icy, winter evening, I found myself between Kandahar and Kabul; using my second gear, my clutch broke.

Knowing that we were not too far from a teahouse, Rahim went to ask for help. He came back with almost forty men who lifted and carried my car for half a kilometer! It was twenty degrees below zero, and arriving at a very small space away from the cold seemed like paradise. It was packed with people. I couldn't believe how they could all fit into such a small space.

They were all sitting on the floor with crossed legs, patiently waiting for some kind of transportation. Some, however, stayed outside, hoping to catch a passing vehicle. After two hours, they called me, and a truck took me home. The next day they towed my car up to Kabul. I had not asked for anything nor promised anything. Rahim only said that I was a man of prayer. When I got down from the truck, one of the passengers kissed my hands and bid me goodbye with the traditional admonishment; "Don't get tired. Conserve your strength."

In 1978, a year before the Soviet invasion, war broke out because the new Regime, installed by the *coup d'état*, was opposed to the religious traditions of the country. The police became political, and the functionaries had to hide how they really felt. But the Afghans will always be the same, even if, as it turned out on one occasion, a course in communism was substituted for the time of prayer. Also, during this period, one of my parishioners from the international community was imprisoned for allegedly spying. The Consul of his embassy was not having much success in arranging a visit to see him and was in desperate need of assistance. It was the time of the hostage crisis in Teheran, and the hostages there were being permitted to receive religious assistance. Fortunately, a visit was finally managed, and the Secret Police agreed to permit a visit on Easter. I accompanied the Consul to a room in a hotel where we were to see the unfortunate man, but he was detained for almost an hour before he was led in, being instructed as to what he could and could not say to us. I had brought Holy Communion with me and was trying to figure out how I was going to administer it to the prisoner. He finally arrived accompanied by four agents. One, who was from Eastern Europe, was the instructor of the group. The Consul made conversation, discussing with them the small problems related to the salaries of the persons who worked for him assisting the prisoner. When it was my time to speak, I took from my pocket a little box with a Host inside. "Gentlemen"—I said—"at Easter, in my religion, we have the custom of sharing bread." As I opened the container, one of the agents grabbed it, taking me by surprise. One yelled—"Take it to the laboratory." I jumped toward the Host and retrieved it. I broke it in two and consumed one half and gave the other half to the prisoner. The agents were surprised but understood that it was not poison nor a means of communicating with a spy. They got up, indicating that the visit was at an end, and told us to leave. One of the men, who accompanied us to the door, whispered to me, "Excuse me, Father."

 These words overheard during a later political climate would have been enough for that agent, himself, to have been thrown in jail. But hospitality is part of the Afghan nature. I indicated by a small gesture that I understood.

 Although the new regime did not like the Afghans to pray, they could not forbid their going to the mosque on feast days. War would continue to ravage the land for twenty more years. The day after the bombing before Easter, I received two visitors. I was busy trying to fix some of the damage done by the missile and was placing a plastic cover over a window of a room. The *mullah* of the door was not on duty and my shadow, Bengi, kept barking. I wondered why and walked toward the street. There,

I encountered an Afghan who appeared to be passing by and looking at the ruins. When he saw me, he somewhat nervously advanced in my direction and whispered: "Father, I was sent by the Commander of the Resistance. I had to find out if you were still alive. Our thanksgiving to Allah is great. Tonight, the Commander will release one hundred prisoners as a sign of gratitude."

During the war years, when I could do it through my helpers, I gave rice to any family that needed it, even to those of the Resistance. They were now reciprocating by exhibiting the joy they felt for my having been saved. A little later, another visitor came. This one appeared more self-assured and belonged to the new Regime. The dialogue went something like this: "Father! You are alive!" "As you see, yes, thanks be to God!" "Father, the President is so happy and grateful that he has given orders to the market that they must give you all you need free of charge for a week. Take any food you may need. It will be given gladly with joy."

The fact that my life would be important politically does not explain it at all. They were not obliged to demonstrate their pleasure. It is simply the fact that we had created a friendship during the years and, also, it was their nature to be always hospitable.

To experience the hospitality of the merchants is entertaining and exciting at the same time. If you want to buy a carpet, you must not ask the price, right away. Greet! Watch! Don't pay too much attention to what you want most. The seller will greet you and invite you to take tea.

There is an exchange of polite conversation that gradually works around to the important question of why you are there. But the reason why you are there is only the beginning. If the seller tells you the price and you accept, he will not sell it to you.

You must not spoil the fun of his bargaining. The hospitality of the vendor obliges him not to charge you too much. If you understand prices, ask for half of the amount he stated. The vendor will say that the buyer should not treat the vendor like this. The buyer repeats the same words. And, in this way, you will arrive at an honest price, leaving both buyer and seller happy.

Finally, speaking of hospitality, one must not forget music. Even in their music, there is God. The invitation to prayer is musical. They will show you their instruments, whoever knows how to play, must play. The tambur has 18 strings, the Turkic rabab, a little less. There's the tabla with its percussion, two small drums held between crossed legs and played with the hands. The night before I left Afghanistan, the tablazan played a fine piece of music he had created simulating the sound of galloping horses in the desert and mountains of Afghanistan. I shall remember it forever, this great attachment to hospitality.

Drugs and Goodness

On the east side of Kabul, at the foot of the Bemaru Heights in the Sherpur quarter, one can find the Christian Cemetery (established in 1879 during the British occupation). Up to the time of the retreat of the Soviet troops, the cemetery had been respected by all the diverse administrations of the city. In the cemetery, I buried many drug addicts who found death in Afghanistan. This memory brings to mind two words: drugs and goodness. Unfortunately, their meanings exist simultaneously in daily living, although they present an absurd and illogical combination. Drugs are produced in abundance in Afghanistan, and the Afghans extend a hand to the victims of their products. In a few short words, I will tell of the subject at hand. The goodness of which I speak lies with diverse groups of Afghan society: ordinary people, doctors, policemen, judges, jail wardens, and finally, drug merchants. Even they became compassionate in certain very painful cases.

At the beginning of the '70s, Nepal, until that time a drugs' paradise, made it difficult, economically, for drug addicts to enter the country. India, besides Nepal, had borders that were impenetrable by all, except for the British and Swiss. The genius of the drug addicts made them find methods of falsifying passports for the two mentioned countries.

There were many unfortunate cases, but one in particular came to my attention. A hippie and drug addict from South America was hospitalized in a very grave condition. He called for me because he wanted to go to confession; he also told me his real name. A very kind Afghan doctor took care of the youth and helped him to get well. I visited him every day and saw his progress, but on one occasion, I also noted in the hospital garden a group of young people who appeared to be spying on the young man. I learned that they visited the boy after I did. They were afraid the young man might tell me about the false passports or where they obtained drugs. Time passed, and he was well on his way to good health. I realized, however, that the one in the bed next to him did not appreciate my visits or my conversations. After ten days, the doctor called, asking for clothes for his patient because he was well enough to leave the hospital. I arrived at the hospital one hour later, only to find that the young man was dead. While the Good Samaritan doctor was calling me, the conniving addicts had given the boy a lethal injection. The police arrived at the same time as I. No one in Afghanistan was from the young man's country, so the police asked me to help simplify matters. I wrapped the body in a plastic bag and had it carried on a cart to the Christian Cemetery. The custodian of the cemetery called the gravediggers.

All involved were very moved by the death and were very kind. I erected a cross at the grave and added the young man's name that only I knew. I found myself standing beside an Eastern European who began to cry and said: "At least, they have buried you with your real name." He (the young man) had not lied to me. He had had some contact with his people, and the address he had given for his family was correct. Before my next morning Mass, I found about 50 young people in my church. They wanted to know where I buried that one! I looked at them with compassion and tolerance. Among them there was perhaps the killer. I gave the cemetery key to an Italian friend and asked him to kindly conduct the boys to the grave in the cemetery. The next day, the custodian called me. The youth's friends had taken away the cross and in its place had put a pipe used in smoking hashish. All around the burial plot they had scattered leaves of the drug they took, and cigarettes of the same substance. Of course, I removed everything and placed the cross once again at the head of the grave. However, the behavior of all involved, the police, doctors, custodian, and others showed a bounty of spirit that is usually not seen in such circumstances.

It was a time in Kabul when cheap hotels frequented by drug addicts sprang up like mushrooms. The point of reference when they were ill or dead was the only priest in the country: me. My sense of smell became so sensitive to the odor of the drugs that I could distinguish each of the drugs used in the little restaurants or hotels I passed. I could tell the emergency room doctor what particular drug the victim was suffering from. What availability they showed toward these strangers! A part of the Afghan society created their ruin, and a small group of good Muslims served with their competence to help the poor, disoriented Christians.

Four young boys from the new world died one night, suffocated in their van in front of the statue of the large Buddha in Bamiyan. An Afghan from that district brought me their corpses, and the police gave me their documents and small possessions. In one bag, I found a letter in which the author wrote that he had had difficulties, but had found himself in Nepal—a paradise. A policeman involved in these matters asked me: "How can these people think there is a paradise on earth?"

The arrest of the hippies with drugs almost became a ceremony. A jail warden explained the situation to me like this: In a narrow street in the commercial section where wares are displayed outside of store fronts, a drug trafficker would offer hashish or other substances to whomsoever. A few paces along the way, a conspiring policeman would stop the hippie and find the drugs on him. The policeman would then take the addict's passport with the promise to return it for a certain sum of money. The addicts had no recourse. Whatever money they had went to pay for drugs, therefore, only jail remained. The conditions of the jail were third-world level, but the jail wardens were really fraternal toward these unfortunate hippies. Normally, those jailed did not find it difficult to find someone to bail him or her out. Actually, it was more fruitful for the heartless drug traffickers to have them on the outside.

Many of the hippies, who were in transit in Afghanistan, disappeared. Drug dealers from nearby countries kidnapped some, and others, without names, were found dead. A few parents, through my references, could at least retrieve their children's bodies. The compassionate Afghans always collaborated whenever they could. When we thanked them, they always referred all to the mercy of God.

The Houses Within the House

In the city, it is no longer like this, but in the outlying districts, where tradition prevails, the walls of a large domain for one family enclose four different families. This has come about because the Qu'ran allows the Afghan male to have four wives, according to the Prophet Mohammed. This reality is played out according to the economic and cultural status of both the man and the woman. The leaning toward monogamy has gained strength and has been recognized by all member states of the United Nations. What still has not changed, so far, is the free choice by the bride of her spouse (and vice versa). The choice is still left to the parents of each potential spouse. The approach of the opposite party is slow. It is the man's father who makes the various visits. Even if the parent likes the girl and the family, he does not rush the engagement. First comes a courtesy visit. If the father of the girl appears not to understand the meaning of the visit, the man's father will not take tea and will promise to come back at a later date. Other visits follow and, a little at a time, the contract is set up. This is not only the responsibility of the man's father but also of the girl's father. He must assure the other family that his daughter's moral and physical attributes are worthy of the future husband.

For a Westerner, this poses a question: How can they love each other without knowing each other?

The answer shocks us: We love each other because we have married. Thus, we see again, that the will of the father is an expression of the Will of God, and a manifestation of respect for the one who will later be the mother or the father to the children; therefore procreation prevails over physical rights without excluding affection for each other. In the West, we can brag that we marry because we love each other. But the ever-greater number of separations of spouses puts in doubt the truth of that assertion.

In those matrimonies in which I participated, I was only placed with the men and I had to have everything written down for me, especially the women's parts of the ceremony.

All appeared quite involved. The Afghan proverb for the woman says: "The wedding day is ordained by God and comes only once." That is very fortunate, because weddings in Afghanistan are very expensive. On the wedding day, one is not permitted to ask anyone to leave who is there without an invitation. It would be a shame! A disgrace! The night before the wedding, there are feasts in both houses. About midnight, a group of women and men with lanterns and music go to the girl's house. That night the future husband is called king. The door remains closed in front of the courtyard. There must be a loud, clamoring noise before it can be opened. Even in this ceremony, the bride maintains a ritual shyness.

The rites demand that loud noises and protests are heard before the group gains entrance. As the people enter, they see a throne in the center of the main room. The groom, however, does not allow himself to be found easily; he has to hide in order to have the others find him, as one who has come from far away. When he is found, they have him sit on the throne with a page nearby. The marriage ceremony does not take place at this time, but follows two days later. The groom must tell the father of the bride three times that he consents to marrying his daughter. The word he repeats three times is: yes! This is similar to the 'I do' which is repeated in Christian marriage ceremonies. They affix immediately all the personal property that the husband will give to the bride (without administrative rights). This is done in the event that later the bride becomes a widow. The *mullah* signs the document that will also be signed by the witnesses. The following dawn, the groom sits with the bride after she has been presented to him, veiled, and seated on the small throne that is traditionally covered with rugs and cushions. A large mirror is placed in front of the bridal pair, and the bride's mother tells her to lift her veil and look in the mirror, where the groom, also looking in the mirror, will see her for the first time. Even in this ceremony, the bride will adhere to the strictest rituals.

It can be seen from these rituals what patience a groom must endure before seeing his wife-to-be. It is also curious to note the discussions about money with the groom's father. At the beginning, the groom must put on the floor a stone symbolizing the amount of money that is considered. If the father of the bride demands too much, the groom's father says that the stone is too heavy and he cannot lift it. The future father-in-law, however, may insist, and so they will enter into a Muslim fraternal discussion. The bride's father's heart is sweetened with the cone of sweets that the future husband's father brings to him. Then, the future husband's father is also the recipient of a cone of sweets. After a silent prayer, the cones will be smashed against each other. All the grains of sugar will signify the well being of the marriage. At this moment, the father of the groom will present his son as a slave of the bride.

Even if religion is present in a clear manner, cultural differences are honored. A problem remains as to the religious status of the woman. There should be less severity for the woman and more mercy from the man. Actually, the man lives in a privileged state. Not only is he free to divorce if he chooses but also can take four wives. Many choose monogamy, but there are still many men living with more than one wife. Because I know so many of the multiple families, I marvel at the order that reigns in such places. There is an internal, unwritten law that accords each wife her place with exact rulings and with a sense of hierarchy that is easily accepted. The children behave as if they had the same mother and father, although their mothers may be different. On feast days when a whole family is seen at a park (sometimes they will number about twenty), one cannot help but notice the love that exists among all the family members. This comes about because, in his very heart, the father has accepted the Will of God.

I would like to make known two curious facts. A foreign woman consented to marry an Afghan who was a politician (though not an important one). She had, of course, cultural difficulties but boasted that she was a pioneer in this and that other women might follow. After some years, she returned to her country. Her experiment had failed. A few months after the Soviet invasion, some of my Afghan students at the United Nations, where I also taught, were absent for some days. They were about 13 to 15 years of age. I asked for their absence notes when they came back to school. Simple! They had all married. The new Regime established that every family could have only one house. The Afghans promptly made their girls marry. The families multiplied, and the houses did not become property of the state. No comment!

Under the Same Shade

It is said, "He who finds a friend finds a treasure." We could add, "He who finds a good neighbor finds a treasure." When Jesus tells us to love one another, he is saying to love your neighbor.

There is a sort of symbiosis in Afghanistan between a friend and a neighbor.

Whoever is living next door, or working next door, or taking a trip and happens to be with you at a place at the same time, or in the same caravansary at the same time, is said to be "under my shade."

In isolated countries, shade is as precious as is water in the desert. This is not only a saying. It holds a profound meaning. In some cases, entire families living nearby become affiliated with the clan or the tribe. This rapport among good neighbors extends even to one who may be a foreigner and has shared bread and salt with the Afghans. This relationship does not only include a greeting; it is deeper than that. It encompasses favors that are exchanged as needs arise during the time spent together.

My special Afghan friends were those who worked in the Italian embassy. My house was attached to the embassy. They were important and special because their relations with us were watched closely—we being Christian and not Muslim. The local administration kept their eye on our Afghan staff and sometimes also obliged them to spy on us. In spite of this, our relations were cordial, and we exchanged professional and social help with one another. We took turns in being interpreters, scribes, and messengers for one another. In Afghanistan, the scribe is still in vogue. He copies all manuscripts by hand. You may still see the scribes sitting on the trunk of a tree, against a wall, or on a bridge writing feverishly from morning until night. Many from the country who do not read or write seek out a scribe when they visit the city. On occasion, I used a scribe for State letters or for assistance to Afghan families who wanted to communicate with distant relatives. If the letter had to be written in a language of the West, I became the scribe. I mention this neighborly activity because it was not only inter-confessional but also inter-religious, creating a continuous dialogue between the parties. The correspondence implied a reciprocal trust and exchange of confidence, exposing personal problems and, at the same time, providing another venue for expanding my understanding of that exotic culture.

Afghanistan has two official languages: Dari (the Afghan Persian) and Pashto (the language of the Pashtun, Afghanistan's largest ethnic group). But there are also dialects. Perhaps only a small number, but they exist. There are the Dardic dialects in Nuristan (Land of Light), the name given to the old Kafiristan after the people of that remote mountain region were converted to Islam. We add also Tajiki and Turkic dialects. Because my pastoral work took me to faraway places, I needed interpreters in order to supply the needs of those living there.

At the teahouses where I stopped during my travels, there was always near me one who offered to explain the conversation as it unfolded in those languages unknown to me. My work as interpreter consisted mostly for those foreigners who wanted to make purchases but could not communicate with the shopkeepers. Among the people who helped me with rare dialects, there never seemed to be a personal interest but solely the desire to be available to one who did not share their shade. The isolationism that the Afghans experienced made many of them introverts. Their problems, physical or moral, were always kept inside of them. Only if a close neighbor of great confidence could be told the problem would there be a remedy sought. They, many times, told me of their physical problems. I asked for details in order to consult a doctor for them and obtain remedies. They had great simplicity in explaining to me what disturbed them. I was a special neighbor to them because they knew I lived alone and would not communicate their confessions to anyone. They had, in this Christian priest, total confidence.

Sometimes it was necessary to function as a messenger of the physician and upbraid someone for not adhering to the law, for example, breaking the Ramadan fast, if need be. My message would not be taken lightly. They would respond that they knew the law and would do it. They told me how they were progressing. Sometimes, it was I who had the problem. I would refer it to them and although it was difficult to explain my complicated travel duties, and to enjoy some freedom while respecting the limits set by Afghan Laws to a non-Muslim minister, they always had solutions for my little problems.

In a book published in 1937, there is mentioned an incident involving one of my predecessors, Father Caspani. Father never proselytized but was allowed to administer the Last Rites to some Catholics living near the bazaar, without having the Afghan authorities take any measure.

I compare my attitude in similar circumstances and feel that it comes out in my favor. I have never proselytized, because I was asked not to, but I experienced a great tolerance toward the openness with which I tried to perform my religious duties and that transformed my pastoral work into an apostolate of presence. Reaching such understanding did much good, at least for me.

Not a Stranger, Not an Infidel

The vast majority of my parishioners who lived in Kabul felt quite at home. They enjoyed the country and lived well. This was the situation not only when the city was somewhat of a paradise but also even when the war began to leave it in a mound of ruins. Some friends have asked: "What does Kabul have to cause one to be so attached to it?" We have already spoken of the hospitality of the people. Even if I sound repetitious, I must say, again, that Kabul was a welcoming city. (Unfortunately this is not true anymore.)

If one pulls out a few weeks in summer, during which time the sand of the desert is almost suspended in the air, the welcome of the city is offered every morning. At dawn, the sun does the same thing—it rises behind the Suleiman Mountain and for six months it paints the Hindu Kush in pink and orange. For the rest of the year, the mountains do not attract attention. Instead, the flowers of the gardens, especially roses, inspire our awe and admiration.

Even though Kabul is at an altitude of two thousand meters, and it may have the aspect of a city lying at the bottom of an old lake, the mountains that circle her, dividing her in two, do not take anything away from her. It is an airy, open city that is very cordial. Nature, it seems, adjusts to the people who live there. They are Muslims. They are needy people. They can no longer separate themselves from strangers and infidels. Since Alexander the Great, many foreigners have tried to colonize the country. The British, from their vantage point in India, tried without success to add Afghanistan to their empire. The Russians always seemed to have coveted Afghanistan. Their last attempt to control Afghanistan began when the Soviets arrived on a snowy Christmas Eve in 1979 with three division-sized units and took control of the airfields in and around Kabul. They ultimately failed in their mission, as did the many others, and after ten years of battle and leaving Afghanistan a virtual wasteland, their tanks and personnel carriers rumbled up the Salang Pass and finally across the ancient Amu Daria, in full retreat.

Needless to say, the many invasions retarded progress in Afghanistan and even helped to fuel war among the Afghans themselves, dreaded civil wars. Afghanistan, when there is no war, is a very cordial country. The people, if we exclude those who love to wage war, consider the stranger a charming guest and the infidel a poor devil who really is not to blame for not having the faith of the Afghans. They do not have complexes, neither of superiority nor inferiority. They are themselves. If you respect them, they will be friendly, and you may get to know their mysterious, but distinctive, Asian spirit.

Going to market was always an experience for me, and a visit to the small alley behind the great mosque where they sold birds, their food and cages, and charming unglazed pottery vases was virtually a spiritual retreat for me. Regardless of whether I was covered with sand or mud, depending on the season, I was always greeted with kindness and respect. One old man from whom I bought little things every year, always invited me to sit and have tea with him; he seemed to enjoy my comments and observations, in addition to those of the passersby. I, as a Westerner, could sit for an hour in one of those corners and never hear a complaint, a curse, or a bad word, not even an angry tone from anyone I encountered. Others I would see just in passing by their shops greeted me with: "Good morning, priest sahib, aren't you buying anything? It's time for you buy a little canary from me! (A canary was worth two months' salary of a laborer). A lot of mud, eh? Too much sand! Allah understands!" (The verb "understands" was used for "knows.") Faces serene, smiles discreet. It is a lived life that is transmitted to others.

When I accompanied a friend or acquaintance to the bazaar to help with purchases, writing paper, socks, rugs and small necessities, the merchant would always give me some little thing in gratitude for giving him an opportunity to sell. I had friends comment, on returning from one of these excursions, that they had taken a bath of serenity with the simple merchants who were so cordial and wise. Perhaps it was their wisdom, united with their own strong faith that made me and the stranger not feel what we were—strangers and infidels.

A little at a time, the foreigner becomes accustomed to Afghan ways. March 21 was Nawroz, New Year's Day, in Afghanistan. On that day, as I mentioned, every Afghan plants a tree. Of course, I had to do the same. It was a true spirit of New Year's, and a far cry from the ugliness that makes one feel that since tomorrow is uncertain, why not enjoy yourself today, create a hilarious time and forget about tomorrow. It was a celebration in which everyone confirmed, and knew with certainty, that they were in the Hands of God, and that with the spring came rebirth and contribution of life. There was no thought of not being around in the New Year.

Adjusting to the Afghan cuisine was also not difficult. Above all, every large clan had included in the family all who had studied in Europe. All who were invited, even westerners, were royally received. The Afghans took great delight in presenting their cuisine. Although different from Western fare, it bears a well-studied balance easily enjoyed by all gourmets: rice, stuffed foods, roasted meats and yogurt, *boulani* (small spicy potato and onion pancakes), and an endless array of other delicious specialties that combine to create a festive, welcoming atmosphere. Perhaps what really bonds, fraternally, an Afghan and a stranger, a Muslim and a Christian is *naan*, a distinctive bread that is prepared in special underground ovens with openings above ground. During the night, the aroma of *naan* baking in these primitive ovens subtly permeates the air, conjuring up images of industrious bakers kneading their dough, shaping it into elongated ovals, and throwing it at the cylindrical sides of the ovens where it would bake and be rescued by the baker's paddle before it would drop off the oven sides and onto the hot coals below. When one is seated, cross-legged on rugs, after having heard the invocation in the Name of God and the wish "Pleasant Eating," we look at the large golden bread feeling perfectly at home. Wine is not used, but tea is enjoyed universally in Afghanistan. In the sharing of tea and *naan*, a rhythm of fraternity is created that makes one forget differences of religion or nationality.

The Minar-I-Chakari

On the very crest of the Shakh Baranta mountain chain about eight miles south of the Kabul plateau, stands an ancient 88-foot Buddhist minaret, the *Minar-I-Chakari* (Tower of the Wheel), which archeologists estimate dates to between the second and third centuries, AD.

The Wheel, as used in the name of the *Minar*, is symbolical and refers to the Buddhist's Wheel of the Law, the Law of Births, Deaths, and Rebirths, which the Buddha set in motion while teaching the *Dharma*. From the minaret at its lofty altitude of almost three thousand meters, one has a panoramic view of the entire city of Kabul. It is believed that the *Minar* was part of an ancient Buddhist monastery. On this day in memory, the long climb up the crumbling stone trail leading to the *Minar* put me in a very prayerful mood almost as though I were on a spiritual retreat. The wild tulips that bloomed for a month in Kabul, and then disappeared, decorated the stark landscape, their colors kept fresh by the water that trickled down from the melting winter snows. The tulips gave joy to all for that one month and especially to me that day. Men and things are all subject to the Wheel of Time. Only faith gives sense to this Wheel.

The Kabul plateau is surrounded by Afghan cemeteries. Seen from afar, they are impressive for their simplicity. Every deceased is placed so that he faces Mecca. On the tomb, nothing is placed, no name or inscription, except two ribbons of stone. The name given in the call to prayer is gone. It fits in with the logic of the Centrality of God. In the face of death of a loved one, Muslims express their grief with the affirmation "God is Great" or, alternatively, with the expression from the Qu'ran "We belong to God and to Him we must return." Of course, a Christian finds himself, in turn, comforted on such occasions with Job, Tobit, the Psalms and all of Christ's teachings. It was always the Wheel of the Buddhists that made one think of the Muslims' funerals.

The visitor who comes to pay his or her respects to a deceased sits for a half hour in complete silence, gives his condolences when it is his turn, and leaves when the time is up. The silence is a sign of mourning. One hears only the expression "God disposes" which is said to each new arrival. Near the deceased, there is a little lamp, and passages from the Qu'ran are recited.

The meditative walk from the minaret, among the tulips that would die in a few weeks, gave rise to thoughts of the transience of life, but also of the efforts of the living. Even at the funeral and during the forty days after the death of a family member, it is the custom to give alms and food, especially rice, to the poor. The custom of giving alms, particularly in a poor country, was followed only on feast days and at funerals. Beggars were not seen on the streets because the Afghan clans took care of their own. Beggars did begin to emerge during the Soviet stay, and it was easy to see why; they were spying for special interests. After the Soviets' arrival, it was no longer possible to leave the capital. Therefore, I couldn't make my customary climb to the Wheel and enjoy a day's spiritual retreat. It was also on that same peak where the cannons and missiles were placed, and it was from there that, every day, the city was bombarded. The Tower of the Wheel became the venue for the dispensing of death.

I saw the Wheel of Time in the hands of ruin, of jails filled with political prisoners, of the tortured and dead that multiplied by the day. Just as with every other regime, the new regime promised the Afghans heaven, but more than ever, they believed only in the other world. I remember once having a very animated religious discussion with some strangers as we hiked up to the minaret. It was a place that always obliged me to focus on what life is all about. We were a group of three different religions, making our joint ascent to the *Minar*: Buddhist, Muslim, and Christian. I was asked, "Father, can we refuse to believe that religion, like politics, divides us?" I replied that if we go to the essential part of all religion, it does not divide us. They all agreed with this statement. As we stood near the Tower of the Wheel, we were all of one accord.

"Where do the divisions come from?" Another question. The diversity of Masters could be a cause. Buddha, Jesus, and Mohammed were all different. And people come from different latitudes and longitudes. Therefore, what is the fundamental point in diverse cultures? The divisions among men, I am firmly convinced, have to do with their culture. Divisions flow from a fundamental misunderstanding as to how to arrive at the heart of the matter. Religion is a seeking of God, not a seeking of Self.

If they have as a goal to seek God, and He is the main focus of their lives, religious men would find themselves in harmony with one another. The difference between a fanatic and an ecumenical man is a matter of opinion, or lack of it, in a discussion. The ecumenical man is open to the universal reality that is God;

the fanatic is enclosed within himself and with a God that is only for him, in a nest alone, where he feels comfortable, without worrying about God, unless life turns that way.

We kept watching the tulips as we talked and walked; we enjoyed the music of the cascades of water rushing toward the plateau below. We smiled. There was little more to say.

A little farther along, we met some Afghans who invited us to tea. I felt a certain displeasure because in the common seeking of the Lord, many as yet were not guided by Jesus for the simple fact that they did not know Him. But continuing to think about Jesus, I felt His great openness and understood the universal truth of His saving death. My friend, who objected before, seemed to have read my mind.

"Are you happy Father, that you are a Christian?" "Yes, I'm grateful," I told him, "and I hope that the Wheel of Time will one day bring all of humanity into one big family." The breeze made the tulips move as if they, too, wanted to answer "yes." You may laugh, but I'm sure it was not only poetry.

Taken by the Nose

Whatever may be thought of the Muslim woman, one must understand that she is not inhibited.

The legislation in the Qu'ran leaves the woman in a state of disparity as far as the man goes. But in everyday living, her nature and good sense temper that disparity or inequality. During my 25 years in the country, I saw what an Afghan woman loses outside of her home. She has no rights, as far as the social life is concerned. Let's say, did not have. Afghan women began receiving more recognition in the 1960s, when the Civil Movement was in full swing. One could see women filling jobs in administration, schools, banks, and hospitals, and even as policewomen. For some years in the 1970s, the Minister of Education was a woman. But, in the social ambience, the woman is almost forgotten. In the interior of her home, it is another story. It is known that the last Afghan king had to discuss all affairs of State with his mother and the Queen. Those elderly men in the Assembly of the People proclaimed the female counsel they received in the home.

Perhaps it was in foreign circles that the Afghan woman showed her lack of shyness most. There were two international cultural institutions in Kabul. The Society of Amateur Dramatics of Kabul and The Musical Society of Kabul. The Afghan women were represented as organizers, members of the choir and orchestra and as performers, producers, and more. We don't know what natural gifts cause Afghan women to excel in linguistics, but they learn languages rapidly and well. All were impressed by the relaxed camaraderie that existed among the international members of the various groups. To illustrate the free spirit of the Afghan women, a specific instance might be more helpful here than a mere statement of fact.

Let's begin with the veil, also known in the West as the *chador*. We need to let go of our prejudices; after all, references to the *kimono* worn in Japan and the *sari* worn in India do not cause pain when we hear them mentioned. Perhaps it is the veil over the face that makes us prejudiced against the *chador*. At any rate, the *chador* is a tradition with Afghan women, and it is an adjunct to their femininity. When one sees the colorful, pleated *chadors* hanging on clothes lines in the little alleys of Kabul, it is as though the city is dressed for a feast in every season of the year. A woman walking in her flowing *chador* does appear to be the epitome of grace, and yet, her vision is restricted having to peer through a veil.

And there is also the nagging question about preference. Is she bound by custom and tradition, or is she more comfortable in her colorful, pleated *chador*? In any case, the decision as to the fate of the *chador* does not lie with the West. It lies with the women whose culture embraces it. In spite of her discreet, hidden external appearance, I must emphasize that the Afghan woman is not inhibited. She will ultimately prevail in this matter, in her own way. But why is *Taken by the Nose* the title to this little chapter? You ask. The response is simple. It describes an incident that could help us to understand the Afghan woman.

In 1973, when King Zahir Shah was overthrown in a *coup d'etat*, he was replaced with a new republic that was supposed to be modern, if not democratic. Those who orchestrated the overthrow were from the Union of the North. One understood immediately that this new regime was transitory. At first, the anti-government protests were permitted, but were later prohibited. Well, the soul and victims of these demonstrations were the women.

One day, while driving to the International School, I found myself surrounded by university students who were demonstrating in the street. Since I was delayed by the demonstration, I had time to take stock of the statistics. In the cheerful line of students, numerous, but composed, were the female students. They outnumbered the opposite sex. The slogans were very moderate, but in a Muslim country they seemed almost out of place. It was only spring but the day was very hot.

The sun, at two thousand meters, beats down hard even though there is plenty of snow still around. It was uncomfortably hot in my car so I opened a window searching for a little breeze. The demonstration had halted at a monument erected by King Amanullah. He was a favorite of the students because he did much to modernize the country and tried to help the lot of women. Regrettably, his ideas were too modern for his day, and he was forced into exile. At the side of my car were some young female students who were talking to me: "What do you say, guest?"

I smiled. One thanked me and, with superstitious spontaneity, put her hand through my window and nicely took hold of my nose. "Excuse me," she said while watching me. "Maybe this is the first time that an Afghan woman does a gesture of this kind. Do you think I could be making history?" I smiled.

It was not yet time for that history-making. That day there were no incidents, but the next day on the university campus some student fundamentalists went around the paths of the school and threw acid in the faces of the girls who were not wearing their veils. It was these youths who would later become the rebel chiefs of the worst fundamentalist groups of the Resistance.

What that fundamentalist group did not succeed in doing during 1972 to 1978, the Soviets accomplished during their stay. In spite of the fact that the young Afghan women had been attacked with the acid, they continued to dress decently with a scarf over their hair but not a veil over their faces. The regime imposed by the great empire of the North to modernize Afghanistan, forced the country to return to Religious Nationalism. The men who had been wearing jackets and ties went back to turbans, and the women, back to the veil. The hand that took me by the nose made me reflect often on the star-crossed pattern of Afghan history, a history made of spurts, little jumps forward, stops, starts, and then terrible steps backward.

Unfortunately, the most destructive steps backward took place in the 1990s.

The war continues, and I cannot understand even remotely why it is so. Here, I must mention the *Taliban*. They say they are theological students and want to impose the Islamic *Sharia*. They began their attempt in this direction by closing all schools to women. These theological students want the women to get married as soon as they reach puberty, have children and stay at home. There has been a strong reaction in the international community to the suffering of Afghan women under the Taliban. According to the Taliban, the economy and religion make it necessary that women have only a domestic role in life. These excuses resonate with no one. Quite the contrary; the sacrifices of the Afghan women have the power to shake the conscience of human society. They have found their voice and are beginning to be heard once again in Afghanistan. Can the free spirit of the Afghan women forge a fair place in society for themselves, as well as a better life for all Afghans, especially the children who for so long have been deprived of their youth? I believe that the Wheel of Time is ready for that miracle. Would not the chieftain of the nomads say that it is what God wants?

The Social Scientist

"The Human Terrain System develops, trains and integrates a social science-based research and analysis capability... to enable sociocultural understanding..."
— from the US Army's Human Terrain System website

I met Sam Stryker, Doctor Sam J. Stryker, at a two-day selection event for the US Department of the Army's Human Terrain System near Ft. Leavenworth, Kansas. The event itself was memorable, and it provided a great opportunity for mapping the human terrain of the typical candidate for this kind of program. The array of characters was a training ground in *sociocultural understanding*.

Social scientists, analysts and prospective team leaders, all coming from different regions and backgrounds, would meet to see if they made the cut. The most hilarious moment came when about 20 of us met in a conference room to be screened for *IQ* and psychological profiles and were requested to file a pre-screening questionnaire of potentially disqualifying lifestyle factors. The looks behind the room said it all. At first glance, you would have to be Mother Theresa to qualify for any position. We even had doubts Mother Theresa could answer no to all of the 55 damning questions. Questions went from "Have you ever lost your temper with a member of your family?" to "Have you ever had a relationship of a sexual nature with a foreigner?"

When asked if any of us had any questions regarding the questionnaire we could not hear a fly buzz. People kept looking elsewhere, staring at imaginary focal points in corners of the ceiling. Finally one slight woman in her early 30s put up her hand and courageously came up with the question everyone wanted to ask, but did not, for fear of being profiled as the individual who had something to hide. "Will we have to undergo a polygraph interview during this weekend?" When the facilitator answered "no," we heard a loud sigh of relief coming out of the room. All of a sudden, everybody became a Mother Theresa.

During the course of the two days, Sam struck most participants as a natural communicator. He is a natural storymaker and storyteller. He is the kind of guy one ends up having a profound battle-zone friendship with. He has served in the military and has been employed as a teacher, consultant, director, military liaison and intelligence field operative. He has completed a tour in Iraq, primarily overseeing the training of third-country national soldiers in base defense, as a military liaison and aiding the Provincial Reconstruction Team in Mosul, Baghdad, and Taji. While serving two tours in Afghanistan, as a human terrain specialist, he was a social science field operative, helping NATO, NGOs, and government agencies understand the Afghan culture and apply this understanding to achieve objectives and enhance security, development, and governance. He has been personally rewarded and recognized for his work with village stability and with the ANA to reduce attrition and corruption.

We met for dinner, six of us in all. Sam took center stage. When we started talking about this book, he volunteered a few stories he had written for the benefit of his family. He was happy to see the stories published, and he hoped that this kind of quantitative narrative, less than the typical Human Terrain reports he had to produce, would help the public catch a glimpse of Afghan spirit. Sand and Wind. The sand cannot lie and the wind will tell all secrets… if we but listen…

Sam Stryker

WHITE STONES

Someone asked me once, "What are those white stones up there?" gesturing at the nearby hill.

I was attending a Counter Insurgency Leadership Course outside Kabul, AF at Camp Julien. During one of our breaks between lectures, we found ourselves gazing at the barren, steep hills surrounding the base. Up on the hill near its summit were many large, white stones in stark contrast to the brown hill and blue sky.

At first I thought they were sheep dotting the hillside, such was their distance; or perhaps distance markers set by Coalition Forces to gauge the ranges in case the enemy attacked from that direction. Several other theories drifted around, most being of a tactical nature, as you can tell. I was surrounded by military men and women. I was intrigued, so I asked an Afghan officer in my horrible Dari.

"They mark the passing of loved ones. When someone dies, their family places a large white stone on the hill for all to see." he replied, cordially. I thanked him and stood there contemplating the cultural implications, but soon we were called back into class where yet another PowerPoint slide show awaited. The white stones were soon forgotten as I began to fight the effects of PTSD (PowerPoint Traumatic Stress Disorder).

My next mission took me to a district far removed from any semblance of civilization. No electricity, no clinic, no schools—just farmers and fighters. Stepping back 1,000 years in time is an occupational hazard in my line of work. My mission goal was simple—to see if it would be feasible to recommend a certain program be started in the area, enabling the local population to protect themselves from insurgents. It was standard operating procedure for the Coalition Forces to visit during the day and interact with the people. But at night the insurgency would come and threaten, kill, or steal from the defenseless villagers. Infamous "Night Letters" would be placed on mosques and schools, threatening death to whoever sought aid from the Coalition or the Government. Teachers would be driven off, village elders kidnapped, and any who defied them would be beaten… or worse.

In my usual exacting nature, I met with the military entities who could give me some ideas of places that may be ready for such a program or that were in great need of security. *(I regret I cannot go into details, but specifics of my report have been classified and its particulars cannot be shared.)* One village was mentioned and, above all others, its praises were sung highly—so much so that I doubted its truth.

My usual untrusting nature assumed there was an ulterior motive. Perhaps a favor owed to a local Malik? Or a contractor hoping to score some easy money? It really didn't matter—I would find the truth of it.

I geared up, looking like just another heavily armed soldier, mounted into a Stryker and headed for the fabled "perfect village." The village was actually several villages dotted along a picturesque river. A place where tourist hotels might be were it not for the little detail of a war-in-progress. As soon as I exited the vehicle into a village of mud huts and walls, children ran among the soldiers freely. There was no fear on their smiling faces, just a burning desire to steal my pens and touch everything. Even the dourest soldier could not help but smile at the bright, grimy faces running everywhere. Shortly, elders came up and shook hands with smiles of their own. They guided me down to the river and sat us down in the shade. *Chai* tea was served with small candies, the sign of welcome to friends who had come to visit.

I took off my vest and helmet, removed my sunglasses, and we spoke like men in the shadow of peace. I learned to relish these moments, for they are rare indeed out in the hinterland of Afghanistan. I learned how these people refused the insurgents' threats and passed information freely to the US soldiers stationed nearby. I asked about security, aid, and other issues. We talked of schools for the children. I saw hope and heard of possibilities.

After several such visits to other local leaders, the story was the same. Somehow these people remembered what it was to be free after 30 years of subjugation. They craved it still and guarded it jealously. They desired to be able to protect themselves; to stand once again as men in charge of their own destinies. Needless to say, I began to wonder where this fire came from. Who was the kindler of hope? I had met many leaders, but none seemed to be the wellspring. In Afghanistan charismatic leadership was the one form of leadership people responded to. One name did come up in conversation time and again. He was considered a man of action and respect by all I spoke with. Virtually all elders mentioned him with a kind of reverence reserved for the truly heroic. I had found my charismatic leader. Of course, I had to meet this man.

In the land of Afghanistan, corruption is a pervasive art form; Illegal checkpoints, graft, stealing from your employees, skimming from your employer, and bribery. The newly formed government was no different. I secretly believed it to be the unseen second front in this war. I wondered if he was one of the many warlords who ruled by the iron hand. Or a fundamentalist *mullah* bent on his own personal gain; any one of a hundred scenarios where the powerful prey on the weak. Maybe he was just a friendlier version of the usual despots.

I was astounded to find out he was a low-level government official! He was a hero to the people because he fought for them against the Soviets, the Taliban, and now the insurgents. He actually used his small local police force to protect those of his village and the other villages in the area. He suffered no bribes from his subordinates. The police walked as freely among the people as I did! This amazing accident defied logic. This culture was rooted in government corruption. There was no trust for the government in Kabul. It was a nation of post-traumatic stress. Everyone was in survival-mode. Higher ideals had no place in Afghanistan. The people who survived learned long ago to bow to the will of the one with the rifle… And yet, here was evidence to the contrary. Maslow would be scratching his head at this one: A people united against tyranny and striving for something greater.

His home was simple. Carpets covered the dirt floor with comfortable pillows all around. No visible sign of excessive wealth. He invited me in and talked with me for several hours, a great honor. We discussed the intricacies of a security program at the village level and how it would be implemented. In short order, I gauged his loyalties and judged his character to be true. The man was genuine. He regarded the safety of his people as a point of honor and took it very seriously. We spoke plainly of those insurgents caught in the past and the rule of law, fragile as it is, in a land where the central government does not have the reach. We spoke of the incredible difficulties his people faced to achieve their success so far.

"*Drop by drop a river is made,*" I responded. It's an ancient Afghan saying and really the only one I know, but it seemed appropriate. He agreed. But the shock I received came from the woman passing through the room to retrieve more tea. She stopped at my words and looked directly at me. Green eyes regarded me for a moment, and then she whispered something to her father. He smiled and nodded in my direction.

In Afghanistan, the honor of the family resides in the women. Rarely do they speak with strangers. They usually are veiled, head to foot. I do not ask about them because it's considered an insult to inquire about someone's women. I have grown accustomed to ignoring them over the months so as not to offend my hosts. The simple fact she was interacting modestly with her father while he entertained male guests was most unusual. But this woman was different. She took more liberties, spoke plainly, and had her father's abject love. I pondered this for a moment as I sipped tea and came to the only conceivable conclusion: it was her! She was the wellspring of this most unusual and progressive situation in the hinterland of one of the most oppressive places on earth! Her expressive eyes could not hide her fire. They betrayed an intensity that spoke volumes. She was keenly interested in my presence. Though respectful and quiet, she bowed to no one. *Here* was the force of personality to move men's hearts… and she had to move only one man's heart.

She, having her father's ear, convinced him of following his heart. Of setting aside fear and making a line in the sand! I had heard the implications of honor being called into question by another man in Afghanistan, but a woman is ten times more compelling! A hundred times! She was the driving force behind this leader—of that there was no doubt.

Over the next several visits I began to piece together the family's story. Father, a hero during the Soviet invasion, rose to prominence. When the Taliban came, he withdrew his people and acquiesced to their demands but never stood with them. His daughter, Farishta, was young and full of fire. He secretly taught her to read and write during the Soviet occupation, something expressly forbidden by the Taliban regime. When she was 18, she was taken by a Taliban and forced into marriage. Her father feared for her life because she was vocal and headstrong—not the qualities a Taliban looks for in a woman, but beauty clouds judgment.

She had two sons while very young. It seemed her future was set much like any other woman in Afghanistan. When the two boys were around the age of ten, the father began to use them for intelligence gathering. They would inform on those within certain villages that had rather un-Taliban sentiment. They would walk around markets and eavesdrop on men talking, then report their words to the father. He would turn in those his children identified to advance his own standing in the regime.

Farishta was not quiet. She fought her husband until he realized simply beating the woman would not keep her silent. He could no longer suffer her insolence concerning the two boys and sent her back to her father, exiling her from her children. Within two years she heard of their deaths. It was at the hands of those they informed on, or perhaps the families of the unjustly accused. Here vengeance is written into the code of conduct. The Code of *Pashtunwali* is uncompromising and demands vengeance for those wronged by others.

Her husband had no interest in her and probably feared her wrath if he saw her again. So Farishta resided with her father and in no small amount of grief. 2001 brought *badal* (vengeance) to her. Her husband died at the hands of the Northern Alliance in the beginning of the War on Terror.

Farishta remained in the village of her childhood, helping her father with good counsel and using her female networks to every advantage. He rose quickly in prominence and galvanized the population to choose sides. They chose to stand with the Coalition Forces and never looked back, though I daresay, over the last eight years, they had good reason to question our resolve.

We spent much time talking, and Farishta took a liking to me, though none but my interpreter knew.

I, of course, threatened him with all manner of death if he betrayed our confidence. I would not want any harm to come to the father and daughter because of any undue familiarity. At least that's what I told myself. Truthfully, I began to like this *Joan d'Arc* of Afghanistan.

I admired her resolve. Her quiet strength. I became fond of her. I visited often, using his hospitality to talk to other elders and staying longer to discuss issues with Farishta and her father. Her father was the one who actually spoke of a time when our countries and cultures could come together in a time of peace. He even expressed a desire to visit America… as did Farishta—carefully worded, of course,

"I would be honored to show you and your family America."

Things unspoken can be more powerful than words.

In short order, I concluded my findings and returned to give my report. My thoughts often drifted to that strange and unusual family by the river. Such open hospitality and honest discussion moved me deeply—deeper than I thought possible considering my circumstances.

I happened through that same village several weeks later. Actually, I purposely diverted there to *reassess atmospherics*, but that wasn't my only reason. I wanted to see Farishta and her redoubtable father. I missed their frank and open discussion of possibility and promise. I missed green eyes and the laughter of children as well. Perhaps it was the irrepressible spirit, or maybe my own desire for a kindred spirit.

The children overran our lines as usual. The father met me at the boundaries of the village, a sling upon his right arm. I approached, "*Salamaleykom, rafiqeum!* How is your family?" I said as I removed my helmet and dark sunglasses. It was then that I noticed his grim expression. He regarded me for some time and then simply pointed to the hill. A white stone shone stark against the dark rocks. I stood and stared for what must have been a long time. He only had one family member… Farishta. When I turned back, he was gone.

The patrol leader came up to me, wondering why I wasn't proceeding into the village. "Lieutenant, what happened here?" I asked.

"TB (Taliban) came across the river three weeks ago. Tried to take out the leader you were just talking to. He fought them off—tough bastard. But they killed his daughter. But we got the phone call and got 'em all," he said matter-of-factly.

Before I enquired as to the *second order* effect, I noticed several of the village men walking around with weapons. No smiles this time—just hard stares of resolve. The father did not wait. He had armed the villagers himself. The insurgents would not come here again. They tended to prey only upon the weak.

The strength of Farishta had done its work.

"Let's get out of here." I walked back to the Stryker.

Though I only saw her eyes, she was one of the most beautiful souls I've ever met.

I wondered long after how many other quiet heroines and heroes were out there… and how many more would be sacrificed before Afghanistan found itself.

Sam Stryker pictured without helmet

Hazara Girl (courtesy of Penelope Price)

The Accidental Angel

"Ordinary people can occasionally achieve extraordinary things..."
— Vogue magazine article on Mary MacMakin by Rebecca Johnson, 2001

In 2010 I decided to fund the filming of a documentary that could depict the eternal dance between opposite forces in Afghanistan through the use of visual effects and interviews with people who had been in Afghanistan for a long time and had a story to tell.

The choice of filmmaker was fairly easy. Penelope Price is a native Arizonian whose work focuses on human rights. She began making her own independent films in 1985, and her work has screened and won awards nationally and internationally.

In the year 2000, her first documentary won the top award at the San Francisco International Film Festival and consequently screened at the United Nations conference Against Torture in Washington DC.

Her film, *Artist of Resistance*, was released in 2006 and screened in festivals across the United States, Canada and Europe, and she is the founding director and faculty member at The Film School of an Arizonian academic institution. She has developed and is currently teaching a documentary course called, "Lights,

Camera, Activism: Documentaries for Social Change." She was the right person for the job. It was clear from the beginning that her job would not be easy. Storytelling from a number of *Quissa Mar* with the limited help of words and the primary aid of a camera is an art in itself. She did a great job. The title of the documentary became: *Between Light and Darkness*.

The first and most important *Quissa Mar* that Penelope had to interview was Mary MacMakin, a legend, the *Accidental Angel*. I had known Mary for a few years already and fallen in love with her almost at first sight. The emotional and spiritual strength in this octogenarian is infectious. From the '60s to the '80s, Mary worked as a physiotherapist in Kabul hospitals and, after experiencing the desperation of widows and generally women under the Taliban rule, she started a number of underground schools for girls. For her work in support of women's emancipation under the oppressive Taliban, she was jailed with a number of her female staff. Eventually, after strong pressure from the United States Department of State to release her, she was exiled to Pakistan and stayed there until the Northern Alliance offensive in 2001.

She crossed the snowed-in border, riding a horse, right behind the Northern Alliance advance and settled back in Kabul, where she was instrumental in setting up the Beauty School of Kabul, a slap in the face to the *chadri* enforcers with the black turbans who had exiled her a few years before.

She owes the *Accidental Angel* title to a biographical article that *Vogue* published about her. I drove Penelope to meet Mary in Bisbee, Arizona, a town that suits Mary's spirit. Mary happened to be there for one of her visits to the United States. She had come over to care for her ailing husband. Three years later, I met her again in Kabul. Her husband had passed away, and Mary was free to live for the rest of her life in her beloved Afghanistan.

When I met her in January 2013, she told me that she was residing in an apartment right next to the Christian Cemetery in Kabul, and she was adamant that it was there that she wished to be buried when she passed away.

I knew Penelope, the filmmaker, would be great fun to work with when I saw the light in her eyes while she was interviewing the grandmother of *Quissa Mar* (by the way, Mary would kill me for calling her a grandma) and because, over lunch, she called my *gazpacho* soup *Gestapo*. Anybody that can confuse an *Andalucian* cold tomato-based vegetable soup with the National Socialist *Geheime Staatspolizei* (the secret police of Nazi Germany) is a welcome guest at my table, and I will happily pick up the tab.

You could tell that Penelope was enthralled by Mary. We had lunch and three cups of tea, and then two of the most fascinating American women I met—the *Accidental Angel Quissa Mar* and the filmmaker, who confuses soups and secret police, opened up in one of the best interviews I have ever witnessed. The two women had met barely two hours before.

Mary: Just, I take milk and yogurt and cheese. I don't take any supplements. I don't take any pills. I do take iodine. I do have iodine insufficiency, and, if I don't take iodine, I get very tired in the afternoon.

Penelope: You don't want to be tired. You have a lot of work to do.

Mary: That's right.

Penelope: Okay, we're ready. So let's start with the story about them coming to your door.

Mary: Yeah. The word went out in Kabul about this foreigner who was living down the street there. She'd help widows and all, so one day there was a ring at the door, and I went down. It was this woman with two sort of teenage girls, and I liked her right away; so we chatted a little bit, and she asked if we had any extra food. I got some bread and some cake that we happened to have and I gave it to them. And I thought about them quite a lot after. Then they came back again, and I asked would the older girl like to work for me and of course, she would like to, so she became one of my monitors, one of my project managers. And she did a very good job with that. And finally, bit by bit, I got their story together, all the pieces of it. And it turned out that, about two years before, an army or maybe an Air Force general had decided he wanted to be king so he started staging a coup. And so he got his pilots together; he got the planes armed with bombs. I don't know where he got the bombs. And he flew over Kabul and just dropped some bombs. Not a lot, but he dropped some, and one of them fell right on her house. Her mother was in there, her father, her uncle was there with other people and just destroyed the house. Mud houses will just crumple down when a bomb hits them, and, as soon as the planes had left, the neighbors started coming around to see if they could help. Nalita's mother was calling from underneath all of the bricks and rubble so they started throwing bricks away and getting the rubble out of the way, getting the clay and everything, the dry clay, and finally they came across her hand and they seized on her hand and all these guys, they started hauling away, and, of course, with her body still under part of the rubble, there was this huge strain on her shoulder which ruptured the medial epicondyle, the ulnar nerves.

So her left arm became paralyzed but, anyway, apart from that, she was grateful to be rescued, and to be alive, and to see that her girls were alive; none of the others, none of the kids, got hurt except Nalita.

The blast was so strong that she couldn't escape unscathed; she was deaf for about three or four days after that. In fact, she was deaf in one ear, partially deaf, and I don't know if it was from a childhood illness or if it was from this bomb, but she didn't hear very well from the one ear. So the family now were nomads.

(By now I knew I was in the presence of myth. I could hear an Afghan, talking but the words were coming out of an elderly American woman.)

Mary: They had no home, and the relatives couldn't take them in. Their homes were all crammed full except one, so they started this really pathetic search around town to find places where they could stay, to spend the night. And they went to one of their distant relatives, and he said, "Well you can stay one night here." And next morning, they were ushered out the door, which is a very shameful thing. Anyway, they went from place to place for 18 months. Then, at one point, they ended up in a compound where there were other widowed women. The compound was housed on the site of a destroyed house.

Luckily, it was summer; there was grass there, so they started eating grass. They had nothing else to eat and no money. I have it written down. I've got to find this notebook I had. So place after place for 18 months. They found one man who let them stay in a little room for about six months, so that was the place they stayed at the longest. You know, they'd spent two weeks in a place to then be kicked out, spent one month somewhere else to be kicked out, spend three days somewhere to be then kicked out again. It was terrible.

I could picture myself with my little girls shuffled from place to place with no opportunity to get a job or substantial help. In the United States, we get social services, unemployment benefits;

in Afghanistan you get other people's support, but three single females are too much of a burden.

So after this 18-month odyssey of being shoveled out from one house to another, they finally came to me, and, two days after meeting Nalita, I gave her a job. Then they were finally able to pay rent on a little room, but it was a very, very poor room. The floor had no carpet, nothing, no throw rug. Just an old piece of canvas they had on the floor, but they had been able to save some of their stuff after the bomb had destroyed their home, so they eventually began to build up their life a little bit at a time.

Nalita's mother, Reyma, made money also by making dolls in spite of her left hand being partly crippled. She had been a seamstress before, so she continued in her trade, and she made these little Taliban dolls for the *madrassa* students. That little Taliban doll I have is one that Reyma made.

Penelope: And then did you sell these dolls in your stores?

Mary: Oh, yes. I paid her close to five dollars for each of the dolls, maybe too much, but all of the widows that made dolls got more pay for them.

Penelope: Who were your customers? Who bought the dolls?

Mary: Well, in Kabul there were foreigners living there. There were other NGOs. In the Taliban times, there were about 25 international NGOs, which meant that they were maybe in each office. And when the Christians were there, they'd been there all during this time; there were about a dozen more of them, and they were good customers, too. So there were some two hundred to five hundred foreigners living in Kabul at that time. Expats we called them, expats in Kabul. Plus there were the Taliban students, who were not really allowed to get any figurine or anything else of that kind, but the allure of being pictured was too much, so they bought their little Taliban dolls.

Penelope: Mary, tell us how you worked with the taxis; you would have a whole group of taxis come; and everybody would go to the different homes to check on things. We heard that the Taliban were tolerant of your network because it had been sort of peaceful—you'd actually even signed a permit. You'd gotten a permit from Omar.

Mary: Alright, in order to carry out our work in Kabul, we had to have transportation, and busses weren't sufficient, so most of the organizations would buy a car, a jeep or a van. I decided I didn't want to hassle with having to buy gasoline and worry about whether I could obtain fuel or not. I did not want to bother with getting tires or batteries, or anything else. So I just rented cars, I rented taxis. For me, that was the perfect solution, because I didn't have to bother if the taxi didn't work. I didn't have to get it fixed up. The owner drove it and took care of his taxi. That was a good system. So our taxis took our female staff discreetly to wherever we needed them and then drove them back again. The Taliban appreciated our discretion in managing things. Other organizations did not understand the unwritten behavioral codes.

The World Food Program (WFP), for instance, was far more reckless than we were but had powerful backing and protection. They employed a lot of women at their bread bakeries. They were supplying bread to a lot of people, so they hired a lot of women both in the bakeries making bread and then distributing it. Well, the Taliban were very upset about this. They didn't like it especially when the WFP, which was right on the main street, would advertise for female workers; so you would see a lot of *chadri*-clad women, all lined up outside the wall of the WFP compound. All of them waiting to be interviewed.

The Taliban would drive by in their cars and see this hoard of women, and they were just horrified—"What are all these women doing out?" So they had several meetings with the WFP and pretty much cancelled the hiring process.

Well, we were right nearby, too, and we started getting observed, too. The Taliban started even disliking all these women in taxis. So, one day, we were about to get into a taxi to go out somewhere, and the police across the street, the Taliban police, stopped us and said: "Now come to our police station."

We were taken to this house converted into a police station and we ended up spending all day there. The Taliban head policeman, his name was Amanala, was trying to carry out his duties and, of course, that meant to see what in the world this foreign woman was doing with all of these Afghan women.

At the end of his investigation, he informed me that my presence with these Afghan women was very bad. I was polluting them with my presence, with my words and with my ideas and thoughts. It was too much for him to bear. There it was, this young guy—yes he was quite young—and like so many Taliban, unconsciously he was just dying for contact with women. They are meant to be chaste until they get married. Some of them are even like these Christian monks who vow celibacy for life, yet they cannot bear to be without a woman any longer. Here is this guy yearning for women, and here I had two women with me. During our long day, another woman was brought in on charges of prostitution. Who knows what had really happened with her. We waited around, they fed us lunch and, in the meanwhile, word that we had been arrested got out.

Someone, the usual rumor mill had told the Western organization who oversaw the NGOs in Afghanistan that an American woman and some of her staff had been detained. One of the Western representatives rushed to the police station to visit us and see if we were all right.

The visit accelerated the Taliban's need to get the "truth" out of us. So they kept probing us. They wanted to know where these women, who were with me, lived and they kept saying: "Oh, we don't know where we live. We can't write, we're illiterate," and we all kept telling these outrageous lies, and we held on quite remarkably. While my girls were being interrogated, I got talking to another one of the Taliban there, and I found out that Amanala wasn't married. So the next time Amanala showed up to question me, I got right up to his young face and I said, "You know, Amanala, I know why you want the addresses of these young women. Because you want to go visit them. You want to marry them." He was silent. He didn't say anything. He just got up and got two pieces of paper and a couple pencils for my two girls and he said, "I want you to write down on this paper that you will never, ever go into a foreigner's office again." So, the girls, after having said they were illiterate, here they were writing this note, "I will never go into another foreigner's office again." I'm not sure what they actually wrote, and we all signed it. And then unmarried Amanala gravely said: "Alright, you can go now." So we went out of the police station across the street, and all three of us went into my office.

These young men, these Taliban, they were very simple, very naïve. They really didn't know what they were doing. They did not really know how to enforce their own rules when prevented from using violence.

So we continued to use taxis. Then we were told we couldn't use the taxis any longer. We did not listen a bit, but, when we got stopped, the taxis were impounded. We felt bad for the taxi drivers, so we spent weeks pressuring the Taliban trying to get our taxis back. This even included me sending a letter to Mullah

Omar in Kandahar because, frankly, the Taliban police in Kabul were starting to get on my nerves.

One of our electrical engineering teachers was a Pashtun man from Kandahar; we sent him down with one hundred dollars and my personal note to Omar: "Dear Mullah Omar, we are an NGO of women, and we want to carry out our work helping people, etc, etc, etc…" Well, anyway, the guy we sent, I forgot his name, went down to Kandahar and it took him a month before he was able to see Omar. Mullah Omar just read the note and stopped on the line where it said that we were women. He said, "Oh, a group of women," and wrote on the note with his personal signature, "Help these women find a place to work." He addressed the entire note with his personal remarks to a ministry in Kabul. So they had to do it as it was their boss who had ordered them to find us a place. They're obedient boys, these Taliban.

They found us a nice office, and we had to spend some money fixing it up. It was in a compound with four other homes. It had been owned by a businessman who had had enough money to build four homes for his brothers, sons and family members. So he had the second floor of one of these houses. It had been slightly damaged in the fighting but not too badly. So we were very happy there. This was in January 2000.

The Taliban in Kabul could not forget how we outmaneuvered them, and the Arabs, who were more and more numerous, egged them on. One day, Taliban officials from the Morality and Vice Ministry, the ones that clamp down on women not wearing *chadri*, came over to the office claiming that our unveiled staff was visible from the street. I'm not sure whether they were using field glasses to watch us or what.

They stormed the building, took a look at our academic material, and came up with the accusation that we were teaching Christianity. If they only knew how bad of an apostate I am, they might have cleared me of missionary activity, but I would have gotten in trouble anyway. I said, "No, we're not teaching Christianity; you can't even read English, that is why you do not even know what these books are about." They left all frustrated but aware that they had looked quite pathetic.

The second time they stormed the building was more serious. It happened after lunch in July 2000 and I was preparing to go somewhere. I was at the top of the stairs, and I saw all these Afghans starting to run up the stairs and I said, "What are you doing here?" The man in charge was the minister himself, so, anyway they didn't pay any attention to me. They went in and looked in the rooms and the women were just cleaning up after lunch, still washing the dishes and doing their prayers and whatever else.

I thought the visitors might get very impressed with that and leave us alone, but they carted all of us over to a detention facility.

This place was previously another large home that had been converted into a prison. It was very solid, with a big stone foundation and it had a number of fairly large rooms. There were already other women there. In total there were about seven or eight of us. We were all told we had to stay there until further notice. We had not been permitted to take anything with us. Of course, we had no toothbrushes, no toothpaste and no change of clothes. We had nothing but the clothes we were wearing. We were so ticked off that although we spent only four days in captivity, we managed to cause a little trouble while I was there.

Nobody had told us why we were detained. No charges were brought against us. We were taken to inadequate facilities as the place was mainly a detention center for young boys who had been caught stealing or were having family troubles. There were about 60 to 70 boys all dressed in gray *shalwaar kamiz* and eight women in a walled-off section from this big compound, in a separate house, of course. So although we were fed, of course it was jail food, Afghan jail food. We had little water to wash with. Two of our drivers had been jailed with us and did not even get that.

Again, words, the rumor mill, got out that Mary was in jail. So right away there was a whole horde of cars, foreign NGO vehicles, outside the wall of the compound asking what had happened to Mary. On the second day, I guess someone who spoke Arabic was able to get in and she brought toothbrushes, toothpaste and feminine supplies. By the fourth day, I stole the pots, pans and a ladle that the jail cook had put out in the sun to dry. We started this massively loud concert: bang, bang, bang, bang and the boys joined in making a lot of noise. Pretty soon a couple of Taliban ran to the gate of our compound and, yelled, "What's the matter?" and I shouted back, "Well, what am I doing here?" You know, I actually said, "What the heck is going on here?" and I thought I was not getting any success at being heard so I kept banging the pans incessantly.

We kept going until the minister showed up and just said, "You can go home," and I said, "Well, are you going to let the other women go?" and he said, "No," and I said "Well, I'm not going either," and that infuriated him so much he took my bag with what little I had grabbed from the office, including my little, tiny computer. I had a camera, he pulled the film out of the camera and threw it away, but I went back into the compound with the women and the other women who were there, too.

They were fascinated by our desire to stand up to their abuses. In jail, they wanted to tell me their stories, and they were trying to share a room with me. Although the jail warden kept saying that the foreigner should stay in isolation, they all snuck in. I heard the most fascinating stories. I had them written down. I got to write that up. I got so many things to write up. So anyway, then on the fourth day, they did let us all go.

Two days later I was told, in no uncertain terms, that I should leave. I reserved a seat on the ICRC plane that would take me to Peshawar. Just before I left, I went to see one of the officials in the Afghan Ministry of Foreign Affairs, who was a nice guy and liked me. "Mary, wait until the dust settles, wait a month or two and then apply to come back, and we'll see what we can do," he said. I had trusted him in the past. This time, it would be different.

I was exiled to Peshawar until the opportunity to sneak back in occurred.

Penelope: And it was right at that time when 9/11 happened right? Were you still in Peshawar?

Mary: 9/11 happened, and I had now been there for more than a year. I was really tired of Peshawar, and I wanted so much to get back to Afghanistan so, just before 9/11, I went to Islamabad where the United Nations had a plane that flew up to Panshir, which is up in the Northeast corner that was still in the hands of *Massood*. The Taliban hadn't gotten there, so I just had to get away from Peshawar and finally got into Afghanistan again.

I stayed in the Panshir Valley, which housed a sort of shadow government. The Northern Alliance had set up a little guest house for foreigners. We were a very diverse bunch, a few filmmakers, humanitarians, intelligence types and journalists. We got to know each other pretty well. One of us was present when *Massood* was attacked and eventually killed by the two Arabs who claimed to be news people.

While I was staying in another valley at the guest house, our woman friend showed up, but she did not tell us that *Massood* had been killed. She just told us that he had been taken to a hospital in Tajikistan. Suddenly, all these news people started to arrive, so my friend Nasreen and I looked at each other and finally figured out what was about to happen. So this little house was now just bursting with foreign news people, and all beds were taken; people were sleeping on the floor.

I actually went to bed early. I took a bed that was somebody else's. We had a generator and we watched 9/11 unfold on Turkish Television. These planes slicing like a hot knife into butter, into these buildings.

I couldn't believe it. I kept watching. They'd play it over and over. For us it was just disbelief. Is this really happening? The next few weeks were a whirlwind of events. I had to get to Kabul fast but Northern Alliance helicopters were ferrying fighters primarily. The front was closed, so I took a helicopter to Peshawar again, and then I hired a pick-up truck and two young guys.

They had to take me to the border, and we were going to use a mountain pass. I passed through the border riding a horse, and the pass was snowed in, as it was September, and it was freezing. There was this little tiny staging post on the Afghan side, and there were a lot of Afghans in transit every day going in both directions.

There was no government; nobody would check your passport. Just a bunch of people passing back and forth by horse or mule. I was riding a horse on one side and going over what I had done, I had rented a horse. Anyway, so the night before crossing the border, I was crammed in this little stinky place. They fed us supper, and the place was so packed with all these guys and one foreign woman that I could not find a few spare inches to sleep on. Finally I went into the kitchen. I found a shelf there to sleep on and then the next morning, off we went.

My escorts had the only horse, and it was cold. Here it was September. It was quite cold and then, as we went up the mountain, it got colder and then the snow started falling, and I got very exhausted and cold. I didn't think I could make it. One of the boys loaned me his gloves, and I had a jacket. He kept reassuring me, saying, "Well you know at the top there's a Pakistani military post, and they have tea. You can rest up and have some tea." Well of course when we got up to the top, there was no post, no Pakistani soldiers, nobody. So I just clenched my jaw and endured the rest; at least, from then on, it was downhill.

We went through a snowstorm and as we went lower it turned into slush and then, pretty soon we got down to the little village at the bottom; the sun was shining, and it felt like the September sunshine and the crops being gathered were a sign that there is a beautiful dawn after a long night.

*Mary MacMakin, 2001 (*Vogue *magazine)*

*Mary MacMakin between the author (left)
and Yasin Farid (right) in Kabul, 2013*

Bamhyan gorge (courtesy of Yasin Farid)

Time

*"Men and things are all subject to the Wheel of Time.
Only faith gives sense to this Wheel."*
— Father Angelo Panigati

Y*OU HAVE THE WATCHES, we have the time*—the Afghans often like to repeat.

The saying is correct, it carries a very deep social meaning, and it is accurate, too. Cultures, nations, people can be defined by their relations with time and time keeping.

First, it is good to observe the way cultures identify themselves with time periods. For instance, I was lucky to live in three different countries: Italy, England and the United States. I observed that Italians might well be stuck in the present, the Brits in the past and the Americans in the future.

Italians take few lessons from the past, with the exception of lost wars, and are absolutely obstinate about not wanting to plan for their future. The *carpe diem*, let's enjoy the present because one cannot be so sure about tomorrow, dictates social policies, lifestyle and planning. As long as there is food on the table and money for summer holiday, there is no need to worry about the rest. The British still live like they have an empire, with their Queen, their James Thornton's *Rule Britannia* chants at football games, their gentlemen's clubs and their taking the Commonwealth seriously. The Americans are in a constant hurry. Hungarian writer Márai Sándor described New York as an interesting city, a pity that it wasn't built to be inhabited by human beings. Try stopping on a New York's sidewalk in rush hour and you will be stampeded to death. Everybody is running somewhere. American hurry is contagious. I have witnessed it in Beverly Hills. Even the Persians, who are not known for being in a hurry, feel compelled to go heavy on their car's horn if one has had the misfortune to idle a few extra milliseconds when the traffic light turns green. I saw this woman literally obliterating eardrums in order to pass a car and then park 19 yards in front of the car she was anxious to overtake.

Afghans live neither in the past, present nor future. They are on their own time. Time that cannot be described or categorized by Western standards because it is in a different dimension: the *Inshallah* time.

Life expectancy in Afghanistan is 44 years; in the United States, it is 78 years. They know they will live less and, at times, they wish to live less, yet they take it very easy. We, on the other hand, keep wishing to live longer, and then we go through life at crazy speed.

One could catch a glimpse of the Afghan region's concept of time in the renowned book *Three Cups of Tea* by Greg Mortenson and David Oliver Relin.

In the book Mortenson mentions: *We Americans think you have to accomplish everything quickly. We are the country of thirty-minute power lunches and two-minute football drills. Our leaders thought their "shock and awe" campaign could end the war in Iraq before it even started. Haji Ali (a Balti village chief) taught me to share three cups of tea, to slow down and make building relationships as important as building projects. He taught me that I had more to learn from the people I work with than I could ever hope to teach them.*

The way this passage could be read is that we might be departing Afghanistan without learning a most important lesson about time. Mortenson's words might be telling us that we spent the entire time trying to teach something about the need to achieve things quickly instead of learning to slow down.

In the same book, Mortenson mentions Helena Norberg-Hodge. Helena is a renowned advocate of the impact of the global economy on cultures around the world. She is a pioneer of the localization and counter-development movements.

The counter-development idea centers on the concept that preserving a culture's traditional way of life brings about more happiness than trying to "improve" standards of living with unchecked development. Mortenson mentions Helena's words: "*I used to assume that the direction of 'progress' was somehow inevitable, not to be questioned. I passively accepted a new road through the middle of the park, a steel and glass bank where a 200-year-old church had stood… and the fact that life seemed to get harder and faster with each day. I do not anymore. In Ladakh (Pakistan) I have learned that there is more than one path into the future, and I have had the privilege to witness another, saner 'way of life,' a pattern of existence based on the co-evolution between human beings and the earth… I have seen that community and a close relationship with the land can enrich human life beyond all comparison with material wealth or technological sophistication. I have learned that another way is possible."*

Mortenson built his dream humanitarian organization, with the help of a few visionaries, during the course of 18 years. It took no more than *60 Minutes* to destroy his credibility and the ability to raise money for a lot of other NGOs that operate in the region.

Entertainment-addicted cultures, especially those who are heavily exposed to television and videogames, have shorter attention spans. Television programs are tailored to cater for this eventuality, so it was natural that an *expose* of Mortenson's misdeeds should take only 60 Minutes. Sixty minutes of sensational media tore apart 18 years or more of someone's life. Essentially, the charges were that Mortenson is not a storyteller but a storymaker, quite a liberal one in his representation of reality and, more importantly, an embezzler.

Alarmed at the repercussions that the entire scandal might have caused to the reputation of other organizations present in the area, a few executives operating from Afghanistan voiced their opinions. Marnie Gustavson is an American woman who has settled in Afghanistan, one of those hardcore *Scorpions*. She has been willing to reside in Kabul and stands by her promise to work side by side with the Afghans for a very long time. I asked her to contribute to this book, and she asked me for a few days to think about it. Punctually, a few days later, Marnie's email came, addressed to three people:

> *Dear,*
>
> *We may not be able to talk by phone, but I woke up this morning compelled to write down my thoughts on the Greg Mortensen "scandal." I want you to be aware that I did not see the* 60 Minutes *piece and do not have details about the accusations. I do have a lot to say about the context of the issues uncovered in the "scandal." My first commentary is not on Greg but on the US culture, and supposedly "investigative journalism." I assert that*

60 Minutes *did not conduct that piece with the intent of finding out the truth but went into the story with the ending already told. I experience a significant gap between what it is to live and work in Afghanistan and what the US media portrays as the situation here.*

Additionally, I am well into my seventh year, and I continue to be astonished by the American public's belief in the media. I encountered it in my own very-well educated family in the first years of living here. I had to defend my working here often because of what the media was portraying re: violence and instability. Finally, I asked them "Would I have my husband and sons here if I thought they would be killed?" and they stopped asking. With the barrage of negative media, it is still hard for them to maintain this perspective with beloved family based here.

Second, by being such a distance from my own culture, I have discovered that Americans get very confused by human complexity. This was my own cultural learning curve. For us Americans, black is black, and white is white—A bad guy cannot be good and a good guy cannot be bad. I also learned that, to find anything close to the truth in Afghanistan, I may need to ask 17 different people in the same village. And then you might have an approximation of the truth, but it will lean toward what you wanted to hear.

I did a survey in Northern Afghanistan, checking in on Aga Khan's seed banks. In one village I received the following answers: "There hasn't been a seed bank here for 20 years," "Last week they came but they only gave seeds to the Ishmalis!" "Yes, there is a seed bank here but no seeds in the bank," "We don't know how to plant the seeds, so we feed them to the cows." And on and on....

Given how much trouble I have doing adequate research in Afghanistan—being fluent in Dari—I cannot believe that the people investigating this case received any information other than what they wanted to hear. Afghans hate to say, "I do not know"…and will always opt to say anything, even if it is not the truth, so as not to disappoint the questioner.

I am extremely disappointed that this story has made such headlines; what the US government policies and implementation agencies are doing is so much more of a problem for those of us working here and for the Afghan people, and these stories contain corruption, deliberate misinformation, ambition and cover up. It is upsetting to have Greg the focus of the American public's frustration.

I predict that if anyone is going to try to unravel this story, they will find mistakes, not deliberate deceit, greed, and indifference to the Afghan people as I experience with the programs overseen by the US in Afghanistan.

A colleague, and respected lawyer, Mike Smith, has spent his last six months attempting to bring issues relating to the US development to the attention of the people governing the projects, including the head of USAID, and his attempts have resulted in nothing.

Alex Their (Mike, is the head of USAID mission in AF) refused to meet with him and they are professional acquaintances. I am digressing here, back to Greg and the scandal: non-profits are funny animals usually led by people who have been deeply moved by a cause. I lived in Afghanistan in the '60s, and you couldn't pry me out of here and take me from my work because of my heartfelt commitment to Afghans. But that sense of mission does not *give us the skills or competence to run organizations. We have to learn on the job.*

Greg's credentials are not non-profit management, and neither are mine. I have put in over 25 years learning how to manage non-profits, and then learning how to manage in Afghanistan, which is something almost none of us know how to do…and I say that after six hard years of learning. During the "on-the-job" training, most of us make mistakes, usually financial (or these are the ones that the board usually gets called in on).

Whether he wanted it or not, his book resonated deeply with the American public, and, as a result, he has become an icon. He provided the American people an unusual window into the Afghan culture that portrays the generosity and sweetness that goes along with the fierceness and independence of their character. Americans donating to his charity could feel a sense of being able to give to the Afghan people in a meaningful way. I thank him for that.

As for the accusations? He is going to spend the next decade trying to recover from that, and, really, I say we owe him the space and opportunity to do so. Having watched these phenomena with other non-profit leaders I have surrounded myself by young competent Afghans who I promote and we work as a team and they take responsibility for problems and successes by my side. I have no desire to take all of the credit or blame. I also live here, and I am not planning on leaving, and leaders of orgs who view Afghanistan as home make different decisions.

We are also part of a community here and we work together.—I wish Greg had been able to take the time to meet us…he would find understanding allies if he did and badly needed support at this point. His organization is US-based, not Af–based, and those of us that run non-profits from here do not recognize that as a very sound organizational principle in Afghanistan, especially if you have projects in the provinces.

Canadian Women 4 Women's strategy is an example of a strong strategy—they partner with local organizations. They provide funding and technical assistance to partners as their primary objective. They do not come here and try to conduct direct services without a local partner. Because of the strong network they have developed, they have the capacity to know what is going on in their projects relatively accurately, and to hold their local partners accountable. They are also supporting "emerging Afghan leaders" who will be able to expand and take over projects creating a sustainable future for their work.

I learned the most amazing lesson last week. For six months a new director with ARCS (Afghan Red Crescent Society) Marastoons had taken an attitude against us and was using every trick in the book to get us evicted from the Marastoon where we have lived and worked for the past four years.

He was obnoxious. He would enter our Scout meetings and tell all the children to go home. "This NGO had no permission to do this program." Our Afghan country director had more patience with him than I did. We kept calm and countered every accusation (teaching Christianity, stealing Marastoon donors, etc.) with a measured response and the truth as we knew it as well as support from our donors and colleagues. Last month he sat down with Yasin and apologized for his behavior and pledged support.

Since then, we have experienced unprecedented goodwill and help from ARCS. I learned two things: "Bad" guys can be good. (Or maybe the story is more complex.) As leaders our measure is taken not by our successes, but by how we respond in times of crisis and failure. I predict that Greg will carry on that tradition of good non-profit leaders and survive this crisis.

I hope that at least this gives you a little background on my perspective on the issues. At least your question allowed me to sort out how I see it.

Warmest regards,
Marnie

PS…I also recommend Julia Bolz, a lawyer who has spent the last ten years building schools and supporting educational programs in the northern part of the country for a perspective on this. Like Greg, she is based out of the US and is well respected in Afghanistan for her work. For reference on our organization and our work—we were featured alongside Greg and his foundation two years ago in Christiane Amanpour's CNN documentary "Generation Islam."

Did CBS take the time? Did they take the time to really know? Know where they pressed by the inexorable *battle rhythm* of US news and its commercial need to broadcast something sensational with impossible frequency? Did they apply US timelines when investigating deeds in a region that requires a different approach and extra due diligence?

In 2007, I ventured into a remote village outside Bahmyan to provide relief to the numerous family of a widow, a family that consisted of seven women and no men. We trekked a few miles uphill and were honored to be welcomed in the woman's very modest abode.

When the winter snow comes in and overwhelms the village, entire families stay locked indoors, feed on stowed provisions and warm themselves with animal dung fires whose acrid smoke exits the dirt-floored huts through small openings in the ceiling.

Families live in the solitary confinement of smoke-filled habitations for months at a time without *CNN,* the *Disney Channel,* DVD players or Xbox. The snow literally piles outside the entrance to the habitation and it becomes an amazing challenge to venture outside. Five, six days at a time confined in a space half the size of the average American garage.

How do they manage? They manage well because they are on a different time. In rural Afghanistan, time stops and assumes a surreal dimension. Months fold into months, years into years, lives into lives. They go about their daily chores rhythmically and ritualistically. Life stops being a chore and becomes a ritual.

Lighting a fire, warming up the room, melting snow and cooking becomes a slow endeavor that assumes the meaning of life. How many times have we taken a shower without remembering the way we soaped our bodies? How many times have we cooked food in a microwave oven and forgotten its taste?

In that little house in rural Hazara-jat, life would come to a standstill to the point that everything, even the smallest detail, assumed extraordinary importance.

Is it possible that, in Afghanistan, we are fighting what we perceive as insurgent elements in two different time zones? Is our time zone, which requires quick victories, results and a quick transition to Western-styled governance, applicable to a medieval region?

Is Afghanistan really willing to abide by our sense of time? Are the majority of Afghans really convinced that they want to embrace our governance, rule of law and progress?

In this land, is the Afghan concept of time making our need for speed irrelevant and obsolete?

Between the end of World War II and the present day, our lifestyle has accelerated dramatically. During the same period, Afghanistan's rural life has stayed the same. We are now affecting the timekeeping of the larger urban areas, and we are increasing the time gap between the big cities and the rural areas. Insurgents use both time zones to their advantage; they know when to accelerate, and they know when to slow down and wait. We seem to know only how to accelerate.

In April 1948, after defeating the Third Reich, the Allies started the European Recovery Program, commonly known as the Marshall Plan. The Second World War in Europe took seven years of ruthless, active, bloody combat and 52 million deaths. The United States lost half a million military personnel, an average of 13,900 casualties per month. The Marshall Plan, nominally implemented for only four years, required an industrial, commercial and military involvement that lasts to this day—64 years.

The Vietnam War spanned a 20-year involvement and seven years of active combat, with 39,587 US casualties, an average of 472 deaths per month.

In Afghanistan, the crossroads of Asia, as of January 2013, there have been a total of 3,255 coalition casualties over 11 years. As of January, the United States has lost an average of 16 military personnel per month. What has changed?

In the past two generations, our time has accelerated dramatically. Our patience and stoicism have diminished in an inversely proportioned effect with time acceleration. Our need for quick resolutions and success have increased. Afghan's time has stayed the same. Is there a lesson here?

The progress of technological advance and the need for entertainment dictates that the shelf life of stories has reduced dramatically. Media needs to move on to keep the public entertained, and public support is vital for the military cause. We need new stories, and Afghanistan is an old one. Despite our increased lack of tolerance for casualties, three deaths caused by a roadside bomb have ceased to make the news.

We have run out of our time now that the watches are running our lives. Faith is definitely what gives sense to the Wheel of Time.

Back in time (courtesy of Penelope Price)

Conclusion

For a number of personal reasons, I have been ambivalent about keeping journals, but I cannot deny that they often come in useful as they allow one to recall important details that otherwise might be forgotten.

What Is Past Is Prologue

Often, when we are caught by the incessant rhythm of everyday life, we forget the way we felt about things, our moods, happy memories and other meaningful details of the past.

I had to go back to reading one of my rare attempts at keeping a journal to corroborate two of the stories contained in this book. My diary about a 2007 trip to Afghanistan was instrumental in remembering the name of the area where I managed to drive a minivan into a roadside ditch; it was somewhere in the Ghorban area, an area that, in 2013, is indicated as at high risk of insurgency activities.

Localizing the accident and reading the details brought back the more delicate moments of the event. In hindsight, those moments are tough to trivialize with the addition of humor—moments that caused sheer terror in two of my traveling companions. In the diary, I describe in detail their shrinking and almost blending with the fabric of the minivan's seats.

After reading the journal, I realized that my recollections of events at the airport were somewhat different from the woman whose story I reported. I did offer *baksheesh* but only to avoid that a number of Afghan knives, which the humanitarian volunteers had purchased at the bazaar, could be confiscated by the border police.

Even the Qu'ran debacle was resolved a lot more amicably, without the use of a bribe and with a show of impeccable compassion on the part of the devout Muslim policeman. The diary helped me remember when finally shaking the guard's hand in gratitude, I whispered to him: *Allahu akbar!* (God is great!) and the man, being pleasantly surprised, had tears in his eyes.

My point is that the events occurred as recently as 2007, five years ago, and stories differ somewhat. Readers might have accepted my traveling companion's version as accurate or might be even more inspired by the second rendering.

Which one is the true story, then? I hope that the answer this book delivered, the one of many Afghan *Quissa Mar,* is clear: *It really does not matter.* Accuracy is not important—the overall lesson is.

A story, in the end, is just a story. Stories are recounted at a precise time for a precise reason.

Things in life do not happen by chance. I believe we all are, and always have been, part of a beautiful project. Every meeting, event, occurrence is meant to teach us something important. The ultimate lesson is the betterment of our own life and of the lives of those we touch.

We shall learn from successes and, most importantly, from mistakes. We shall learn from winners and from losers alike. We shall learn from the stories that each one of us embodies. 9/11 and our involvement in Afghanistan did not just happen.

There is a reason for it and an important lesson behind it. If the memory is fading, then it is an opportunity to learn. We owe those who died fighting on our behalf and, more importantly, those we killed, the obligation to pause, slow down and listen.

The ritual should not only be reserved for funerals and memorials for the fallen. It should be a continuous state of mind. We owe ourselves the opportunity to learn from others, without judging or rushing through. After all, *La Storia Siamo Noi*, (we are the ones making history).

Acknowledgments

As soon as I finished the first draft of this book, the lyrics from a 1983 Italian song by Loredana Bertè suddenly came to mind:

"Dedicato a chi si guarda nello specchio e da tempo non si vede più, a chi non ha uno specchio e comunque non per questo non ce la fa più"… (dedicated to those who look at themselves in the mirror and cannot recognize who they have become and to those who have no mirror and yet are struggling as much).

It seemed so fitting to the Afghanistan dilemma and the paradox of life.

I have to thank my friends Michael Freiberg, Sam Stryker, Marnie Gustavson, Maria de Longy, Kelly Bender, Mary MacMakin, George MacDonald and all the faceless heroes at the Human Terrain Program of the U.S. Army who have provided me with the inspiration, stories and documentary support to make this book possible.

I owe a lot to the Afghanistan desk of the NATO CIMIC Fusion. They are a great group of tireless professionals.

I tried to personally thank Lane Hartill many times but did not succeed. Lane, if you read this, please know that I am very grateful to you.

I would like to thank Yasin Mohamed Farid, my brother from an Afghan mother. May God keep you safe and happy.

A big thanks goes to Meranda Keller, a very talented artist with a big heart.

Finally I would like to thank my publisher. Because of her, my guardian angel, I have learned a great deal about life, patience, and a number of other very important matters.

Gennaro Buonocore
1 April, 2014

About the Author

Gennaro Buonocore is a native of Naples, Italy, spent his formative years in Rome and more than a dozen years of his 24-year career in the investment banking sector in London, England. As an investment banker, he has operated in 28 different countries, specializing in capital markets and development finance. In addition to investment banking, he has served as a military reservist and fulfilled a number of tours as a Civil Affairs officer in both Iraq and Afghanistan. A modern day renaissance man, he has a keen interest in world affairs and diverse cultures, speaks several languages and has held key positions in non-profit humanitarian organizations. In 2012, he co-authored the book, *Failure of the European Multiculturalism—The Islamist Crusade*. He is an alumnus of Regent's University London European Business School and Webster University's George Herbert Walker Graduate School of Business and Technology. In 2006, he was awarded a Dottorato in Economia e Mercati by the Universita' di Roma III.

CPSIA information can be obtained at www.ICGtesting.com
Printed in the USA
LVOW05s1016250714

396015LV00002B/58/P

9 780985 576226